Petra

Maria Giulia Amadasi Guzzo
Eugenia Equini Schneider

Petra

Translated by Lydia G. Cochrane

The University of Chicago Press • Chicago and London

The University of Chicago Press, Chicago 60637
The University of Chicago Press, Ltd., London
© 2002 by The University of Chicago
Originally published in Italian, © 1997 by Electa, Milano. Elemond Editori Associati.
All rights reserved. Published 2002
11 10 09 08 07 06 05 04 03 02   1 2 3 4 5

ISBN: 0-226-31125-2 (cloth)

Photo credits: Double's photographic agency, Milan; Franca Speranza photographic agency, Milan; Overseas photographic agency, Milan; Ricciarini photographic agency, Milan; White Star photographic agency, Vercelli; Mondadori photographic archives, Milan; Scala photographic archives, Antella (Florence); Bibliothèque Nationale de France, Cabinet des Médailles, Paris; Federico Borromeo, Milan; Eugenia Equini Schneider, Rome; Musée du Louvre, Paris; Archaeological Museum, Amman; Petra Museum; Pergamonmuseum, Berlin; Soprintendenza archeologica delle provincie di Napoli e Caserta, Naples; Rolf A. Stucky, Archaeological Institute of the University of Basel; Jane Taylor, Amman.

Library of Congress Cataloging-in-Publication Data
Amadasi, Maria Giulia.
  Petra / Maria Giulia Amadasi Guzzo,
  Eugenia Equini Schneider; translated by Lydia G. Cochrane
      p. cm.
  Includes bibliographical references and index.
  ISBN 0-226-31125-2 (cloth : alk. paper)
  1. Petra (Extinct city) I. Equini Schneider, Eugenia.
  DS154.9.P48 A45 2002
  939'.48—dc21
                                        2002017350

Contents

El Deir Petra
March 8th, 1839
David Roberts

Introduction

Places, and the language that is their own, are the best narrators of the past. They stand beside the historians, ancient and modern, the geographers, and the writers, enabling us to restore the features of a civilization through patient investigation and careful readings of the physical documents as they come to light. In this way, it is possible to decipher the real identities of ruins often obscured by time's accumulations, if not by abandonment, and to rescue them from provisory and inadequate interpretations and from commonplaces of reconstruction.

Scholars are not alone in their fascination with Nabatean civilization and history and their study of the Nabatean capital city: their passion is shared by everyone who has ever, in any way and at any time, encountered the city of Petra. After lying forgotten for nearly six centuries until its almost chance "rediscovery" in the early nineteenth century, Petra has elicited increasing interest and enthusiasm. The power of suggestion of that caravan city nestled at the heart of a basin reached through narrow gorges carved by the watercourses that modeled its mountain masses and deep valleys—a city where monumental rock tombs of a lively and refined architecture line the cliffs in superimposed rows—and the mystery that seems to shroud the beginning and the end of this civilization have attracted hundreds and hundreds of travelers, lovers of ancient things, and the simply curious. Even today anyone who ventures into this impressive stone landscape or who penetrates the muffled silence of these monuments worked in the living rock is struck by this special atmosphere. Both sacred and grandiose, the site seems to have valued death over life, eternalizing it in lasting constructions. The very concept of survival assumes a special significance here as the ability to perpetuate personal memory for a never-ending posterity continuing indefinitely through time.

The theme and the principle of the *attolli super ceteros mortales* are common to other Mediterranean civilizations—we need only recall the Etruscan rock necropoli of Italy; in Turkey the necropoli of Lycia, Paphlagonia, and Phrygia; or the Cyrenaic tombs in Tripolitania—but the structures of Petra are unequaled for their magnificence and their monumentality. More clearly than any other testimony that has come down to us, they reveal the level of wealth and the refined lifestyle that Nabatean civilization achieved in the course of its history.

For the better part of the nineteenth century, these exceptional ruins called out to travelers, exerting an attraction that often made for fascinating reading. In more recent times, however, genuine scientific exploration and controlled investigation of the monuments and their surroundings have given rise to a large number of studies and research projects. Bit by bit, the historical physiognomy of the territory has been pieced together, starting with the formation of the Nabatean state in the late fourth century B.C.E. and continuing through the late Hellenistic era to the age of Roman domination.

The Nabatean kingdom, which extended east of the Jordan River and included the Sinai Peninsula, the Negev, and northeastern Arabia, managed to maintain its independence under the Ptolemaic rulers of Egypt and the Seleucid kings of Syria and to coexist (albeit with conflicts and problems) with the Hebraic world. It established peaceful relations with the rest of the Arab world, expanding and reinforcing its territory even after Rome's direct intervention in the Near East, when for some time it was the only "client state" of Rome west of the Euphrates.

Thanks to Nabatea's function as an intermediary in the commercial trade between Arabia, the East, and the Red Sea—the principal support of the Nabatean economy—the territory was enriched by cultural importations of various origins and provenances. Petra, the epicenter of this exchange of material and artistic goods, became a center of production as well, and for at least two centuries practitioners of a variety of trades and occupations worked together or in competition with one another in a city that gradually became a great cosmopolitan metropolis.

Even today, however, it remains difficult to define many aspects of Nabatean civilization. Although excavations in Syria, Jordan, and the Negev have helped to clarify some of the characteristics and the problems of both sacred and civil Nabatean architecture, in the capital city of the kingdom only a few monuments have been studied with scientific rigor. For the most part, scholars have focused on the rupestrian architecture of Petra; only a few of the market complexes, temples, palaces, fountains, and residential areas—the public and private buildings that the city undoubtedly had and in which daily life took place—have been accurately identified and studied in detail.

The present volume obviously does not aim to fill this gap, nor does it claim to resolve problems that still remain open. The reader will not find here an exhaustive analysis of the Nabatean civilization. Our intention has been to offer a summary of what is known; to make available to the reader a general panorama of the history, the religion, the society, the language, and the artistic culture of this people, as these are reflected in the city of Petra; and to pave the way for more in-depth study.

This aim risks producing a book that is too challenging or boring for some, too generic for others, and too superficial for specialists. We have attempted to keep ourselves *in media via,* although we are fully aware of the criticism that this method invites. A documentation that is so uneven, that offers a wealth of information on certain aspects of the topic and a dearth of material on others, necessarily imposes choices, omissions, and changes of perspective.

MARIA GIULIA AMADASI GUZZO is responsible for: The Region; The Nabateans: The Problem of Origins; The Nabatean Kingdom between Arabia and Syria: From the Origins to the End of the Roman Republic; Nabatean Society.

EUGENIA EQUINI SCHNEIDER is responsible for The Nabatean Kingdom between Arabia and Syria: The First Century of the Roman Empire, The Roman Province of Arabia, Petra and the Caravan Trade; The City of Petra.

In the section Monuments and Written Documents, Eugenia Equini Schneider has written the material relating to archaeology; Maria Giulia Amadasi Guzzo has written the material regarding epigraphy.

The Region

The region constituting the Nabatean state at the time of Alexander the Great's successors and in the Roman era varied in size from one period to another. In the absence of clearly defined natural borders, its boundaries changed according to the power of its rulers in relation to the surrounding states (Judea in particular), growing, for example, as the Seleucid dynasty in Syria and Ptolemaic dynasty in Egypt weakened. In all probability, the Nabatean state was formed between the end of the fourth century and the beginning of the third century B.C.E., though clear historical data is lacking. Its end coincided with the Roman conquest of 106 C.E. At its height, the Nabatean state extended from the eastern part of the Nile Delta to the Sinai, the Negev, and what later became the Transjordan; north to south it reached from the Syrian region of the Hauran all the way to the Gulf of Aqaba; in Arabia proper, Nabatean domination included the Hijaz to Hegra (now Medain es-Saleh). Some Nabatean inscriptions have even been found in the oasis of Dedan (now al-'Ula), which was not part of the Nabatean state. The eastern borders of Nabatean territory lay in desert lands, which means that they are difficult to define, but it is known that those lands contained routes that extended toward Mesopotamia. From the Negev, one route reached the Mediterranean, where the Nabateans controlled ports such as Rhinocolura (now el-'Arish) and Gaza.

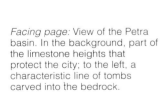

Facing page: View of the Petra basin. In the background, part of the limestone heights that protect the city; to the left, a characteristic line of tombs carved into the bedrock.

Right: View of the city of Petra. The great obelisks of the Zibb 'Atuf, which seem to symbolize divine protection of the place, dominate the landscape. Scholars still disagree about the interpretation of these gigantic, roughly squared stones, their sacredness, and the deity they may symbolize. They are most commonly connected with Dushara and al-'Uzza.

Thanks to commerce—in particular, trade in spices and aromatics from Arabia and the East, a trade in which the Nabateans were long the privileged intermediaries—Nabatean merchants were present from the mid-first century B.C.E. in both the Near East (at Sidon, according to an inscription dating from 4 B.C.E. [*CIS* II, 160]) and the West. Two Nabatean inscriptions discovered in Pozzuoli (*CIS* II, 157 and 158) provide evidence of a Nabatean community there, and the second of these records the construction and renovation of a sanctuary, perhaps in honor of Dushara (an inscription in Latin letters, *Dusari sacrum*, names that deity). A bilingual funerary inscription in Latin and Nabatean found in Rome itself (*CIS* II, 159 = *CIL* VI, 34196) has been attributed to the latter half of the first century C.E., and a second fragmentary bilingual inscription in Latin and Nabatean on a marble slab, clearly of a dedicatory nature, was found in the sanctuary of the Magna Mater on the Palatine.

The territory we have summarily defined presents a great variety of geographical characteristics and climatic conditions, but despite these difficulties it was crisscrossed by caravan trains moving to and from the Mediterranean, Egypt, and North Africa, or Mesopotamia, northern Syria, and the Red Sea. From the geographical point of view, the territory stretches north to south along the rift valley of the Jordan

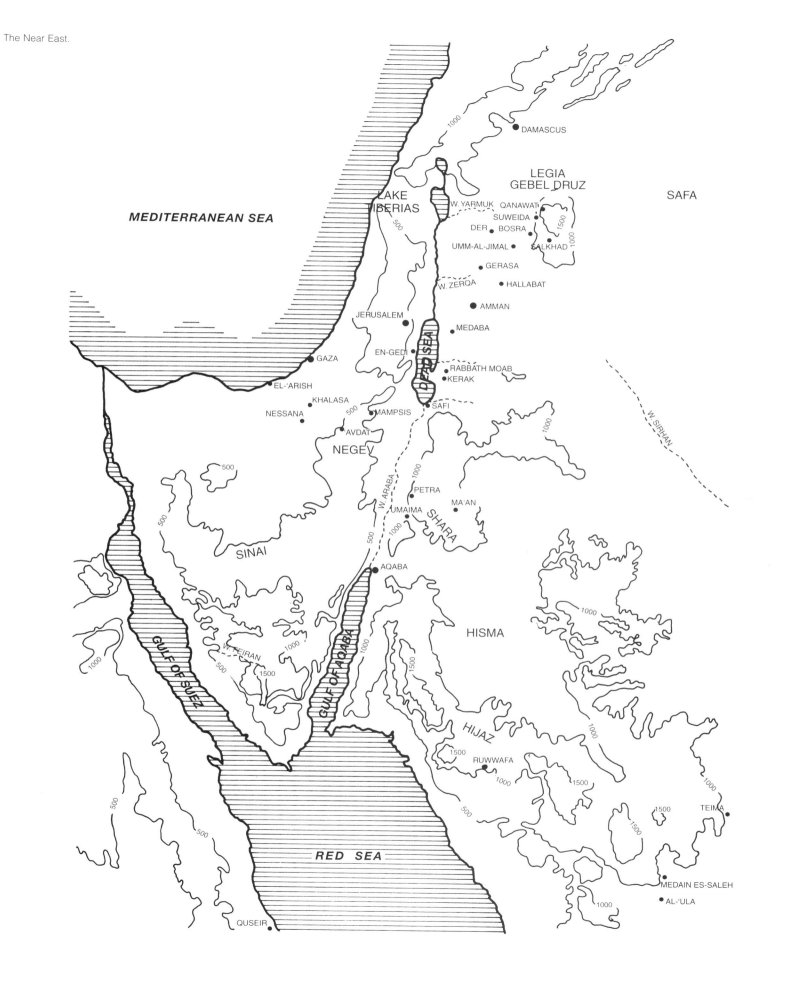

The Near East.

MEDITERRANEAN SEA

DAMASCUS

LEGIA
GEBEL DRUZ

SAFA

LAKE
TIBERIAS

W. YARMUK   QANAWAT
            SUWEIDA
DER   BOSRA
UMM-AL-JIMAL   SALKHAD

GERASA

W. ZERQA   HALLABAT

AMMAN

JERUSALEM

MEDABA

EN-GEDI

DEAD SEA

GAZA

RABBATH MOAB
KERAK

EL-'ARISH

KHALASA

SAFI

MAMPSIS

NESSANA

AVDAT

NEGEV

W. SIRHAN

PETRA

W. ARABA

MA'AN

UMAIMA

SHARA

SINAI

AQABA

GULF OF SUEZ

GULF OF AQABA

HISMA

W. FEIRAN

HIJAZ

RUWWAFA

RED SEA

TEIMA

MEDAIN ES-SALEH

AL-'ULA

QUSEIR

View of the Petra basin with the Qasr el-Bint. This view, taken from the heights of Umm el-Biyara, shows that the gorges cut by the wadis provided relatively easy means of communication for those familiar with the topography.

River, parallel to the Mediterranean coast, between the Lebanon and the Anti-Lebanon mountains. Two depressions in the valley contain Lake Tiberias (the Sea of Galilee) and the Dead Sea, which lies below sea level. South of the Dead Sea, the bed of the Wadi Araba winds its way toward the Gulf of Aqaba.

The Jordan highlands, the northern part of the region to the east of the Dead Sea, is a vast limestone plateau that contrasts strongly with the basalt outcrops that border it to the north and form the tablelands of el-Leja and the massif of Gebel Druz. This plateau is cut perpendicularly by a series of wadis running from east to west. The northernmost of these, the Wadi Yarmuk, was traditionally considered the southern boundary of Syria. Moving southward, the next is the Wadi Zerqa, which passes north of Amman and once marked the northern limits of the biblical region of Moab. Next comes the Wadi Mujib, which cuts through the Moabite region, then the Wadi Hasa, which marks the northern boundary of the ancient land of Edom. South of there, the high plains end in a steep slope followed by a flat, desert zone of clay and limestone.

The communication route between southern Syria and southern Arabia followed the valley of the Wadi Sirhan, to the east and to the south of that region. The route crossed the Jordan plateau, making the zone a busy transit route for traffic coming from the south, from the internal areas to the east, and from the coast. Jordan could also be crossed following the course of the Wadi Yarmuk. Thanks to easy communications, relatively favorable climatic conditions, and, especially, sufficient precipitation for growing crops, the western portion of the Jordanian highlands was always the part of the area best adapted to stable settlement, and it was in fact the site of Gerasa, Philadelphia, and Petra.

The southern portion of this territory is higher, rising to around 1,300 meters then descending abruptly toward the region known as the Hisma. The highest peaks bear the name Shara, a term that may be the origin of the name of Dushara, the principal god of the Nabateans. Crossing this region, then the Hisma, was the preferred route to Aqaba rather than the one that followed the Wadi Araba, where temperatures might be excessively high. The coast of the Red Sea could be reached by crossing the high plateau of the Hijaz rather than by sea from Aqaba, a site on a gulf that was particularly insidious for navigation. Thanks to these routes, connections always existed between southern Arabia and the sedentary peoples east of the Jordan, which is why it is supposed that the Nabatean Arabs originated in this region.

West of Petra and southwest of the Dead Sea lies the region of the Negev, a land that was arid but could be cultivated by irrigation techniques known to ancient peoples. In Nabatean times, in fact, the region was much more thickly inhabited than would seem possible today. Substantial centers existed at Nessana, Khalasa, 'Avdat, and Mampsis. The Sinai, still farther to the south, was instead a genuine desert, and its role was to serve as a route for land communication between Syria and Palestine and Egypt and North Africa.

Although sedentary populations lived on the Jordanian plateau from ancient times, there were always nomadic groups of shepherds on the fringes of settled areas. These shepherds moved according to the seasons but usually remained in the same general territory, shifting place on occasion, probably in search of better pasture. The history of the region has constantly been marked by changes in the relations between the sedentary inhabitants of the urban centers and the nomad groups living at the margins of the region, but also by continual exchanges between the two groups and fluctuations from one type of life to the other as the historical situation changed. The formation of the Nabatean state should be seen within the framework of these relations, although by that time (in distinction to the second millennium B.C.E.), camels had made it possible for nomads to travel long distances in the desert.

Top: A view of the peaks surrounding Petra, known as "the Rock." Differences in the composition of the limestone bedrock of the uplands and strata that react differently to weathering have created rock formations that give the landscape an often spectacular variety.

Bottom: A detail of the limestone strata that make up the rock walls around Petra. Variations in color, often tending toward red or pink, form veins and shape these typical features.

The Nabateans: The Problem of Origins

Greek and Latin texts seem to make no distinction between Nabateans and Arabs, and they often refer to the inhabitants and the king of the state whose capital city was Petra as "Arabs" or "Arabian." Many Nabatean proper nouns are in fact of a type than can be defined as Arabic, even if the language used in inscriptions belongs to the Aramaic group, a family of languages related to Arabic, its northern varieties in particular, but distinct from it. Moreover, in the period preceding the first historical information regarding the Nabateans, the nucleus of the future state—the mountainous territory to the south of the Dead Sea, the depression along the Wadi Araba, the land both to the east of there, and, in more fluctuating fashion, to the west—seems to have been occupied by a population of varied origin that the Hebrew Bible calls "Edomites," their land being called "Edom." The Edomites, according to biblical accounts that were often reworked and are difficult to evaluate as reliable historical sources, were frequently in conflict, first with David (around 1000 B.C.E.), then with the kingdoms of Judah and Israel in the following centuries. They formed a state that remained independent for a relatively short time—flourishing between the late eighth century and the seventh to the sixth century B.C.E.—and which probably was absorbed into the Babylonian Empire under Nabonidus around 550 B.C.E. (information on the conquest is lacking). Up to that time the Edomites had left little direct written evidence, but what does exist shows the use of a language classified as Canaanite—that is, a language that belongs to a group distinct from Aramaic for several characteristics and that displays affinities with Phoenician and Hebrew. It also displays a type of onomastics in which the divine names of Qos and El are common. As was true throughout the ancient Near East, Aramaic, the language of culture and the instrument of communication in the Assyrian Empire and later in the Babylonian and Persian empires, eventually replaced the local Edomite dialect. The historical period between the ninth century and the sixth century is well attested in archaeology, especially at Buseirah, at Tawilan, at Umm el-Biyara, near Petra, and at Tell el-Kheleifeh, on the Gulf of Aqaba.

The next period, which was marked politically by the Persian occupation, then by Hellenistic domination, is poorly documented, and scholars have been unable to establish a secure archaeological continuity between the Edomite settlements and the Nabatean ones that can be distinguished by fine ceramics with painted decoration showing schematic vegetal patterns. It seems certain that Edom formed part of the Fifth Satrapy of the Persian Empire, but there are archaeological sites that furnish contradictory evidence. Still, excavations at Tawilan have produced a tablet that mentions a "King Darius" (not definitely identifiable as one of the three Persian sovereigns of that name) and jewels of an Achaemenid type. John R. Bartlett rightly insists on the continuity of settlement in the zone, albeit on a simpler level. The impoverishment of the area seems to have resulted from a lack of interest on the part of Persia, which tended to prefer the trade routes that cut across southern Arabia to Gaza via the Gulf of Aqaba and thus isolated Petra.

Archaeological data are scarce, but various indications show that the population of the region changed between the fifth century and the third century B.C.E. as an increasing number of people of Arabic origin settled in the land. There are two contrasting views of this historical development: Ernst Axel Knauf reconstructs the rise of the Nabateans in terms of conflict between nomadic and sedentary populations in which the nomadic element gained the upper hand because it enjoyed greater autonomy and had superior combat techniques. The other view, held by the majority of scholars (in particular, in recent years, by Bartlett, David F. Graf, and M. C. A. Macdonald), sees the emergence of the Arab element as the result of a combination of peaceful infiltration and domination of the sedentary inhabitants in a period of power vacuum and a decline in prosperity in the urban centers. Mixed marriages also played a role in this peaceful takeover.

We have evidence of Arab tribes on the periphery of the Near Eastern sedentary states as early as the seventh and sixth centuries. Some of these attestations point, somewhat ambiguously, to two ethnic

The tower tombs or "djin blocks" of the zone of Bab el-Siq. These are among the oldest monuments of Petra, perhaps dating from the first century B.C.E. The later populations of the city thought these massive structures to be water reserves (sahri) or the dwellings of genies. The first scholars of Petra called them "pylons." They provided a tangible memorial to the dead, whose cult was important in Nabatean religion, although we do not know whether the Nabateans believed in survival after death.

Nomads of various "Arabic" groups were known to the Assyrians as early as the seventh century B.C.E. This relief from Nineveh shows a typical "bedouin" camp made up of tents supported by posts. Outside the camp are livestock: sheep, from which this population got meat and wool, and camels, which provided them with a means of transportation over vast reaches of steppes and desert.

The region around what later became Petra was inhabited by populations that the sources call Edomites and, more to the north, Ammonites and Moabites. Seals were a form of artistic production with a fairly broad distribution among these peoples. This red carnelian seal has been classified as Ammonite; it dates from the seventh century B.C.E. The inscription notes its proprietor (Paris: Musée Biblique de Bible et Terre Sainte, no. 6053).

groups, the Qedarites (or Kedarites) and the Nebaioths, as having had something to do with the rise of the Nabateans in regions within Syria and Palestine. Kedar and Nebaioth are mentioned in various places in the Bible: they are twice listed as sons of Ishmael, the son of Abraham (Gen. 25.13; 1 Chron. 1.29), and we are also told that Esau, first of the Edomites, married Mahalath and Basemath, sisters of Nebaioth, son of Ishmael, son of Abraham (Gen. 28.9, 36.3). Other sources of a variety of literary genres, prophecy in particular, depict the Qedarites as people who lived in tents or in villages, but they give no further information about their precise location.

More specific information can be gleaned from the Assyrian annals, which record several revolts on the part of the Qedarites and the defeats they suffered. There are also mentions of their king under the reigns of Sennacherib (690 B.C.E.) and Ashurbanipal (668–627 B.C.E.). The latter is credited with having conquered the Nabayati, defeating their king, Natnu,

during a three-month campaign that began in the area around Palmyra, continued on toward Damascus, and ended in the southern part of el-Leja.

Later, during the Babylonian period, Jeremiah (49.28–33) tells of a campaign by Nebuchadnezzar against the Qedarites. 2 Chronicles gives other references to Arabs in the Persian epoch. Some important information also comes from Herodotus (3.4–5): in 525 B.C.E., Cambyses II called on Arabs at the southern borders of Palestine for help in his Egyptian campaign. Herodotus (3.97) also describes the empire of Darius II (522–486 B.C.E.), naming the Arabs among the peoples who did not pay tribute to the Persians, but the fact that he states that they offered gifts to the king consisting of a thousand talents' worth of incense, an enormous quantity, suggests that these were in reality tribute in the form of merchandise. Herodotus also speaks of an Arab guide in the Egyptian Delta from whom he gathers information on the cult of the gods Orotal and Alilat.

One figure, whose mention perhaps reflects direct sources, is cited in Nehemiah (2.19, 6.1ff.): an Arab named Geshem (Gashmu) who was among those who opposed the governor of Judah (Nehemiah himself) in the year 447 B.C.E. A silver cup from Tell el-Maskhuta, in the eastern Nile Delta, datable to the fifth century B.C.E. is inscribed: "[This is what] Qaynu, son of Gashmu, king of Qedar, has offered to Han-Ilat" (the goddess who appears in Nabatean inscriptions as Allat). Finally, an inscription in Lihyanite from Dedan records a person of the same name, son of Shahr, and a "governor" of Dedan. This may of course be a simple case of homonyms, especially as the name "Gashmu" was fairly common. To end the list, among the northern-Arabic documents found at Gebel Ghunaym, southwest of Teima and northeast of Hegra, there are mentions of wars against the *Nbyt*, a people seemingly located south of the Qedarites.

These mentions raise two main problems. The first is indirectly connected with the Nabateans and regards the real political power of Qedar; the second is the possibility of grouping together the Nabayati of the Assyrian sources, the Nebaioths, the northern-Arabian *Nbyt*, and the Nabateans. The population that we call "Nabatean" may have derived its name from a founding father named Nabaṭu. The phonetic similarities shared by the people cited in the Assyrian annals, the tribe of the biblical Nebaioth, the northern-Arabian *Nbyt* people, and the Nabateans is obvi-

ous. We can add to this list a note in Pliny (*Natural History*, 5.12) that connects the Nabateans and the Cedrei and seems to reflect a link between Nebaioth and the Qedarites. This connection poses a problem of a phonetic order, however, that appears to be insurmountable. The dental consonant written as *ṭ* in the name "Nabaṭu" is articulated differently from the *t* in the name given in the Assyrian sources, the Hebrew Bible, and the inscriptions from near Teima. The dental in the Nabatean name is emphatic; in the Assyrian name, the biblical name, and the name from Gebel Ghunaym, the dental is simple. The names in the sources and inscriptions cited derive from *nby*, not *nbṭ*, which makes it impossible to equate them. In spite of this difficulty, which is stressed, in particular, by Jean Starcky and Israel Eph'al, both Bartlett and Graf remark on the similarity between the two populations and do not exclude a possible identification, or a secondary connection, among these names.

We can say, however, that the sources available reflect the growing presence of an Arab element in Palestine in the Persian epoch. One important confirmation comes from hundreds of ceramic fragments inscribed in Aramaic found in centers in southern Palestine (Arad and Beersheba) and in unspecified sites in ancient Edom, published in past decades, most recently in 1996. These ostraca are accounting documents pertaining to agricultural operations, and they contain traditional Edomite names (which are often compounds in-

Below, left: In Jordanian archaeological sites, a Nabatean presence is typically revealed by highly refined, thin-walled ceramics having a characteristic pale slip. The oldest examples date from the beginning of the first century B.C.E.; the latest, from the early second century C.E. These bowls were found in Petra and date from the first century C.E. (Amman: Archaeological Museum, J 1982 and J 1983).

Below, right: Between the period of Edomite occupation (late ninth century–seventh century B.C.E.) and the era of the Nabatean kingdom, the region of Petra is not well known archaeologically. Very few finds can be dated to the Persian epoch, when the zone must have lost population and undergone a steep decline. None of these characteristic terra cotta figurines of "knights" have been found in the Petra region. These examples come from a tomb at Maqlabien, south of Amman, and date from the seventh century B.C.E. (Amman: Archaeological Museum, J 879).

cluding the name of the god Qos), generic Aramaic names, Hebrew or Phoenician names, and typical northern-Arabic names, in particular those of the Nabatean type. These names testify to a mixed population, but they also demonstrate that agricultural life continued in the region under a well-organized administration. The documents in Aramaic are often dated by the year of reign of a Persian sovereign, thus showing a connection with the imperial administration. In a few cases the inscriptions mention a king named Alexander, twice identifiable as Alexander the Great. Even though some uncertainty remains, this identification has enabled André Lemaire, who has published a portion of these documents, to posit an administrative continuity in the territory during the Hellenistic period despite changes in political regime.

In northern Jordan, the Persian period is documented by findings in a tomb at Umm Udheinah, to the east of Amman. This bronze bowl, datable to the sixth century B.C.E., is shaped like examples from Syria and Palestine. A portion of the Ammonite inscription incised on the border, which indicates the object's owner, has been conserved (Amman: Archaeological Museum, J 14653).

Beginning in the early fourth century B.C.E., Arab groups whose names characteristically ended in -*w* seem to have settled in the area that was to become a part of their state a century later. From the documents cited above, it seems that these Arabs settled gradually, mixing with the local population, as can be seen from inscriptions of the Nabatean era in which Aramaic names persist. There is also evidence of the preservation of preexisting cults, in particular that of the Edomite god Qos.

The problem of where these Arabs originally came from has been taken up on several occasions. For a variety of reasons, some scholars have proposed southern Arabia as the zone of origin; others (J. T. Milik, for example) prefer northern Arabia, on the west coast of the Persian Gulf. It is posited that the Nabateans

moved from there into the region around Petra, settling first at Gaia (el-Ji), then at Reqem (Petra). From Petra they traveled into the Hauran, where they were already present in the mid-third century B.C.E. (as demonstrated by the Zenon papyri), and into the south, around Mecca. An alternate theory has the Nabateans coming from northwest Arabia. This version is based on the name of the Nabatean national god, Dushara, which probably means "the one of Shara," a place name identified with the mountain chain south of Petra. For now, it seems impossible to resolve the question definitively, although the last solution seems the most probable. The ways in which these incoming Arabs assumed political control are debated as well. According to Knauf, in particular (and Lemaire seems to agree with him), the Nabateans

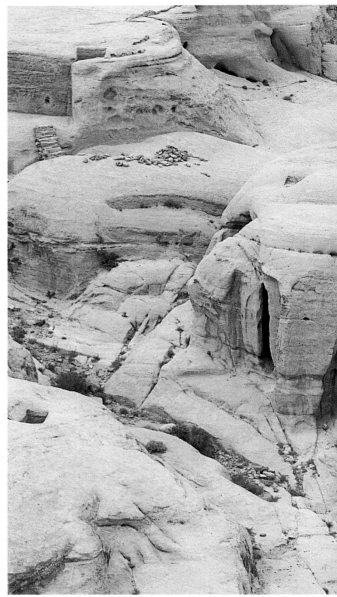

were part of the confederation of the Qedarites; by force of arms, in Persian times, they took control of the Transjordan, in particular, the territory that had been Edom. The most recent analysis of the sources, by Graf, favors Milik's hypothesis that this population originated in northeast Arabia. Graf sees the affirmation of the Nabateans as a progressive migration without notably violent clashes. Choosing among these hypotheses seems complicated, because the available data are insufficient and subject to varying interpretation. What is certain is that Arabic peoples were firmly settled in an Aramaic environment as early as the fifth century B.C.E.; the problems of what might be called their "primitive seat" and of precisely how a group that called itself Nabaṭu took the lead in constituting an autonomous state remain open.

One Petra monument that represents traditions handed down from the distant past and deeply rooted in the Syrian geographical area is the "Lion Monument." A large sculpted block four meters long and two meters high, it stands by the road leading to highest point in the zone of the Wadi Farasah. Traces of channeling over the feline form suggest that a fountain may have been placed here. This animal may also be connected to a female deity, perhaps al-'Uzza. The Syrian goddess Astarte, who shares some characteristics with al-'Uzza, is often associated with a lion.

The city of Petra has no monumental buildings that can be dated reliably to the early period of Nabatean settlement. This curious monument, of uncertain date but perhaps fairly ancient, is in the necropolis of eth-Thurra, southwest of Petra, behind a group of "pylon" tombs. The monument is generally considered to be a tomb, but its true function is unclear, and it may have been a cult building.

The Nabatean Kingdom between Arabia and Syria

From the Origins to the End of the Roman Republic

The Sources

Reconstruction of Nabatean history, especially in the period before the Roman intervention in the Near East, is imprecise and incomplete due to the nature of the available sources. The direct, written documents are inscriptions in Nabatean (in some cases in Greek or, in the later period, in Latin) carved into monuments or rock and a handful of papyri, many of which are fragmentary and difficult to read. The inscriptions and the papyri give no information regarding political events, but they do communicate the language and the written script of the Nabateans, and they relate specific episodes connected with the redaction of the text in question. The monumental inscriptions are for the most part religious in nature—that is, they are dedications to deities or funerary formulas—which means that the information to be gleaned from them regards those contexts. The many graffiti on rock faces recall single individuals or invoke the protection of a god. Even if these inscriptions give no information about historical events, when they are combined with other data they permit us to reconstruct the succession and chronology of the Nabatean kings. The texts are in fact often dated by the year of reign of the sovereign, which means that we can reconstruct not only the line of succession but the genealogy of the ruling house, given that in some cases other members of the royal family are named.

Epigraphic data on the Nabatean dynasties are completed by a series of coins inscribed with legends giving the names of sovereigns and a date during their reigns; comparison of these legends can give an indication of the minimum duration of the reign of the sovereign who coined any given series. The type and weight of the coins enables us to put them in chronological order. In a few cases, the inscriptions include dual dates, one for the year of reign of the Nabatean king, the other for the year of reign of the Seleucid king (an era that began in

312–311 B.C.E.). This synchronism permits us to establish some benchmarks for an absolute chronology, which in turn makes it possible to draw up a general framework in which individual data can be arranged in temporal order with some certainty, although some problems exist. For example, we can reconstruct the list of Nabatean kings from Aretas I (accession ca.170 B.C.E.) to Rabbel II (accession 70–71 C.E.), at whose death Cornelius Palma, the governor of Syria, was ordered by Trajan to annex the Nabatean territory. Dedicatory inscriptions, data derived from archaeological investigation of cult centers, and rare indications in the works of ancient authors, both classical and Islamic, provide a general picture of Nabatean religion, while funerary inscriptions tell us not only about the dead and about burial customs, but also about a number of norms and laws concerning tomb ownership. Not least in importance, we can learn much from personal onomastics: names help us reconstruct the origins of the Nabateans and describe their traditions. On occasion, inscriptions cite the trade or function of the individuals named, thus providing some information on the structure of Nabatean society. Dating formulas in the inscriptions often give the month, which enables us to recreate the Nabatean calendar. Finally, the geographical distribution of the inscriptions falls into patterns that show, at least in general terms, the dimensions of the Nabateans' territory and the ample range of their commercial activities.

The corpus of direct, written sources intersects with literary mentions of the Nabateans and their relations with other states. These are, essentially, a number of passages in 1 and 2 Maccabees that mention the Nabateans or Petra in connection with persons and events in the history of Judea and passages from the works of Flavius Josephus (a writer of Jewish origin) for the period preceding the Roman conquest, of Diodorus Siculus, and, somewhat later, of the geographer Strabo.

The Beginnings of Nabatean History

The oldest literary mentions of the Nabateans refer to 312 B.C.E. and are contained in several chapters of book 19 of the *Bibliotheca historica* of Diodorus Siculus (ca. 80–20 B.C.E.), in which Diodorus recounts the vicissi-

17

The oldest Nabatean coins date from the second century B.C.E., perhaps from the reign of Aretas I. The attribution is uncertain, however, because the coins lack a legend giving the name of the king. This example can be attributed to Malichus I (ca. 50–30 B.C.E.). The king is represented here with his head circled with a diadem, following the Hellenistic scheme. The king's name and the year of his reign are inscribed on the reverse of the coin.

Facing page: The facade of the building known as the Khazneh el-Far'un, "The Pharaoh's Treasury," one of the most elaborate archaeological facades of Petra. Its name derives from a popular legend that an Egyptian pharaoh deposited his wealth here.

tudes of the Diadochi, the successors of Alexander the Great. As he narrates contacts with this unfamiliar population, Diodorus furnishes a picture of its customs from the late fourth century B.C.E. His source, Diodorus tells us, was Hieronymus of Cardia, an eyewitness to the events related. In chapters 94–100, Diodorus describes the attempts, first of Antigonus Monophthalmus, then of his son Demetrius Poliorcetes, to conquer and subject territories to the south and to the east of Palestine, perhaps in preparation for an invasion of Egypt.

In 312 B.C.E., "now that Antigonus without a fight had gained possession of all Syria and Phoenicia, he desired to make a campaign against the land of the Arabs who are called Nabataeans" (Diodorus, 19.94.1). He sent two expeditions, but they failed to procure the easy success he had hoped for. Diodorus relates (19.95.1–5) that the first of these expeditions was led by one of Antigonus's generals, Athenaeus, to whom he gave "four thousand foot-soldiers and six hundred horsemen . . . and ordered him to set upon the barbarians suddenly and cut off all their cattle as booty" (19.94.1). The plan was to surprise the Arabs, who had gathered for an annual feast day, leaving their possessions, their old people, and their women and children near some rocks (a word given here as *pétras*, elsewhere in the text in the singular). These "rocks," which we can identify as Petra, are described as impenetrable but unfortified. The Nabateans were indeed taken by surprise, according to plan, and when Athenaeus's soldiers went to the "rock," they captured prisoners and garnered a booty that included incense, myrrh, and five hundred silver talents. The Nabateans, however, pursued the Greeks, falling on their camp by surprise and wiping them out. On their return to the "rock," they sent Antigonus a message "in Syrian characters" (*syríois grámmasi;* 19.96) complaining of Athenaeus. Antigonus responded diplomatically, but he also ordered his son Demetrius to move against the Arabs and exact revenge for the defeat.

This time the Nabateans were determined not to be caught unprepared: the sentinels they posted as guards used smoke signals to warn of the approach of the new attack, and the Nabateans in the meantime had already dispersed their flocks to hidden and scattered sites so they could not be captured. After various negotiations Demetrius withdrew. He was unable to conquer Petra, obtaining only hostages and gifts.

Jean Starcky (*DBS*, cols. 903–904) draws a connection between this first encounter between Greeks and the Nabateans and a note in Stephanus of Byzantium, a grammarian of the first half of the sixth century C.E., who writes: "Motho, a village in Arabia where Antigonus, the Macedonian, died at the hands of Rabilos the king of the Arabs, according to Uranius, in his fifth book. . . . In the language of the Arabs [the place name] means 'place of death.'" Antigonus is often corrected to read "Antiochus," and the passage is connected with Antiochus XII, who defeated the Nabateans at Kana but lost his life in the battle, as Flavius Josephus reports (*Jewish Antiquities*, 13.391). In reality, the Nabatean king who took part in that battle was an Obodas, which suggests that the "Rabilos" mentioned by Stephanus was not the Nabatean king, but the leader of the troops who defeated Athenaeus in the age of Antigonus.

The next mentions of the Nabateans date from the mid-third century B.C.E. and consist in information contained in two papyri of the Zenon archive, found in Egypt at Gerza, also known as Philadelphia, in the Faiyum. One papyrus of 259 B.C.E., year 27 of the reign of Ptolemy II Philadelphus, names "the people of Rabbelos" in relation to a shipment of grain. A second contemporary papyrus speaks of Nabateans in the Hauran. This mention is important because it shows that the Nabatean penetration in that northern region had already occurred in the third century B.C.E.

It is possible, as G. W. Bowersock states, that in the same period the Nabateans had already partially settled in the Negev. The oldest known Nabatean inscription, now lost, came in fact from Khalasa, the ancient Elusa, a settlement on the caravan route from Petra to Gaza. The graphic and photographic documentation of the inscription, although not of the best quality, shows a notably archaic script, still close to the Aramaic writing of the Persian era, and a language that is also archaic in comparison to what might be called classic Nabatean. The text states: "This is the [sanctified?] place / built by / Natiru / at the time of / Aretas / king / of the Nabateans." The "Aretas" mentioned here (written *ḥrtt* in Nabatean) is perhaps Aretas I, who is mentioned in 2 Maccabees. Milik, on the other hand, basing his opinion on the archaic form of the letters, considers the inscription to refer to a previous sovereign, and he dates it to the third century B.C.E. (See *Journal of Biblical Literature*, 1955, p. 160, n. 25.) Starcky dates the inscription to about 200 B.C.E.

Between the end of the fourth century and the third century B.C.E., various sources show the Nabateans already present in the localities that were to be their territory in later ages, when historical information and direct sources become more abundant. Diodorus Siculus, still drawing on Hieronymus of Cardia, describes the customs and lifestyle of the population in this early period. The Nabateans, he states, were pastoralists who had no

houses, but lived in the open, raising sheep and camels. They were a people used to surviving in the desert, thanks to their skill in creating underground reservoirs and hiding them from outside eyes. They were also merchants: some of them became wealthy thanks to trade in incense, myrrh, and other spices that they procured from the populations of Arabia Felix (Diodorus, 19.94.5). Hence at the end of the fourth century B.C.E., the Nabateans were already functioning as intermediaries in the conveyance by land of merchandise from the east and from the south to the Mediterranean ports of Gaza and Rhinocolura. The Nabateans must have already held a degree of monopoly on the sale of asphalt from the Dead Sea, which may be why Demetrius failed in his attempt to procure that commodity after his defeat: he was immediately attacked by six thousand Arabs and forced to withdraw.

The Nabatean Kingdom: Second Century B.C.E. to Augustus

The next mention of the Nabateans in literary sources derives from their relations with the Maccabee brothers (ca. 170–135 B.C.E.), members of a Jewish family, the Hasmoneans, known by the nickname ("Maccabeus") given to Judas, one of the heads of the revolt (which led to a period of Judean independence) launched by a conservative faction among the Jews in 168–167 B.C.E. against the Seleucid Syrian king, Antiochus IV Epiphanes, who ruled

Judea as a subject territory. The Maccabees' participation in this revolt is narrated in the four books of the Maccabees, only the first two of which (conserved in Greek, although the original texts were certainly in Hebrew) are considered canonical by the Roman Catholic Church and thus are included in the Bible. The mentions of the Nabateans are in 1 Maccabees 5.25–26, 9.35–36 and 2 Maccabees 5.8, 12.10–12. These passages give information on specific events, but they fail to present a clear historical framework for the Nabatean state in that period. It is likely that the Nabateans, like the Judeans, sought to take advantage of the political and economic decline of the Seleucid dynasty to augment their own power and regain possession, as far as possible, of portions of the territory held by the Syrian kings. We know of a king named Aretas in this period, by convention called Aretas I (170–160 B.C.E.), the sovereign mentioned in 2 Maccabees 5.8 as the tyrant of the Nabateans, whom scholars tend to equate with the king named in the Khalasa inscription, basing their identification on the archaic nature of the written signs in that epigraph. 2 Maccabees 4.23–29 tells us that in 168 B.C.E. Menelaus outbid the high priest Jason for his charge and replaced him. 2 Maccabees 5.8 relates the end of Jason's career: "At length he met a miserable end. Called to account before Aretas, king of the Arabs, he fled from city to city, hunted by all men, hated as a transgressor of the laws, abhorred as the butcher of his country and his countrymen. After being

View of part of the theater with the city of Petra beyond. When the Nabateans had achieved a notable degree of autonomy and prosperity, in part thanks to the decline of the Hellenistic powers, they embellished their city with the monuments that make it unique. At the same time, they sought to extend their territories at the expense of nearby states that had also gained autonomy, Judea in particular.

View of the orchestra and the
stage area of the theater.

Facing page: The cavea and
part of the stage area, as seen
from inside a rock dwelling. The
theater's plan is typically Roman,
and its construction can be
dated to the reign of Aretas IV
(9-8 B.C.E–40-41 C.E.).

driven into Egypt, he crossed the sea to the Spartans."
The Greek version has Jason fleeing "from city to city,"
but in the reading given in the *Vetus Latina*, L and X, the
city to which he fled was Petra.

1 Maccabees 5.24–27 states that after three days'
march through the desert beyond the Jordan, Judas Maccabeus and his brother Jonathan "met some Nabateans,
who received them peacefully and told them all that had
happened to the Jews in Gilead." The references to
Gilead and to a three-day march both lead to the supposition (supported by Bowersock) that this meeting took
place in the Hauran, where a Nabatean presence is attested, as we have seen, from the mid-third century B.C.E.

A passage in 2 Maccabees (12.10–12) parallels the
earlier account but tells of a violent encounter between
nomads, generally identified as Nabateans, and the
Judeans. Given the contrast between the hostility in this
passage and the friendly attitude described in 1 Maccabees, we can suppose, with Bowersock (*Roman Arabia*,
20–21), that the hostile nomads described here were of
another northern-Arabian ethnic group. A few years
later, and in the context of encounters near Medaba between the Jews and the Seleucid general Bacchides, 1
Maccabees 9.35–42 speaks of a genuine alliance between Jonathan and the Nabateans: Jonathan calls the
Nabateans "his friends" and leaves baggage with them,
then attacks another Arab group defined as "the sons of
Jambri" after they raided his baggage deposit. This is all
highly likely, given that the Nabateans, who were sedentary at this point, had at least temporary relations of alliance with their neighbors, the Judeans, whereas such
hostile encounters might easily have taken place with

Tombs in the necropolis at the exit from the Siq. The tombs shown here, part of a group of three structures, present interesting double cornices. Their poor state of conservation does not permit evaluation of the architectonic elements as a whole, but it does display the composition of the rock, as is particularly clear in the structure in the background (Brünnow and Domaszewski, Petra, no. 70).

consisted of perfumes and spices) could sail up the Red Sea coast, dominated by the Nabateans, to reach Egypt directly by ship, and from there continue on to the Mediterranean without having to cross the interior by the Petra-Gaza land route. This meant that Nabatean piracy perhaps derived, at least in part, from a desire to protect their own commercial routes. As early as the mid-first century C.E., in fact, commercial traffic by the land route through Petra was reduced. The episodes narrated in Diodorus and Strabo thus show not only the importance of trade, but also the struggles that took place to gain and hold a commercial monopoly.

This period—that is, before 100 B.C.E.—may quite possibly have been the time of the reign of a first King Rabbel (in Nabatean, *rb'l*), named in a fragmentary inscription on the base of a statue found in Petra, not far from the Qasr el-Bint Far'un. The text records the dedication and the renovation of a statue of Rabbel, "king of the Nabateans," in year 18 of King Aretas. Starcky dates the inscription at 67 B.C.E. The writing style is still rather archaic, and we can estimate that some forty or fifty years elapsed between the erection of the statue and its rehabilitation. Thus it seems highly unlikely that the King Rabbel named here, whose patronymic has disappeared in the broken portion of the inscription, could have been a direct predecessor of Aretas III.

This means that before Aretas III, there must have been an Aretas II who reigned from around 100 B.C.E. That sovereign would have been the first to have hostile relations with the neighboring state of Judea, which was in full expansion. Conflict, with alternating victories and defeats on either side, characterized the history of the two states from that time on. Our information on this period comes essentially from Flavius Josephus, both from *Jewish Antiquities* and *The Jewish War*, at times completed by information from other writers, such as Plutarch and Dio Cassius.

To summarize briefly: Judea under the Maccabees succeeded in obtaining its independence and extending its dominion over some of the Greek cities of Syria, in particular under another Hasmonean, John Hyrcanus, the son of Simon, the youngest of the Maccabee brothers, who was killed in 135 B.C.E. Soon, however, internal revolt broke out, in particular between the parties of the Sadducees and the Pharisees, and discord was especially violent during the reign of Alexander Jannaeus, the brother of Aristobulus I (104–103 B.C.E.), successor to John Hyrcanus. Josephus (*Jewish Antiquities*, 13.358–363) relates that when Alexander besieged Gaza, the inhabitants called on Aretas, king of the

northern-Arabian groups, perhaps brigand bands with whom the Nabateans may have had previous unpleasant experiences. At the end of the second century B.C.E., Diodorus Siculus reports (and his source in this instance was probably Agatharchides of Cnidus, ca. 130–110 B.C.E.) that the Nabateans were active on the coasts of the Red Sea. He describes them as pastoralists with vast herds who lived honestly until the kings of Alexandria (the Ptolemies) opened a trade route in the area, at which point the Nabateans took up piracy, but after some success in that career, they were captured by a fleet of quadriremes and punished (Diodorus, 3.43.4–5). Strabo seems to refer to the same episode when he writes: "These Nabataeans formerly lived a peaceful life, but later, by means of rafts, went to plundering the vessels of people sailing from Aegypt. But they paid the penalty when a fleet went over and sacked their country" (16.4.18). Nabatean piracy has been connected with the new Egyptian maritime commerce that developed as a result of the discovery that the monsoons were seasonal (*Periplus Maris Erythraei*, 57; Pliny, *Natural History*, 6.100, 104). Thanks to dependable winds, merchandise from the East (which mainly

Arabs, for aid, but without success, given that the city was conquered before Aretas could reach it. It seems natural that the Nabateans should intervene in favor of Gaza, one of the principal ports that provided an outlet for goods that the Nabateans transshipped through Petra. Even if Aretas was unable to regain Gaza, we have some indications that the Nabateans flourished under his reign. The first Nabatean coins not struck in the mints of the Seleucids and the Ptolemies are in fact assigned to that king. This attribution is not totally sure, because these bronze coins, which bear a helmeted head on the obverse and a figure of victory on the reverse, bear no dynastic name. Some of them bear a sign that might be a Greek *a* or *l* (α or λ), and two examples show a non-Greek letter that might be the Aramaic *ḥ*, the initial letter of the name of Aretas. These coins have been found in notable numbers, especially at Petra and at Gaza, where they clearly demonstrate the presence of Nabatean commerce in that port city around 100 B.C.E.

Aside from the episode of the siege of Gaza, we know nothing of the events that occurred in the Nabatean kingdom under Aretas II. It is possible that he was the same person as the Arab king Herotimus who reportedly headed a group of formerly peaceful Arabs whose raiding parties were menacing Egypt and Syria. Justin, an author of the second to third century C.E., tells us of Herotimus in his *Historiarum Philippicarum* (29.5), an epitome of the *Historiae Philippicae* of Pompeius Trogus. This information would seem to fit Aretas II, who appears to have headed an expanding state, but it also might apply to the reign of Aretas III.

Information on Obodas I (in Nabatean, *'bdt*), the son and successor of Aretas II and venerated as a god by the Nabateans, is relatively more abundant. First, we have an inscription that dates from the first year of his reign and comes from Petra, where it is conserved today. Near the Siq, the narrow gorge that gives access to the city, there is a space carved into the rock known as the Triclinium. This space, which was divided into a principal chamber and two smaller contiguous rooms with a cistern, was devoted to gatherings and cult-related banquets. On one wall of the principal room a carved dedication in archaic script can be dated, according to the tracing of the characters, to between the late second century and the early first century B.C.E. It is addressed to Dushara, the principal god of the Nabateans, "for the life of Obodas, king of the Nabateans, son of Aretas, king of the Nabateans, year 1." Later inscriptions refer to "Obodas the god" and extend chronologically to the late first century and early second century C.E.

Literary sources also tell us about this sovereign. Flavius Josephus (*Jewish Antiquities*, 13.375) gives information on the conflicts between the state of Judea, under Alexander Jannaeus, and Obodas. In 93 B.C.E., a king of the Arabs of that name defeated Alexander in battle near Gadara, in the Golan, probably as a result of Alexander's attempts to extend his power over the southern territories of Palestine, the ancient lands of Galaad and Moab. These attempts were in part successful, given that around 90 B.C.E. Alexander Jannaeus returned the lands he had conquered, whether because he was pressed to do so by Demetrius III, king of Damascus at the time, or "in order that" Obodas "might not aid the Jews in the war against him" (*Jewish Antiquities*, 13.382). It seems clear from this passage that it was part of the foreign policy of the Nabatean kings of this period to take full advantage of internal divisions among the Jews. But it was undoubtedly the very success of that policy and the growth of Nabatean power that led to a reaction on the part of the Seleucid kings of Syria (see Bowersock, *Roman Arabia*, 24).

Antiochus XII, who succeeded Demetrius III, in fact organized two campaigns against the Arabs, the first in

88–87 and the second in 85 B.C.E. During the course of the second campaign, fought along the Palestinian coast with Alexander Jannaeus as Syria's prime adversary, Antiochus was subjected to a surprise attack near Jaffa by "ten thousand Nabatean horsemen," whom he thought had retreated toward the Negev (*Jewish Antiquities*, 13.387–391; *Jewish War*, 1.99–102). The death of Antiochus XII decided the outcome of the battle in the Nabateans' favor. The Syrians fled toward an unidentified place given as "Kana," where nearly all of them died of starvation. The king of the Arabs was most probably Obodas I, as stated by Starcky (*DBS*, col. 906). Even though he won the battle, however, Obodas seems not to have survived it for long: Stephanus of Byzantium, under the heading "Oboda," refers to a "village in Nabatea [where, according to] Uranius, in book 4 of his *Arabica*, 'Obadas the king, whom they venerate as a god, has his grave.'" The divine status of Obodas is confirmed, not only by epigraphic evidence, but also by a fairly common Nabatean name, 'Abd'obodat, or "servant of Obodas." The village of Obodas (or Oboda), which has been identified as today's 'Avdat (located to the northwest of Petra, on the road to Gaza), is the site of a temple and the source of many inscriptions from the Nabatean era, available, in particular, thanks to the archaeological and epigraphic research of Avraham Negev.

Aretas III (88-85–62 B.C.E.?), called "Philhellene" on the coins that he had minted in Damascus (84–72 B.C.E.), was Obodas's successor and probably his son. Under his reign the Nabatean state reached its greatest physical extent. Called in aid by the citizens of Damascus, who were engaged in a war with the Ituraeans of Anti-Lebanon under the leadership of the tetrarch of Chalcis, Ptolemaeus, the son of Mennaeus (*Jewish Antiquities*, 13.392), Aretas took possession of the city peacefully and retained dominion over it until 72 B.C.E. The proposed dates are taken from the series of coins cited above, which imitated the Seleucid coins. In 72 B.C.E. Damascus was conquered by Tigranes I of Armenia, who retained control of the city until 69 B.C.E., when he was forced to leave Syria after Lucullus's invasion of his kingdom (*Jewish Antiquities*, 13.419–421). Aretas did not attempt to reconquer Damascus: in 70–69, the Damascenes coined their own money, and the city remained something of a power void easily penetrated by Pompey's army not long after.

When Aretas became ruler of Damascus in 82 B.C.E., he declared war on Alexander, invading Palestine and defeating the Jewish king at Adida, near Lydda. Alexander reacted by advancing into the Transjordan and southern Syria (*Jewish War*, 1.104–105) and conquering various inhabited centers, in particular, Gaza, Raphia, and

A series of tomb facades in the theater necropolis so neatly lined up that they almost appear to be buildings along a street.

Rhinocolura, ports on the Mediterranean coast that had belonged to the Nabateans, as well as twelve villages in Moab and Idumea. Alexander died in 76, leaving power in the hands of his widow, Alexandra. According to Flavius Josephus, Alexandra managed to maintain a degree of equilibrium, but within her state the influence of the Pharisees was growing, to the point that they seem to have taken over effective control, constraining Alexandra to do their will and put their enemies to death. The Nabateans opposed the power of the Pharisees by giving refuge to their enemies (*Jewish Antiquities*, 13.409–414).

Alexandra died in 67 B.C.E., setting off a power struggle between her sons, Hyrcanus (who later ruled as Hyrcanus II), the elder son, who had functioned as high priest and was the designated heir to the throne, and Aristobulus (soon to rule as Aristobulus II). The two fought at Jericho, with Aristobulus winning the battle. On the advice of an Idumean named Antipater (who had married Cypros, a Nabatean and the mother of Herod and Salome [*Jewish War*, 1.181]), Hyrcanus took refuge at Petra with King Aretas (*Jewish Antiquities*, 14.4–17; *Jewish War*, 1.117–125), who—again—was hoping to profit from internal discord in the Jewish state. Hyrcanus and Antipater urged Aretas to take up arms against the Judean forces under Aristobulus, promising to restore to him the territories that Alexander Jannaeus had conquered—that is, "the territory and the twelve cities which his father Alexander had taken from the Arabs" (*Jewish Antiquities*, 14.18). Aretas did indeed move against Aristobulus, defeating him and forcing him to withdraw to Jerusalem, which Aretas attacked around Passover in 65 B.C.E. Now, however—and for the first time—Aretas was forced to confront the power of Rome, which was making its presence felt in the East.

In reality, the weakness of the Seleucid state, the rise of a number of autonomous principalities, and the lack of a strong power in the region encouraged Pompey to send his legates, Quintus Metellus and Lollius, to Damascus (*Jewish Antiquities*, 14.29; *Jewish War*, 1.127), where they took power. Another legate sent by Pompey, Marcus Aemilius Scaurus, joined them there from Armenia, where he had fought against Tigranes, but Scaurus set off again immediately for Judea. Each of the opposed factions in Jerusalem sought the aid of Rome for its own interests (*Jewish Antiquities*, 14.29–30). According to Josephus, when Aristobulus sent Scaurus a sum of three hundred thousand talents (*Jewish War*, 1.128), the Roman was persuaded to support him and to demand that Aretas raise the siege, under the threat that if he failed to do so, he would become an enemy of the Roman people. According to various ancient sources (Diodorus Siculus and Strabo, as well as Flavius Josephus), it was not money alone that induced Pompey and Scaurus to support Aristobulus's cause. The fact remains, however, that Hyrcanus was stripped of power and the Nabateans were too weak to stand up to Judea. For that reason it seemed more advantageous to the Romans to defeat the Nabateans in order to hold that part of Syria solidly under their control.

Faced with the threat posed by the Roman army, Aretas broke his siege of Jerusalem in 64 B.C.E., and Scaurus returned to Damascus. Aristobulus then pursued the Nabateans, whom he defeated in a pitched battle at Papyron, in the Jordan Valley (*Jewish Antiquities*, 14.33; *Jewish War*, 1.130).

In the same year, Pompey went to Syria, where he reorganized the region into a new province, recognizing the autonomy of a group of Hellenized cities, the so-called Decapolis. The southern part of the territory was less tranquil, however: in Judea, the struggle between Aristobulus and Hyrcanus had not been definitively resolved, and the Pharisees were attempting to overthrow the Hasmonean dynasty (*Jewish Antiquities*, 14.41–45). In "Arab" territory the situation of the Nabatean state at the time is unclear. Pompey decided to move against the Nabateans, for reasons that scholars still debate (Was he seeking submission? The payment of tribute?). Josephus reports only that Pompey "took the army that he had prepared against the Nabataeans" (*Jewish Antiquities*, 14.48). Immediately after, in 63 B.C.E., he moved against Jerusalem, conquered the city, and then left the Near East at the beginning of the following year, entrusting the province to Scaurus. Scaurus undertook a number of expeditions in Nabatean territories (*Jewish Antiquities*, 14.80), perhaps to raise money: Josephus states that Aretas paid a tribute of three hundred silver talents (*Jewish Antiquities*, 14.81).

On his return to Rome, Scaurus became aedile in 58 B.C.E. Coins struck for the occasion depict Aretas kneeling beside a camel. This was not to celebrate a victory, because one never actually took place: rather, it was a representation of a formal submission. Appian (*Syrian Wars*, 51) tells us that Scaurus's successors, Marcius Philippus (61–60 B.C.E.) and Marcellinus Lentulus (59–58 B.C.E.), pushed back Arab incursions, but Appian, like most ancient authors, uses the term "Arab" unspecifically and does not say whether these were Nabateans or other populations in the area. The end of the reign of Aretas III and the precise year of his death are not known.

Facade of the tomb of 'Unaishu (Brünnow and Domaszewski, Petra, no. 813), who is described in an inscription as minister to queen Shaqilat, the mother and for a time regent of Rabbel II (70–106 C.E.).

We do know, however, that in 56 B.C.E. and perhaps earlier, the king of Petra was called Malichus (I) (in Nabatean, *mlkw*) and that he reigned, to judge from the coins struck bearing the year of his reign, for at least twenty-eight years. He was succeeded by a king named Obodas who died (again, judging by numismatic evidence) in the winter of 9–8 B.C.E. and who had drachmas coined that weigh about 5.5 grams and bear the legend, "Obodas, king of Nabaṭu," followed by the year of his reign. Coins weighing 6.5 grams minted according to Phoenician standards were put out with the legend, "Obodas, the king, king of Nabaṭu year two" (or "year three," "five," or "six"). Some scholars rely on diversities in style to divide these coins between two different kings named "Obodas," suggesting that an "Obodas II" reigned before Malichus at some time between 62 and 56 B.C.E., perhaps between 62 and 60. This chronology has recently been revised on the basis of a Nabatean inscription found at Tell esh-Shuqafiya, in Egypt, that bears a dual dating. It was redacted in the fourteenth (or perhaps the eighteenth) year of the reign of Cleopatra, which corresponds to the twenty-sixth year of the reign of Malichus. When this text was first published, its editors placed it at 37–36 B.C.E., setting the accession of Malichus to the throne at 63–62 B.C.E., thus eliminating the king Obodas who preceded Malichus. Now, however, on the basis of a proposal by Starcky, the same edi-

tors prefer the reading of the numeral as eighteen, thus dating the inscription to 34 B.C.E. This implies that a King Obodas (II), to whom they attribute the drachmas mentioning years one through three of his reign, sat on the throne in 62–61 B.C.E. Malichus would thus have acceded to the throne in 59–58 B.C.E.

It is certain, however, that it was under Malichus I in 55 B.C.E. that Aulus Gabinius, proconsul of Syria, "marched against the Nabateans, whom he overcame in battle" (*Jewish Antiquities*, 14.103; *Jewish War*, 1.178). This expedition, like its predecessors, must have been undertaken in the aim not only of obtaining tribute, but also of maintaining a firm hold on the southern frontier of the empire and facilitating land travel to Egypt. At this point the Nabatean state was unable to avoid the quarrels typical of Rome in the years of the civil war and the triumvirate, and Malichus found that he had to make a choice between Caesar and Pompey, then between Caesar's assassins and Mark Antony, and then between the latter and Octavian. Even in his own territory, rivalries in Judea obligated Malichus to support one faction or the other. Antipater, the adviser of the Nabatean king who had supported Hyrcanus against his brother Aristobulus, continued his operations in these later years as well. He persuaded Malichus to support Caesar against Pompey, then, in 47 B.C.E., to send Nabatean horsemen to reinforce the troops of Mithridates of Pergamum, who had gone to Pelusium to lend support to Caesar. In chapter 1 of *The Alexandrian War*, Caesar tells us that "Malichus, king of the Nabataeans," was there in person.

In this instance, Malichus's choice proved to be a wise one. But Caesar was assassinated in 44, and after his death the war between the conspirators and Mark Antony, who had defended Caesar, was transferred to the Near East. There one of Caesar's former generals, Quintus Labienus, surnamed Parthicus, called on the Parthians for aid. In the meantime, Antipater died, poisoned, in 43; his son Herod (better known as Herod the Great) took his father's place as minister to Hyrcanus, who in the meantime had become both high priest and ethnarch. In 40 B.C.E. the Parthians besieged Jerusalem. Herod, wanting to avoid taking a stand, sought refuge with Malichus, from whom he also requested restitution of loans made to Antipater (*Jewish Antiquities*, 14.370; *Jewish War*, 1.246–247). Malichus refused to receive him, however, and instead lent support to the Parthians. Herod then went to Alexandria, then on to Brindisi and to Rome, where he appealed to Mark Antony, who persuaded the Senate to confer on Herod the title of king of the Jews (*Jewish Antiquities*, 14.379–380; *Jewish War*, 1.267, 274–285). In the Near East, the Parthians were defeated in 39 B.C.E. by Ventidius Bassus, and Malichus sustained heavy taxes as a result (Dio Cassius, 48.41.5).

When the empire was partitioned among the triumvirs, Mark Antony was awarded the eastern portion. On that occasion he came into contact with Cleopatra, then queen in Egypt, who sought to reinforce the power of the dynasty of the Ptolemies and demanded a number of territories from Rome, in particular, Judea and the lands of the Arabs (*Jewish Antiquities*, 15.92; *Jewish War*, 1.360). As far as the Nabateans are concerned, it seems that in 34 B.C.E. Cleopatra succeeded in obtaining extensive lands, but it is not clear precisely what these were: aside from the balsam plantations of Jericho, formerly under Herod's control, Plutarch tells us that among other lands she received "all that part of Arabia Nabataea which slopes toward the outer sea" (*Parallel Lives*, Antony, 36.2). Given that in ancient texts the Mediterranean was called "the inner sea," this is certainly not a reference to Mediterranean coastal zones, but perhaps to an area on the coast of the Red Sea around the Gulf of Aqaba crossed by a commercial route that led to Petra, as Bowersock, in particular, sustains. A less likely supposition is that the expression "outer sea" designated the Dead Sea. Malichus was charged with administering the territories in that region, paying over its earnings, while Herod was named guarantor of the payments (*Jewish Antiquities*, 15.96, 107, 132). It seems that Malichus failed to meet these payments, however, because Mark Antony forced Herod to declare war on him. Flavius Josephus tells us that this led Cleopatra to hope that the two kings would destroy one another (*Jewish Antiquities*, 15.110).

There were two main parts to this campaign. One took place in the Hauran, in the northern portion of the Nabatean territory. Its outcome was indecisive: the Jews won a first battle at Diospolis (*Jewish Antiquities*, 15.111; *Jewish War*, 1.366), but they were defeated near Gebel Druz at Canatha (today's Qanawat) (*Jewish Antiquities*, 15.112; *Jewish War*, 1.366), and Herod chose to make peace. The second conflict, in 31 B.C.E., was launched by Malichus, who had Herod's envoys killed. According to Flavius Josephus, what Malichus had in mind was the conquest of Judea (*Jewish Antiquities*, 15.124; *Jewish War*, 1.371). The Nabatean army was led by a certain Elthemus. The battle took place near Philadelphia (Amman), and it proved to be a serious defeat for the Nabateans (*Jewish Antiquities*, 15.147–152; *Jewish War*, 1.371). Herod was proclaimed "protector" (*prostates*) of the Nabatean people (*Jewish Antiquities*, 15.159).

In that same year, 31 B.C.E., however, Mark Antony was defeated at Actium, which means that Herod's victory had no evident consequences. The Roman policies in the East passed into the hands of Octavian, whose good graces the local states sought to win. Herod, who had supported Mark Antony and who feared that Octavian might return local power to the aging Hyrcanus (who had attempted, with the acquiescence of Malichus, to take refuge in Petra), had Hyrcanus strangled (*Jewish Antiquities*, 15. 170–172). Josephus tells us that Malichus was put to death by Cleopatra (*Jewish War*, 1.440), but this affirmation, which places his death in 35 B.C.E., is uncorroborated. The Nabateans, probably still under the government of Malichus, sent their forces to destroy the ships that Cleopatra sought to put to sea near Suez in an attempt to flee from Octavian (Plutarch, *Parallel Lives*, Antony, 69; Dio Cassius, 51.7.1). Toward the end of 30 B.C.E., Cleopatra committed suicide, and Egypt was placed under the rule of a prefect. As for Malichus, he did not live long: in fact, Obodas, his successor (who died in 9–8 B.C.E.), coined money for at least twenty years, which means that he must have ascended the throne around 30 B.C.E.

The First Century of the Roman Empire

With the Battle of Actium and the Roman annexation of Egypt, the political picture in the Near East changed completely. The kingdoms of Arabia and Judea, which stretched along the two sides of the Jordan Valley, had to deal with Roman legates to the north in the province of Syria, and with Roman prefects to the southeast in the new province of Egypt. For Rome, closing the circle of provinces along all the southern and eastern coasts of the Mediterranean and incorporating Palestine and the Nabatean state was simply a matter of time.

In 27 B.C.E., when Octavian became *princeps* and the Senate conferred on him the title of "Augustus," Herod managed to win favor from the emperor and obtain control of nearly all of the territories of Palestine as an official gift.

In the same period, Aelius Gallus, the first prefect of Egypt, led an expedition into the Arabian Peninsula from spring or summer 26 B.C.E. through autumn 25 B.C.E. in support of Rome's expansionist policies. The objective of this expedition, which included in its forces some one thousand Nabateans and five hundred Jews, was not the Nabatean kingdom, which the Romans were beginning to call simply "Arabia," but rather the kingdom of the Sabaeans, in the southeastern corner of the Arabian Peninsula that was known as Arabia Felix. The Sabaeans had become wealthy thanks to the commerce in perfumes and spices, controlled by the Nabateans, that reached Yemen from India and continued on to ports on the Mediterranean. Marib, the capital of the Sabaean kingdom, was an important point on the incense route between northern and central Arabia and the Gulf of Aden.

Strabo, who was a personal friend of Gallus's, gives a detailed account of the Arabian expedition (16.4.22–24). According to his version of events, Augustus intended to exercise some sort of control over the Sabaeans (and indirectly over trade in the Red Sea and the Indian Ocean) by making them allies of Rome or subjecting their territory to Roman supervision. The expedition ended disastrously, however, in part because of a terrible lack of water. Strabo, not wanting to attribute its failure to Gallus, blames Syllaeus, the

General view of the great "royal" tombs along the western face of el-Khubtha, the large massif that borders the Petra basin to the east.

epitropus (administrator, or prime minister) to King Obodas. He reports that Syllaeus, who served as a native guide for the Roman forces, deliberately deceived them and scattered the members of the expedition. Augustus took no revenge against the Nabateans, however, which probably proves that he did not hold them responsible for the failure of the expedition.

The Nabateans continued their commercial activities in the Augustan age. They controlled the major currents of mercantile traffic that came from the Persian Gulf, through the desert, and from Aqaba. A large number of inscriptions attest to their presence in major Mediterranean ports from Sidon on the Phoenician coast to Pozzuoli, where a Nabatean trading post existed as early as the second half of the first century B.C.E.

The principal problem facing Obodas and the Nabatean dynasty was the growing power of Herod and of the kingdom of Judea, which had spread into the Golan, creating a territory under Jewish control between Syria and Nabatean Arabia. According to Flavius Josephus's account of events (*Jewish Antiquities*, 16.224), Syllaeus, who was well aware of the danger inherent in this situation, attempted to contract a dynastic marriage by requesting the hand of Herod's sister, Salome. Syllaeus, the sources tell us, was a

good-looking man and Salome had no objections, but Herod opposed the union.

In 12 B.C.E., when Herod was in Rome, a revolt broke out in the kingdom of Judea. Because the Nabateans were lending support to the rebels, conflict with Herod broke out again, and it was resolved with the death of a Nabatean general and part of his contingent. Syllaeus himself went to Rome to lodge a protest against the king of Judea with Augustus, describing the situation of his people in particularly dramatic terms: according to him, at least 2,500 Nabateans had died because of Herod's invasion, which, incidentally, had been undertaken without the authorization of Rome.

Obodas died while Syllaeus, his minister, was in Rome. According to Josephus (*Jewish Antiquities*, 16.294), power passed to a certain Aeneas, who took the dynastic name of Aretas when he became king, a detail indicating that he was probably not in the direct line of descent of the royal family. There is a Nabatean inscription that suggests, however, that he may have had some connection with the royal house through Malichus, Obodas's predecessor. The new king sought to diminish the prestige of the powerful Syllaeus and limit his probable aspirations to the Nabatean throne by sending a letter to Augustus in

which he accused the prime minister of a number of crimes, including the death of Obodas, whom he claimed that Syllaeus had poisoned. Augustus's initial reaction to Aretas's accession to the throne was negative, however, because the new king had neglected to ask Rome's permission before assuming power.

The emperor's intention seemed at the time to be to assign the entire kingdom of Arabia to Herod, a move that would have unified the lands on the two banks of the Jordan and ended a situation of eternal rivalry. Instability within the kingdom of Judea persuaded him not to do so, however, and instead he confirmed Aretas (known to modern historians as Aretas IV) on the Nabatean throne. Syllaeus returned to Petra, where (according to Flavius Josephus) he launched a campaign of political assassination that included the elimination of a certain number of Nabatean nobles and an attempt on Herod's life. In 6 B.C.E. he returned to Rome in the hope of regaining the favor of Augustus, but not long after he was decapitated on the order of the emperor, as Strabo reports (16.4.24).

Two years later, at the death of Herod in the spring of 4 B.C.E., the political situation that was developing in the Near East raised a number of problems. Augustus was dissatisfied with the presence of Aretas IV on

the Nabatean throne, but he put little trust in Herod's three sons, among whom their father had divided his kingdom, and he hesitated to assign the title of king to any of them. Herod's son Archelaus (known as Herod Archelaus) reigned as ethnarch in Judea, Idumea, and Samaria; Herod Antipas was tetrarch of Perea and Galilee; another son, Herod Philip, controlled the Transjordan territories to the north, including Auranitis.

After having finally approved Herod's testament, Augustus sent his grandson Gaius Caesar to the Near East with various diplomatic missions on behalf of Rome. One of these was an *expeditio arabica* in 1 B.C.E., of which Pliny the Elder speaks at length (*Natural History*, 2.168; 6.141, 160; 12.55–56). A few years later, in 6 C.E., Augustus put an end to the power of Herod's various successors, transforming Judea into a province governed by a procurator of equestrian rank.

The literary sources for this period are surprisingly scanty, and even Flavius Josephus leaves a good many lacunae. We have numismatic evidence, however, of the reign of Aretas IV (8 B.C.E.–40 C.E.). Confident of support from Rome, Aretas headed the Nabatean kingdom in a period of extraordinary development and great prosperity, favored by a stable situation on the opposite bank of the Jordan and a greater degree of political stability in the central regions of Herod's former kingdom. In Galilee, one of the tetrarchies that had survived the constitution of the province of Judea, Herod Antipas took as his wife one of Aretas's daughters (*Jewish Antiquities*, 18.109), thus realizing the type of dynastic marriage that had been typical of the diplomacy of his grandfather, Antipater, in the age of the Hasmoneans.

For a period of about thirty years, from 1 to 30 C.E., the literary sources relate no historical events in the Nabatean kingdom, but the archaeological evidence is more than eloquent. Economic prosperity and political stability favored an increasing urbanization of the territory and a notable amount of building activity, both in Petra and in other parts of the kingdom. Construction seems in fact to have been one of the aspects most characteristic of the policies and the economic development promoted by Aretas IV. This period saw a notable development of the cities of the Negev—Oboda, Mampsis, Nessana, Elusa, and Sobata—thanks to the Petra-Gaza caravan route, the principal commercial artery and connection between the southern Transjordan and the Mediterranean.

Not only commercial activity remained intense and profitable during the reign of Aretas IV; agriculture, supported by a network of settlements, grew as well. Techniques for collecting and storing water and irrigating the land were naturally among the prime requisites for both agricultural and urban expansion, and it was probably in this same period that a sophisticated system was developed for storing rain water and delivering it to cultivated fields through channels that ran along a series of built-up terraces.

There must have been a deliberate campaign to transform the Nabatean settlement of Hegra, in the Hijaz (today's Medain es-Saleh in Saudi Arabia) into a major Nabatean center. Grandiose rupestrian tombs were constructed in an architectural style very similar to Petra's, and in many cases they bear inscriptions that permit secure dating. All of these constructions belong to the first century C.E., in particular, to the first half of that century. The sudden growth of Hegra in this period suggests that Aretas IV intended to create an outpost in the Hijaz, and the military nature of the settlement is clearly attested by the unusually large number of funerary inscriptions by or for members of the Nabatean army. It is no coincidence that coins give the name of King Aretas, with the titulary *philodēmos*, "who loves his people."

The royal court resided at Petra, where archaeolog-

ical excavations during the last forty years have revealed a surprisingly flourishing city between the latter half of the first century B.C.E. and the first century C.E. During the reigns of Obodas II (III) and Aretas IV, in fact, the most important civic and religious monuments of the city were built: the Khazneh, the Qasr el-Bint, the Temple of the Winged Lions, and the theater. The city's cosmopolitan nature and its cultural atmosphere can easily be seen from Strabo's description of the Nabateans around 25 C.E.: "Petra is always ruled by some king from the royal family." Not only did the king live grandly, but his subjects' "houses, through the use of stone, are costly" (16.4.26). Petra had become an international center: Strabo reports that the philosopher Athenodorus of Tarsus, a friend of his from whom he also received information, declared that "he found both many Romans and many other foreigners sojourning there" (16.4.21). Strabo also tells us that the city contained many gardens and the surrounding territory supplied generous amounts of fruit.

Around 27 C.E., during the last years of the reign of Tiberius, the stable situation that had been created in the Jordan Valley was seriously compromised when Herod Antipas repudiated his Nabatean wife. He had in fact become enamored of Herodias, the daughter of one of his half-brothers and the wife of another half-brother named Herod. Aretas took the occasion to move forward with an invasion of Herod Antipas's tetrarchy (an act he may already have had in mind) in the aim of reconquering traditionally Nabatean territories and such sites as Suweida, Qanawat, and Si' in the Hauran.

It has been suggested that on this occasion Aretas even managed to control the city of Damascus for a short time. In a familiar passage of 2 Corinthians, St. Paul describes his singular escape from Damascus (2 Cor. 11.32–33) by being lowered from a window in a basket. Paul states explicitly that he had to flee because "in Damascus the ethnarch of King Aretas was keeping a close watch on the city in order to arrest me." As the passage is written, it seems to credit the ethnarch with authority over the walls of Damascus, but it is unclear whether this implies a genuine Nabatean control over the Syrian city in the latter years of the reign of Aretas IV or whether the ethnarch had responsibility for the Nabatean colony residing in Damascus, hence for the Nabatean quarter alone.

Whatever the case may be, after his defeat at the hands of the Nabatean king, Herod Antipas presented a

formal protest to Tiberius, who ordered Vitellius, the governor of Syria after 35 C.E., to march on Petra. When the emperor died and was succeeded by Gaius Caesar, now emperor Gaius, known as Caligula, the situation changed. In a gesture of favor toward Herod Agrippa, his boyhood friend and Herod's grandson, Caligula granted him the tetrarchy that had been Herod Antipas's, thus removing it from Syria once more.

We know from numismatic evidence that Aretas himself died three years later, in 40–41 C.E., and was succeeded by Malichus II, who was probably his oldest son and the legitimate heir. This is reported in two inscriptions at Petra, which give the names of the wives, sons, and daughters of Aretas and of their spouses. By all indications, the new sovereign pursued the same economic policies as his father in commerce, agriculture, and a progressive urbanization of the territory.

A passage in the *Periplus Maris Erithraei* shows that some commercial traffic continued to move along the old arteries that crossed Nabatean territory. Although the anonymous author of this text recognized the new importance for trade between India and the port cities of Egypt that the sea route had taken on after the discovery of the seasonal nature of the monsoon winds, he stresses that the Nabateans were still shipping merchandise from Petra to the Mediterranean.

Pliny, too, notes the continuing importance of Petra and its favorable position at the crossroads of two routes, "one leading from Syria [through] Palmyra, and the other coming from Gaza" (*Natural History*, 6. 32.145). With time, the northern route, which went by way of Palmyra to the Persian Gulf ports of Forat and Charax, at the mouth of the Tigris and the Euphrates, acquired increasing importance because it was the shorter route, and Palmyrene merchants profited from the increase in their activities to the detriment of Petra and the Nabateans.

Before he died, Caligula deposed Herod Antipas and assigned Galilee to Herod Agrippa. In gratitude for his aid in securing the imperial throne after Caligula, Claudius rewarded Herod Agrippa with all of the territory formerly of the province of Judea, thus reconstituting, for a short time, the kingdom of Herod the Great. Herod Agrippa died three years later, and in 44 C.E. Judea returned to being a province and the territories of Herod Philip's tetrarchy were once again united to Syria.

The Nabatean kingdom under Malichus II was probably still to some extent informally dependent on Rome, given that Flavius Josephus relates that

Malichus sent a thousand horsemen and five hundred foot soldiers to augment the forces that Titus was gathering in Ptolemaïs in 67 C.E. for a campaign against the Jews (*Jewish War*, 3.4, 68). Nabatean coinage was interrupted during the Jewish wars, and scholars have put forward the suggestive hypothesis that this was because the political crisis induced the Romans to requisition silver in order to pay their troops. This and other arguments have led to the supposition that the Nabatean kingdom experienced a temporary decline in prosperity and increased political and economic weakness during the reign of Malichus II.

One inscription bearing two dates—one Nabatean, the other Seleucid—places the end of the reign of Malichus and the succession of Rabbel II in the year 70–71 C.E. Rabbel came to the throne at such a young age that coins show him with his mother Shaqilat, who reigned as regent for some six years.

The sense of well-being and increased political stability in the Nabatean kingdom is clear in the expression that accompanies the new sovereign's name in inscriptions: "who has brought life and deliverance to his people." The historical situation was favorable. The civil war in Judea and Titus's conquest of Jerusalem in August and September of 70 C.E., after a thirteen-month siege, had definitively eliminated rivalry with the Jewish kingdom. The Nabateans maintained control over their own territory, developed and expanded terrace agriculture in the Negev, and promoted increased permanent settlement in the north of the country.

During the reign of the last Nabatean kings, a slow decline in the commercial role of Petra was accompanied by the gradual development of Bosra, which later became the capital of the province. Thanks to its links with Damascus to the north, with the hinterland beyond the Wadi Sirhan to the south, and with Petra and the Gulf of Aqaba to the southwest, Bosra, a city situated in the fertile region of the Hauran, was a point of crucial importance for Nabatean interests in the northern portion of the kingdom.

The increased importance of Bosra did not mean that Petra ceased to be an international metropolis, nor that Petra did not still fulfill its function as the center of Nabatean power. With wealth accumulated under political stability in its days of glory, Petra's urban plan became increasingly monumental, and construction continued into the early decades of the following century, after the annexation of the kingdom into the Roman Empire.

The Roman Province of Arabia

It is not clear what led Trajan to the decision to annex the Nabatean kingdom in 106 C.E. During the reign of Rabbel II the situation of the Nabateans and of the entire territory on both sides of the Jordan was, as we have seen, particularly favorable and tranquil. Further proof of this is a group of papyri that were hidden in caves to the west of the Dead Sea, near en-Gedi, in 132 C.E., the time of the great Jewish revolt under the leadership of Bar Kokhba, during the reign of the emperor Hadrian. These papyri form the family archive of a Jewish woman named Babatha, daughter of Simeon, who lived at Mahoza, near Zoar (an area formerly in the Nabatean kingdom that had become part of the Roman province of Arabia in 106 C.E.), and whose life was in danger due to family circumstances. These documents, written in Greek, Nabatean, and Aramaic, cover the entire period of the transition from the Nabatean kingdom to the new province of Arabia, and they clearly attest to formal recognition of the Roman Empire and its institutions on the part of the population.

The archive includes four documents redacted during the final years of the reign of Rabbel II. The oldest of these dates from 93 C.E.; the most recent, from the year 99. They describe in detail complex legal negotiations between Arabs and Jews in the borderlands that met at the south shore of the Dead Sea, and they attest to the existence of peaceful and stable relations among the communities of the Jordan Valley.

None of the documents in this archive dates to the year the Nabatean kingdom ended or the years immediately after; the majority of the papyri can be placed chronologically in the period following the constitution of the province, and they regard a series of legal actions initiated by Babatha after the death of her two husbands to assure financial support for the son of her first marriage and to protect herself from demands made by another wife of her second husband.

What is most significant about these texts is the completely Roman character of the law applied in this frontier territory of Greco-Hellenistic and Semitic traditions and the fact that the Greek language is used, beginning with a document datable to 124 C.E. and continuing to the final one, datable to 19 August 132, not only for official letters and petitions to the governor of the province and to personalities of the administrative establishment, but in the redaction of private transactions as well. The documents also report the names of Roman governors otherwise unknown and, more in particular, some information on the status of Petra within the province of Arabia.

Although these documents are exceptionally interesting, they reveal little about the formation of the province and are highly unclear regarding the modalities of annexation. Babatha's documents do tell us, however, that Rabbel II had a son named Obodas, who should have been his heir apparent, hence we cannot hypothesize that annexation came about because the royal dynasty was extinct.

Ancient literary sources are hardly more illuminating on this point. The Byzantine compiler Dio Cassius reports (though there is no way to judge the accuracy of his version of the original text) that the governor of Syria, Cornelius Palma, "subdued Arabia, the one near Petra, and made it subject to the Romans" (68.14). When Ammianus Marcellinus writes about the creation of the province, he tells us that Arabia was "compelled by our laws by the emperor Trajan [*obtemperare legibus nostris Traianus compulit imperator*], who, by frequent victories crushed the arrogance of its inhabitants when he was waging glorious war with Media and the Parthians" (14.8.13). The same events are reported by Eutropius (8.2), Festus (14.3), and Eusebius (*Chronica*, 2118).

It is not clear whether the verb *compulit*, as Ammianus uses it, indicates armed force or peaceful diplomatic negotiations. Nothing is known about the conditions and the characteristics of the annexation except that it involved the participation of the governor of Syria, which would seem to suggest some sort of military action. The legend that appears on later commemorative coins states *Arabia adquisita*, not *Arabia capta*, the usual formula for territories conquered by force of arms. Moreover, Trajan never adopted the title of *Arabicus*, whereas only one year earlier, after the annexation of Dacia in 105–106 C.E., he assumed the title of *Dacicus*. It is highly likely that the occupation of the Nabatean kingdom was not totally peaceful and involved some coercion, but it was not determined by a genuine battle, and the entire operation probably took place after the death of Rabbel II.

With Roman governance, Nabatean silver coins were replaced by the provincial drachma with Trajan's portrait on the obverse and a personification of Arabia

Wadi Farasah, the Tomb of the Broken Pediment. The composition of the facade displays elements typical of the rupestrian architecture of Petra. The broken pediment that surmounts the facade recalls the architecture of Syria in the Hellenistic and Roman ages. A pair of half-pediments caps a tetrastyle facade made up of four pilasters with quarter-columns and Nabatean capitals.

with a camel on the reverse. For the Romans, the annexation of the Nabatean kingdom implied total control over the entire area of the eastern Mediterranean from Egypt to Judea and Syria, a control that was the indispensable precondition for the great expedition that Trajan was planning against the Parthians farther to the east. It also implied the elimination of the Nabateans' function as intermediaries in commercial traffic and the definitive integration of their kingdom into the empire. Immediately after 106 C.E., in fact, work began on the Via Nova Traiana, the many milestones of which all record dates after the year 111.

Trajan's road was some 340 kilometers long, and it stretched *a finibus Syriae usque a mare Rubrum*. During the period of its construction and in the years immediately following, the governor of the province was C. Claudius Severus, who seems to have replaced Cornelius Palma right after the formal annexation of Arabia and to have remained in his post at least until 115. Despite the ostentatiously propagandistic character of the milestones (which proclaimed that the emperor Trajan *aperuit et stravit*—opened and paved—the road), the new road followed a route known and used from the end of the second millennium B.C.E. Improving this artery had a strategic aim, given that Trajan was preparing to invade Mesopotamia, but its prime reasons for being were economic and administrative: it

united upper Galilee with the Jordanian plateau, linking them to Arabia and facilitating communication among cities and villages as well as improving a military route. When the province of Arabia was created, it was under the direct control of the emperor, not the Senate, and it was governed by a *legatus Augusti pro praetore*. Its area coincided roughly with that of the Nabatean kingdom (the central portion of that kingdom in particular), with the addition of a few cities of the northern Transjordan such as Gerasa and Philadelphia (the modern Amman), and with the inclusion of the Negev. The Hauran region was of course an integral part of Arabia. The new capital, Bosra, was in that region, as was the camp of the only legion stationed in the province until the age of Diocletian, the *III Cyrenaica*. The earliest inscription to mention a military unit, a soldier's dedication, comes from Petra and is carved into the southern slope of the Siq. It is probable, however, that at first another legion, the *VI Ferrata*, aided by *vexillationes* from the *III Cyrenaica*, made up the major military force.

A good number of graffiti in Greek and Latin attest to the presence of Roman auxiliary troops from the territory of the Hijaz, in the northwestern part of what is now Saudi Arabia. They refer to an *ala Gaetulorum* and an *ala dromedariorum*, but rather than armed contingents sent to defend the frontiers, these

The Renaissance Tomb (Brünnow and Domaszewski, Petra, no. 229). This elegant pediment structure, with a molded portal surmounted by an arch, overlooks the Wadi Farasah.

43

probably refer to an armed escort for caravans making their way to the port cities.

Although Bosra had become the capital of the province, Trajan apparently had no intention of lessening the role of the ancient city of Petra as an important center in the southern sector of the Arabian territories. An inscription dated to 114 C.E., found along Petra's Colonnaded Street in 1958, can doubtless be connected to the effort to enhance the monumental character of that street, since it refers to Petra as a *metropolis*. The same term appears ten years later in a document in Babatha's archive (dated to 124) that is an extract of the "acts of the Senate of Petra, metropolis of Arabia"—a body presided over by the provincial governor. This does not mean, as has been

supposed, that at that late date the Roman legate still resided in Petra rather than Bosra. As has been demonstrated on several occasions, the legate was responsible for administering justice in all the urban centers of the province. Petra's title of "metropolis" was probably more honorific than political, and administrative, economic, and military power were by then undoubtedly centered in Bosra.

Hadrian pursued many of the same economic policies as Trajan. Given that the projected conquest of Mesopotamia had ended badly, Hadrian set the border of the province west of the Euphrates. After peace was reestablished with the Parthians and the northern trade route reopened, commerce with the Far East revived, but more to the advantage of Palmyra than to

Petra, and it was there that Sextius Florentinus, the governor in 127 C.E., chose to be buried.

Hadrian certainly visited Bosra, and we know that on his way toward Palestine and Jerusalem he spent the winter at Gerasa, where his presence was commemorated by the construction of a triumphal arch.

The major Jewish revolt that devastated Judea from 132 to 135 C.E. does not seem to have had repercussions in Bosra and Petra, and the tranquillity and political stability of the region during the second century are attested by buildings constructed after Hadrian's reign in the cities he had visited.

Even the great expedition against the Parthians led by Lucius Verus in the years 163–165 C.E. had little effect on the southern area, as was also the case with the revolt of the governor of Syria, Avidius Cassius, against Marcus Aurelius. The existence of a temple dedicated to Marcus Aurelius and Lucius Verus by a confederation of Thamudic Arabs at Ruwwafa, northwest of Medain es-Saleh, is proof of the calm that reigned even in the frontier zones. Moreover, the presence of an Arab confederation at the periphery of the Roman province would seem to confirm Rome's utilization of semi-sedentary tribes to control a relatively inaccessible region. Only with the civil wars that brought Septimus Severus to the throne did the history of the province of Arabia enter into a new phase. Another governor of Syria, Pescennius Niger, proclaimed himself emperor at Antioch in 193 C.E. Once again the province of Arabia, as previously in the case of Avidius Cassius, refused to follow the governor of Syria. The *III Cyrenaica* must have done the same, for later the legion was granted the title *Severiana*, clear proof of its loyalty and the emperor's gratitude.

Once he had been proclaimed emperor, Septimus Severus divided Syria into two: Syria Coele and Syria Phoenice (194 or 195 C.E.), thus notably enlarging the northern borders of Arabia. This redistribution of the frontiers can most probably be assigned to the period of the second Mesopotamian War, commanded by Severus, which led to the annexation to Rome of the area between the Tigris and the Euphrates. The successful outcome of the campaign must have created a propitious moment for redefining the borders of the provinces to the west of the new province of Mesopotamia to the benefit of Arabia. Subjecting the frontier areas to order safeguarded Roman economic interests and helped develop a new and more active flow of commercial exchanges and a wider circulation of money.

that of Petra. Hadrian can be credited, however, with reopening the southern caravan route across the Arabian Peninsula toward the ports of the Red Sea, and with the decision to return the Nabateans to a more active role in commerce by encouraging relations between Rome and some of the desert tribes southeast of Petra, integrating them into the Roman system for the defense and control of both the routes and the territory in general.

The province received an imperial visit during Hadrian's trip to the Near East in 129–130 C.E. Given that Bosra had already received from Hadrian's predecessor the honorific title of *Nea Traiane*, Petra was granted the title *Hadriane*, as coins attest. The first governors of the province made frequent visits to

The close connection between the emperors of the Severan dynasty and this part of the Near East derived from special ties linking the Syrian component of the imperial family to the East. Julia Domna was the center of a circle of intellectuals who encouraged the presence at the court in Rome of persons of Eastern origin—Syrians, Palmyrenes, and Arabs. Many cities situated along the frontier from Arabia to the Tigris earned the status of *colonia*: Petra became a colony under Elagabalus, and Severus Alexander conferred the same title on Bosra some years later. Petra continued to be the only city of Arabia to enjoy the title of *metropolis*, however, an honor conferred on Bosra only under the emperor Philip the Arab mid-century. Military dedications carved into the walls of the Siq attest that the ancient capital of the Nabatean kingdom was still a center of some importance.

In the early decades of the third century C.E., the power of the Parthian dynasty of the Aracids was overthrown by Ardashir, founder of the new Persian state of the Sassanid Persians (226 C.E.). From the Roman point of view, the new dynasty's aggressive policies inaugurated a period of great instability in the Near East and an almost continual succession of invasions and retreats, followed by short-lived periods of informal peace. In 242 C.E., the young emperor Gordianus III led a misguided expedition against the Sassanids that ended, two years later, with his death at the hand of his own soldiers not far from the city of Dura-Europos. The troops then proclaimed as emperor of the East Marcus Julius Philippus (Philip the Arab), who was the praetorian prefect of Jordan and perhaps the instigator of Gordianus's death. Philip was an Arab from the city of Shobha, and his origins gave him the advantages not only of a mastery of local languages but also of a profound understanding of the situation in the Near East.

Although fourth-century sources (*Epitome de Caesaribus*, 28.4; *Scriptores Historiae Augustae, Gordiani tres*, 29.1) speak of Philip as a person of low social extraction—*humili genere natus*, the son of a *latro*, or brigand—the family of the new emperor was actually of equestrian rank and must therefore have belonged to the provincial upper middle class.

Philip concluded the war with the Sassanids at the price of great humiliation for the Romans, and he created a new type of military command in the East by naming his brother Julius Priscus *rector Orientis*. The reign of Philip the Arab lasted for five years, until 249 C.E., when he and his son, with whom he shared im-

perial power, were in turn eliminated in a revolt led by one of his generals, Decius Trajanus.

The mid-third century was marked by the conquest of Antioch, on the Orontes River, and by the capture of the emperor Valerian by the Persian king, Shāpūr, events followed by a brief secessionist movement on the part of the Palmyrene dynasty.

The Sassanid invasion of Syria and Anatolia seems, on the surface, to have spared the province of Arabia, which, although it played a marginal role in these events, still enjoyed a vital and eclectic culture profoundly linked to the tradition of eastern Hellenism. Petra was the city of birth of two of the most famous Sophists of the age, Callinicus and Genethlius, and under the reign of Philip or soon after, the *actia Dusaria* (sacred games for athletes and artists) were instituted at Bosra, the center of the imperial cult for the entire province.

The grave political difficulties caused by the Sassanid Persian invasions, the Gothic invasions, and the economic uncertainty they brought to the East, along with the deep-seated impotence of the central government and a general awareness of that weakness, had created in the population of the province not only widespread and profound discontent, but the more fundamental problem of resistance and defense against the invaders.

In the 260s, this overall situation of instability favored the rise of Palmyra as the controlling city in the East, a hegemony first pursued by prince Odaenathus, with the consent of the emperor, Gallienus, and later by Odaenathus's widow, Zenobia, who was responsible for the short-lived secession of the principality of Palmyra. Early in 270 C.E., when a large part of the Syrian territory was probably already under the control of Palmyra, Zenobia launched an expedition aimed at conquering Egypt by marching across Arabia and Palestine, with the ultimate intent of controlling all the transit routes to the Indies. An indispensable precondition for the success of this military operation and for assuring the security of the route to the south was obviously control of Arabia and the entire length of the Via Nova Traiana.

Information on the Palmyrene expedition into Arabia is reported only by the Byzantine historian Malalas (*Chronographia*, 12.299), but what he relates seems to be confirmed by epigraphy. His narration of the massacre of the Roman garrison by Palmyrene troops is reflected in a famous inscription from Bosra that speaks of the reconstruction of the temple of

Jupiter Ammon, which the Palmyrenes—*a Pal]myre-nis hostibu[s*—had destroyed. The Palmyrenes thus seem to have been responsible for the destruction of the camp of the *III Cyrenaica*, a legion devoted to the cult of that god, and for the elimination of a contingent that might have been capable of stopping their advance. Archaeological evidence seems to confirm the accuracy of Malalas's account in another passage: traces of destruction and widespread fire have been attested by excavations in the Qasr el-Bint at Petra, and other sites in Arabia underwent the same fate in the same overall time period.

The extension of Palmyrene power in Arabia was of short duration—about two years—ending when the decisive intervention of emperor Aurelian (273 C.E.) brought the Palmyrene dynasty to an end. With Aurelian's victory, the Near East was again part of the circuit of exchanges operating within the Roman Empire. Analysis of coins furnishes clear proof of the political and economic isolation of the entire area during the mid-third century and confirmation of renewed relations with the East at the end of that century. It is only with Diocletian, however, and with the victory of Galerius (made Caesar by Diocletian) over the Sassanid king, Narses (297 C.E.), that the situation on the Persian front truly changed and the balance of power that had dictated conditions for nearly the entire century was reversed. Diocletian's reform of the provincial territories included broad changes that also affected Arabia. The province was drastically reduced in size, eventually coinciding geographically with the rich agricultural region of the Hauran, an area that was easier to control. The Negev, Aila, Petra, and part of the Sinai Peninsula were incorporated into the province of Palaestina Salutaris (later called Palaestina Tertia). The Nabatean area was administered, for civil matters, by a *praeses* operating under a *dux* of military rank who controlled two or three of the provincial subdivisions.

The removal from the province of the southern territories reveals Rome's concern about the nomadic tribes, and it coincides with Petra's period of decline. The violent earthquake that struck the entire region on 19 May 363 C.E. undoubtedly hastened that decline, given that it destroyed many monuments there, among them the theater and the Qasr el-Bint, which were never reconstructed. It is also interesting to note that Ammianus Marcellinus (14.8.13) does not list Petra among the *oppida quaedam ingentes* of Arabia, recording only Bosra, Gerasa, and Philadelphia. Dur-

ing the second half of the century the porticos of the Colonnaded Street in Petra were turned into shops, and the presence of late-Roman and Byzantine houses reveals a continuity of life in the city at least until the sixth century.

Documentation regarding the spread of Christianity in Petra is scant. As early as the fourth century there was a Christian community in the city, which in the same period became the seat of a bishopric. The records of ecclesiastical councils have preserved the names of a number of bishops: in 447 a Bishop Jason was responsible for transforming a rupestrian tomb into a church. Nonetheless, despite the presence of Christian chapels and cemeteries, the reuse of pagan buildings for religious and domestic purposes, and the recent discovery of a basilica, the attestations are sporadic, seeming to confirm that urban life in Petra was slowing to a halt. Although the

Interior of a chamber (Brünnow and Domaszewski, Petra, no. 468) excavated out of the rock, eastern slope of the Gebel ed-Deir. A niche fitted into the back wall of an otherwise unadorned room has a rich entablature with a Doric frieze, a second frieze with draped busts of figures holding a torch carved near the outside corners, and a small pediment with acroteria. The room has no facade and must have been used for a ritual purpose.

territory of the former province had a certain prosperity in the Byzantine age, with a lively renewal of building activity that is revealed by the richness and the number of the Christian buildings in Bosra and Gerasa, this revival does not seem to have involved the ancient center of Nabatean culture to the same extent. In fact, paganism seems to have survived there longer than elsewhere. St. Epiphanius, who was born in southern Palestine, wrote in 375–377 that the cult of Dushara was still strong in Petra (*Panarion*, 51.22.9–119); Sozomenus (*Historia Ecclesiastica*, 8.5.11), names Petra among the cities where "the Hellenists were still fighting for their temples"; and in the early fifth century the Syriac monk Bar Sauma was permitted to enter into the city, which was suffering from a severe drought, only after he had produced a miraculous rainfall.

After the Arabic conquest of 636, the metropolitanate of Petra was transferred to Rabbath Moab, south of the Arnon River. It was only in the age of the crusades that Petra found itself along a major strategic line for the defense of Jerusalem and recovered a bit of its former prestige. In 1116, Baldwin I erected a number of small forts north of the city as well as the castles of Li Vaux Moïse (now Wu'eirah) and al-Habis.

Petra lay too far to the east of the pilgrimage route to Mecca to be of interest to Muslims, and among the Arabian historians only al-Nuwairi records the visit that sultan Baibars made to Petra in 1276, during a voyage from Egypt to Kerak.

Petra and the Caravan Trade

Although the commercial contacts between the Mediterranean basin, the Red Sea, and the regions of the Indian Ocean date from the age of the Old Kingdom (third millennium B.C.E.), they are better documented in the Hellenistic and Roman periods, when the networks of caravan roads and maritime routes linking the Mediterranean world to the territories of the East were denser.

The ancient sources, in particular Agatharchides of Cnidus (through Diodorus Siculus), Artemidorus (in Strabo), Pliny the Elder, the *Periplus Maris Erythraei*, and the geographer Ptolemy, offer detailed evidence, from the second century B.C.E. to the second century C.E., of the nature, volume, range, and intensity of these east-west relations. To this documentation we can add inscriptions and the references contained in Indian poems and summaries of Chinese history. Before Alexander, Strabo tells us, Gerrhaeans who had settled on the Arabian coast of the Persian Gulf transported cargo on rafts to Babylon, then continued up the Euphrates to Tapsaco to trade with Phoenicians from Aradus (16.3.3). In the same period the merchants of Tyre and Sidon knew a maritime route along the coast of the Arabian Peninsula, if we can believe Lucian (*Rhetorum Praeceptor*, 5), who speaks of a Sidon merchant who promised Alexander, in Persia at the time, that he could show him a shorter route back to Egypt. That southern route, which also used the trails of western Arabia to arrive at the Mediterranean in Palestine and Phoenicia, was traveled most intensely in the Hellenistic age, and it was the route that determined the Nabateans' monopoly of commercial traffic.

The earliest historical reference to Nabatean commerce is in Diodorus Siculus (19.94.4–8), who observes that "while there are many Arabian tribes who use the desert as pasture, the Nabateans far surpass the others in wealth . . . for not a few of them are accustomed to bring down to the sea frankincense and myrrh and the most valuable kinds of spices, which they procure from those who convey them from what is called Arabia Eudaemon."

It is clear from this passage that the Nabateans functioned as intermediaries in a commerce in frankincense and myrrh that was controlled by the southern Arabian kingdoms of Hadramaut and Hymar and by the Sabaeans, who also held a monopoly on production. From Sabbatha, the capital of the Hadramaut kingdom, and from Qana, the principal port of the entire southern coast of the Arabian Peninsula, the caravan route wound its way north, along the western side of the peninsula, to reach Aqaba (in Roman times, Aila), continuing on to Petra.

Diodorus (3.42.5) provides interesting details about the mining and commercial exploitation of asphalt from the Dead Sea by the Arabian peoples who lived nearby, the Nabateans in particular.

In his description of the island of Phocae off the Sinai Peninsula (probably one of the small islands near the entrance to the Gulf of Aqaba, perhaps Sanāfir or Tirān), Strabo (16.4.8) states that the region extended as far as "the land of the Nabatean Arabs, as they are called, to the Palestine country, whither the Minaeans and the Gerrhaeans and all of the neighboring peoples convey their loads of aromatics."

Petra thus lay at a juncture between the route that ran parallel to the Red Sea, which crossed the southern-Arabian territories, and the trans-Arabian routes to the north. The merchandise that left India reached the rich Arabian emporia of the Persian Gulf at Gerrha (near the modern Oqair, on the Gulf of Bahrain) or at Spasinu Charax, on the Tigris delta. From there, goods were transported by camel caravan to Petra, continuing on to Gaza, in Palestine, where they could be loaded onto ships leaving for all the ports of the western Mediterranean.

The Seleucid rulers of Syria and the Ptolemaic kings of Egypt had long struggled to control the territories of Palestine and southern Syria that profited from commerce with the East. Ptolemy II Philadelphus (282–46 B.C.E.) was the first Egyptian sovereign to encourage regular trade with northern Arabia and sub-Saharan Africa, and he promoted the construction of a number of ports on the Egyptian coast of the Red Sea, in the Sudan, and in Ethiopia (an endeavor continued by his successors).

These Ptolemaic projects were at first more military than commercial; they were connected, in particular, with importing elephants for use in the army and with trade in gold, which served to pay mercenary troops and support other military expenditures. Naturally, other goods passed through these ports (and in

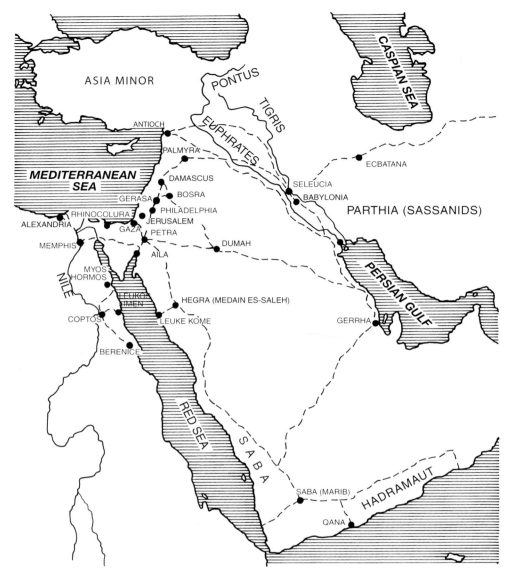

ASIA MINOR
PONTUS
TIGRIS
EUPHRATES
CASPIAN SEA
ANTIOCH
PALMYRA
MEDITERRANEAN SEA
DAMASCUS
GERASA
BOSRA
RHINOCOLURA
PHILADELPHIA
ALEXANDRIA
JERUSALEM
GAZA
PETRA
MEMPHIS
AILA
DUMAH
MYOS HORMOS
NILE
LEUKOS LIMEN
HEGRA (MEDAIN ES-SALEH)
COPTOS
LEUKE KOME
BERENICE
RED SEA
SABA
SABA (MARIB)
HADRAMAUT
QANA
ECBATANA
SELEUCIA
BABYLONIA
PARTHIA (SASSANIDS)
PERSIAN GULF
GERRHA

The Arabian Peninsula, showing the ancient trade routes linking Petra, the Red Sea, and the Persian Gulf to the Iranian plateau and the Far East.

Facing page: The access road to Petra, at the exit from the Siq.

the Hellenistic age, ships paid mooring fees, and boats plying the Nile paid tolls), but the Ptolemies never succeeded in monopolizing commerce with the East, which remained in Arabian hands.

The Seleucids (Antiochus III, 223–186 B.C.E., in particular) attempted to make good use of the northern caravan routes that linked China, central Asia, the Iranian plateau, and Mesopotamia with the city of Antioch on the Orontes and, via the Black Sea, with Byzantium and Asia Minor. Although these routes were preferable for transporting Chinese and Indian merchandise to the Mediterranean, the existence of the kingdom of Parthia rendered them problematic. As early as the late second century B.C.E., Parthia and China under the Han dynasty had established diplomatic relations, but political differences between the Seleucids and the Parthians interrupted the silk road, and commerce with the Middle and Far East was held

up at the frontiers of Syria. This meant that all the traffic in Indian and Chinese products between the second and first centuries B.C.E. went either through Petra, crossing the Arabian Peninsula, or else to Alexandria by water, stopping at the ports of the Arabian Peninsula. Strabo (11.5.12) notes that in the age of the Ptolemies, Greek ships did not dare engage in trade with India, and that navigation between India and Egypt was in the hands of the Indians and the Arabians.

That Petra was an important terminal of the silk road now seems confirmed, and some scholars have identified it as the city recorded in the annals of the Han dynasty as "Li-Kan," which they interpret as a transcription of "Reqem," the name by which Petra was known among the Semitic peoples.

The actual route used to transport spices and other products across Arabia toward the West is still under discussion. There is much archaeological evidence that reflects the presence of the Nabateans in central Arabia, and their expansion along the internal traffic routes is attested by their foundation of Hegra, to the southeast, and of al-Jawf, to the east, near the entrance to the Wadi Sirhan. One of the most frequented and most direct routes from the Persian Gulf region, internal southern Arabia, and southern Syria was precisely that of the Wadi Sirhan, a long depression in the desert with oases at its northern and southern ends. It communicated directly with the Bosra area and was also used to transport goods from the ports of the eastern coast of Arabia. The Wadi Sirhan later played a role of fundamental importance for the prosperity and defense of the Roman province of Arabia.

Control of the areas through which the caravan routes passed implied notable revenues, thanks to a system of tolls and taxes on the merchandise that the caravan trains carried. In the ports that the Nabateans controlled and along the desert routes under their jurisdiction, customs duties might amount to as much as 25 percent of the value of the goods in transit. Fortified installations lined some of the caravan routes to provide protection against attacks by the nomadic tribes, which were frequent.

With the discovery in the mid-first century B.C.E. that the monsoon winds were seasonal, sea trade between the Indian Ocean and the Red Sea increased considerably. The ships that plied the Gulf of Aden at the beginning of the season could take advantage of the favorable southwest winds to reach the Indian

The Dead Sea viewed from Mount Nebo.

Bronze perfume burner with a caryatid support from Umm Udheinah, Achaemenid period (Amman: Archaeological Museum).

coast in some three months, a relatively rapid voyage. They then returned in the autumn, making use of winds that blew in the opposite direction.

Our principal source of information on sea routes is the anonymous author of the *Periplus Maris Erythraei*, a text that exists in a sole manuscript copy at the University of Heidelberg. Its date, much discussed, is now estimated to be in the Neronian or Flavian eras, that is, somewhere between 40 and 70 C.E.

The Greeks and the Romans used the term "Erythraean Sea" for the expanse of water separating Africa and India. They called its two gulfs the *sinus arabicus* (the Red Sea) and the *sinus persicus* (the Arabian, or Persian Gulf). The *Periplus*, written in Greek, describes a long sea voyage from the Red Sea to India. It is a fine manual of navigation and guide to commerce, useful to merchants and apparently written by an eyewitness, since it is clear on several occasions that the anonymous author had visited the places he discusses. His voyage began from the port of Myos Hormos (now Queseir al-Qadim, modern Quseir), on the Red Sea, and after a number of halts, he reached the strait of Bab el-Mandeb. Here two routes lay open: one reached the Indian ports after a long voyage hugging the coast; the other set off across the high seas, taking advantage of the monsoon winds to reach India. Aside from shortening the voyage, the direct routed enabled ships to avoid pirates, a major threat to maritime travel—Philostrates (*Vita Apoll.*, 3.5) re-

minds us that archers accompanied the merchant ships—and also the inhospitable and difficult landing places of southern Arabia.

The text of the *Periplus* provides detailed notes on the progress of the voyage and on the ports of call for commercial maritime traffic, and it gives precise information on the products exchanged in the various ports. It remains a primary source on the role that the Arabian ports played in the economic development of the region in the first century C.E. From Myos Hormos or from Berenice, the southernmost and probably the largest port on the Egyptian coast of the Red Sea (Strabo 17.1.45), ships could sail across the Red Sea to Leuke Kome (in the region of today's Aynunah, now in Saudi Arabia). From Leuke Kome, the *Periplus Maris Erythraei* tells us (in a passage that, among other things, securely establishes the date of the text as within the reign of Malichus II), "there is [a route inland] to Petra, to Malikhas king of the Nabataioi" (19).

The description given by the author of the *Periplus* agrees in general with what Strabo reports (16.4.23–24). According to Strabo, in fact, Leuke Kome, "in the land of the Nabataeans," was "a large emporium" from where "camel-traders travel back and forth from Petra . . . in safety and ease, and in such numbers of men and camels that they differ in no respect from an army." He further notes that from there "loads of aromatics are conveyed . . . to Petra, and thence to Rhinocolura, which is in Phoenicia near Aegypt, and thence to the other peoples." The frontier port of Leuke Kome was certainly a customs station, very probably controlled by Nabatean functionaries. Situated on the caravan route from Hegra that was linked to Petra and, beyond Petra, to the Mediterranean coast, Leuke Kome was of vital importance in commercial exchanges. Throughout the first century C.E., the Nabateans, far from being irreparably harmed by the development of the maritime routes, which never completely replaced the caravan roads, continued to be a massive mercantile presence in the Persian Gulf, the Mediterranean, the ports of the Red Sea, the Nile, and the desert, and they took full advantage of the increased demand for exotic products that followed the Roman annexation of Egypt.

Nabatean participation in the caravan traffic that used the ports of the Red Sea and the Nile is attested by the many graffiti, some of which can be dated to the first century C.E., that have been found along the trails that linked Myos Hormos to Leukos Limen (today's Queseir al-Qadim, modern Quseir), the port closest to the Nile and to the river city of Coptos, which, Strabo tells us, was "a city common to the Aegyptians and the Arabians" (17.1.44–45).

It is not an easy task to extract information from the ancient sources on the complex workings of this commerce. In two well-known passages of the *Natural History* (6.26.101 and 12.41.84), Pliny laments the high cost of the luxury goods imported from India, Arabia, and China. The first of these passages states: "In no year does India absorb less than fifty million sesterces of our empire's wealth, sending back merchandise to be sold with us at a hundred times its prime cost." In the second he states: "And by the lowest reckoning India, China and the Arabian peninsula take from our empire 100 million sesterces every year—that is the sum which our luxuries and our women cost us." Pliny's complaints about the financial hemorrhage confronting Rome might be hyperbole, however: international trade was in fact not exclusively based on precious commodities such as gold, silver, silks, pearls, ebony, ivory, precious stones, and exotic animals, but also included less costly goods such as cotton or consumer goods like incense and myrrh, aromatic products that modern scholars might consider luxury goods, but that in ancient times were used in medicine and for religious and funerary practices.

According to Strabo (16.4.26), the Nabatean economy was not based exclusively on the transport of goods imported from other counties, but also ex-

Amphoriskos and *alabastron* in blue and yellow glass; made to contain highly prized perfumes. From Umm Udheinah, fifth century B.C.E. (Amman: Archaeological Museum).

ploited local products, gold and silver among them, and oils, perfumes, and unguents obtained from resins and plants processed in Nabatean territories and exported to the West in closed containers called, precisely, *unguentaria*.

The political extinction of the Nabatean kingdom and the annexation of Palmyra into the Roman Empire undoubtedly created difficulties for the long-distance, trans-Arabian commerce controlled from Petra. Palmyra lay on a route used with increasing frequency that connected the Persian Gulf and the Mediterranean, and the presence of oases permitted the use of shortcuts through the desert between the coast and the Euphrates. Caravan trains departing from Palmyra went directly east to Dura-Europos, or else they went directly but diagonally to Hit, on the right bank of the river, and from there continued on to Seleucia on the Tigris and to the Persian Gulf.

Relatively peaceful conditions on the eastern frontier during the first half of the second century C.E., after Trajan's war with the Parthians, contributed to the growth and the intensification of commerce throughout the Parthian kingdom and the region of the middle Euphrates. The traffic that Petra had controlled was thus largely ceded to Palmyra, and that city retained its monopoly for over a century.

Nabatean Society

Language and Writing

In Petra, many written documents are inscribed on the bases of statues, altars, and other cult objects or carved into the rock walls of the passageways leading to sacred localities. These are, however, only a small part of what has survived of the written evidence of the inhabitants of the city: we now have more than four thousand documents attributed to the Nabateans, many of them still unpublished. These are almost all inscriptions on stone, but there are a few papyri of a legal nature as well, found near the Dead Sea. There are also ostraca (ceramic fragments, broken in ancient times and used to write on with ink) and fragmentary inscriptions on plaster that have been discovered during the course of excavations. We have none of the literary texts, which were probably written on perishable materials, that would have pro-

vided a more complete understanding, not only of the Nabatean language, but also of the beliefs, laws, history, and social and economic structure of Nabatean society.

Almost all of the inscriptions from Petra are redacted in the local language, Nabatean; a few are written in Greek or Latin or are bilingual. Some finds in Nabatean territory offer side-by-side texts in Nabatean and the language and script of the local northern-Arabian population. The earliest Nabatean document does not come from Petra, but rather from Khalasa (Elusa), in the central Negev; it has been dated to approximately 200 B.C.E. on the basis of the shapes of the signs, or else to about 169–168, taking the "King Aretas" named in the inscription to be the same as the "tyrant" of that name in 2 Maccabees. We also know from Diodorus Siculus (19.96) that as early as 312 B.C.E., the Nabateans used the script and the language that continued to be theirs in later times.

Nabatean is a member of the Aramaic linguistic group. It was used for a long time after the formation of the Roman province of Arabia in 106 C.E.: the latest

Ammonite chalcedony seal engraved on both sides, seventh century B.C.E. The underside shows a bovine passant surrounded by an inscription; the convex top shows some variety of monkey, surrounded by an inscription that refers to the owner, Beyadel, "servant" of Padiel. The zone that later was Nabatean had always been a region of passage occupied by people of many origins, who in time coexisted and in part merged.

Facing page: Detail of the pilaster and the pediment of a tomb facade (Brünnow and Domaszewski, *Petra,* no. 70) in which the veining in the limestone typically used for construction in Petra is particularly evident.

Eighth-century B.C.E. orthostat showing king Barrakib of Sam'al (now Zinjirli, in Turkey) with an inscription in ancient Aramaic (Berlin: Staatliche Museen, Vorderasiatische Abteilung).

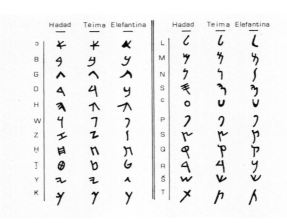

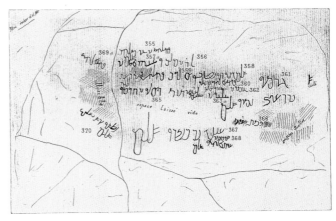

	Hadad	Teima	Elefantina		Hadad	Teima	Elefantina
ʾ				L			
B				M			
G				N			
D				S			
H				P			
W				Ṣ			
Z				Q			
Ḥ				R			
Ṭ				Š			
Y				T			
K							

known Nabatean inscriptions come from the mid-fourth century C.E. (although an Arabic language predominates, despite letters that are still Nabatean in form). Nabatean documents are thus attested—although very inconsistently, both in their geographical provenance and their chronological attribution—for the fairly long period of some five hundred years, after which they were replaced by texts redacted in a variety of Arabic that is the ancestor of classical Arabic.

The family of Aramaic languages of which Nabatean formed a part belongs to the western subsection of the vast ensemble of languages with shared characteristics known as Semitic, a term that derives from the name Shem, one of the sons of Noah, who Genesis tells us was the ancestor of a number of peoples. The linguistic term "Semitic" includes many languages that have been used in the Near East from the time of the origin of written culture to our own times. Place names—in particular the names of rivers and mountains—in fact indicate that these languages must have been spoken in the region long before writing arose around 3000 B.C.E. and before the formation of urban cultures in the area, as is also true of other language groups. Aramaic does not seem to have emerged in Syria as a clearly individuated language earlier than the beginning of the Iron Age (ca. 1200 B.C.E.), when it was introduced with the formation of a series of autonomous political entities that adopted the so-called Phoenician alphabetic writing system, some time around the eleventh or the tenth century B.C.E. Characteristics that were later typical of Aramaic were already present, however, in the area that became Syria. The first phase of the language, known as ancient Aramaic, displayed a number of dialectical variations. Later, from the eighth to the seventh centuries B.C.E., with the growth of first the Assyrian, then the Babylonian supremacy in the areas of Syria and Palestine, the highly diverse dialects spoken and written in the many vassal states were adapted by the imperial bureaucracy into a "vehicular" language of communication. In this manner, a unified written script, now called "imperial" or "standard" Aramaic, was created and used for official documents throughout the periods of Assyrian, Babylonian, then Persian domination.

Although written Aramaic was by then standardized, dialects of Aramaic that differed in varying degree from standard Aramaic continued to be spoken in the various territories, although a common literary tradition renders such differences imperceptible. After the fall of the Persian empire, the bureaucracy adopted Greek as its official language, and a number of local dialects were used in the documents of the various states that emerged during and after the Hellenistic period. These dialects, or linguistic variations, developed individually and were set down in writing styles that were equally diverse despite their common derivation from the chancery script of the Persian empire. This phase of the language, which spanned the early second century B.C.E. and the transition from the second century to the third century C.E., is known as middle Aramaic. This is the period of Nabatean and of the Hebraic Aramaic of Palestine. It was the language of the Qumran texts; it was Palmyrene and ancient Syriac; it was the Aramaic used in the Parthian empire, in particular, in Hatra and Assur between the first century and the third centuries C.E.

ɔ								
ɔf								
B								
Bf								
G								
D								
H								
Hf								
W								

Z						
H						
T						
Y						
Yf						
K						
Kf						

L						
Lf						
M						
Mf						
W						
Wf						
S						
c						
P						
Pf						

S					
c					
P					
Pf					
Ṣ					
Q					
R					
Š					
T					

Compared with other varieties of middle Aramaic, Nabatean presents some rather archaic characteristics that connect it, in part, directly to the Aramaic of the Persian age, and that can probably be attributed to Petra's location at the periphery of the empire. Most scholars agree that the Nabateans adopted middle Aramaic as a written language but spoke a non-Aramaic dialect of a northern-Arabic type. In support of this notion, they point to onomastics (Arabic elements predominate in Nabatean personal names), to certain vocabulary items, and to isolated syntactical habits comparable to Arabic counterparts. Taken in the strict sense of the term—that is, limiting the Nabateans to the group that called itself Nabaṭu—they were very probably of Arabic origin, but they formed a sedentary state in a territory where the dominant language had long been Aramaic. What is more, Aramaic was used by Arab groups in the fifth and fourth centuries B.C.E., in particular by the Qedarites, as demonstrated by bowls inscribed in Aramaic found in the eastern Nile delta at Tell el-Maskhuta, one of which was offered by "Qaynu, son of Gashmu, king of Qedar." This means that we need to reconstruct a particular linguistic situation for the territory of the Nabatean state in which various dialects were used on the oral level but Aramaic predominated. Aramaic probably continued to be used, especially in the cities, throughout the third century C.E., but it is possible that Arabic dialects were used instead in rural areas and were written in scripts of the southern-Arabic type, as seen in a large number of rock graffiti found in the region. We can suppose that the language of culture tended to predominate in the cities as both the spoken and the written language, whereas in country areas the language of groups that had become or remained marginal may have continued to be used, with reciprocal exchanges according to historical circumstances.

The reconstruction of the precise linguistic situation of the country is complicated by a rock inscription found at 'En-'Avdat (to the south of 'Avdat-Oboda), datable to the end of the first century or the beginning of the second century C.E. This text is written in Nabatean characters, but it uses Nabatean for the initial formula and Arabic for the text itself, which is written in verse. There are several possible explanations for the bilingualism of this inscription. The Nabatean inscriptions that we possess are classifiable, on the basis of their content and the type of formulas they use, as dedicatory, donatory (a category that includes the recording of a construction), or funerary. Within each of these categories the formulas that are used remain relatively consistent. Dedicatory inscriptions usually refer to the offering of an object—a statue, an altar, or some other cult-related object—to a specific deity; a gift might also take form as the erection or restoration of a sacred building, as in the case of the Temple of Be'l Shamin at Si'. To date at least, we have no dedicatory inscriptions for the temples of Petra. Throughout the Syro-Palestinian region, however, the scheme that is used is simple and traditional. The object is named first, followed by a phrase indicating who made it ("This is the statue that . . . has made"), then the name of the person making the dedication. Next comes the name of the god to whom the object is offered, at times followed by a special intention, often "for the life"—that is, the health—of the reigning sovereign and, in some cases, of members of his family. Occasionally a date is added in the form of the year of reign of the sovereign, and in a few cases the name of the artisan is given as well.

The funerary inscriptions are of two types. The first are brief indications of the name of the dead person, on

Table showing the development of Nabatean script (from Cantineau, *Nabatéen*, vol. 1). As time passed, the signs tended to become connected and to present differences in tracing according to whether the sign was in initial, median, or final position. This became typical of Arabic script, which derived from Nabatean.

Obverse and reverse of a coin of Obodas II (III). Coins stamped with the name of the king and the year of his reign are determinant for fixing Nabatean chronology. The type of writing is of little help in chronological classification of Nabatean inscriptions.

Reproduction of an inscription dedicating the temple of Be'l Shamin at Si' in the Hauran (*CIS* II, 163). One of the oldest inscriptions from the Hauran, the writing clearly differs from the "classical" script of Petra.

59

occasion preceded by the term *nefesh*, or funerary monument. In some cases this is followed by information about the dead person. The second type consists of long and complex texts on the facades of tombs. These include the name of the proprietor of the tomb, the names of the family members authorized to make use of it, and extremely precise legal information. At Hegra it was customary to specify the fines to be paid to the god or his priest or to the sovereign should these norms not be respected. The only funerary inscription at Petra of this more elaborate type, that of the tomb called Qabr at-Turkman or Turkmaniya, follows a similar pattern.

Few inscriptions deviate from these models. Exceptions include a fragmentary text from the Temple of the Winged Lions that lists a series of laws and the punish-

ments for their transgression; another is the unique example of an incantation text from Horvat Raqiq, in the Negev.

Finally, there are a number of examples of texts inscribed on the rock walls of sacred sites and their access ways. These are brief texts, usually placing the faithful under the protection of the god. The formulas almost always use the passive participle of the verb, "to remember"— "Remembered [*dkyr*]"—followed by the name of the worshiper, but some use the formula, "before the god X." These expressions were widespread in this period, not only in Petra but also in Palmyra and Hatra. They were commonly used in the preceding centuries as well, often with the verb "to bless." Although the precise meaning of these expressions has been much discussed, they are in

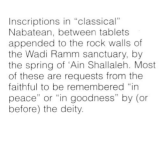

Left: Pink limestone funerary stele (called *nefesh*, a term that originally referred to the living person represented by the stele) erected in the memory of a certain Shullai (Petra Museum).

Middle: Inscribed marble fragment found in an annex of the Temple of the Winged Lions (Petra Museum).

Right: Fragmentary Nabatean inscription on a slab of Italian marble, dedicated to Dushara and dated to 11 B.C.E., found around 1850 at Pozzuoli (*CIS* II, 157). This inscription demonstrates that Pozzuoli (the Roman Puteoli) was an international port city in the Augustan age, the residents of which would certainly have included Nabatean merchants (Naples: Museo Archeologico Nazionale).

any event intended to have an immediate effect: thanks to the force of the formula itself, the worshiper expected benediction or remembrance from the god. A similar power is invested in later formulas of nomination or condemnation.

These texts are redacted in a script that, like all the others used in the states of the Syro-Palestinian region after the beginning of the first millennium B.C.E., uses a consonant alphabet. This means that at least initially, we have no specific, reliable indications of vowel sounds (though after a while, long vowels begin to be shown). Twenty-two characters are used, and the writing reads from right to left. The shape of these characters derived, as we have seen, from the calligraphic writing of the Persian chancery, a good example of which appears in the fifth-century B.C.E. Elephantine papyri. That written style, previously used for papyrus, influenced the stone-cutters' work. Because we do not possess an uninterrupted series of documents from the Persian to the Nabatean age, the development of individual signs is not completely clear. The ostraca from southern Palestine mentioned above and others from unknown sites in ancient Edom can be dated to the last Persian period or the first Hellenistic period. They display a writing style used throughout the region not long before the formation of the Nabatean kingdom. It is a written form of "standard" Aramaic, more or less carefully rendered, that displays a tendency toward the cursive but does not yet present characteristics typical of Nabatean writing.

The writing style of the Khalasa inscription, which also differs from typical Nabatean, is close to the Aramaic style of the fourth-century ostraca. The earliest example of script typical of the Petra texts is the inscription on the Aṣlaḥ triclinium, which dates from between the latter part of the second century and the early years of the first century B.C.E. Here the individual characters begin to show a clear elongation, a specificity of form, and a tendency for adjacent characters to be joined that eventually led to differentiating certain characters according to initial, median, or final position in the word. As time passed, Nabatean writing evolved somewhat and, following Jean Starcky, we can distinguish various periods and regional particularities. There are very few

examples of the archaic period and the earliest developments of Nabatean script before the reign of Obodas II (III), who died in 9–8 B.C.E., when Nabatean had reached the so-called classic, or calligraphic, stage. Aside from the Aṣlaḥ inscription (ca. 96 B.C.E.) from Bab el-Siq, there is the "pebble" from Horvat Raqiq, the painted text of which has been dated to circa 100 B.C.E. by Joseph Naveh, the scholar who published it. This text attests to a cursive variant of the more ancient writing style, an important discovery for the study of the development of writing.

One example of writing incised on stone is an inscription from Tell esh-Shuqafiya, in Egypt, that can be assigned to 77 B.C.E. (if the king mentioned is Ptolemy XII Auletes, as F. M. Cross suggests), or to 44 B.C.E. (if the king is identified as Ptolemy XIII, as Starcky prefers). The inscription on a statue of Rabbel I from Petra is only slightly later than that date. A second inscription from Tell esh-Shuqafiya can be dated to 38–37 or 34 B.C.E. After that period and before the end of the reign of Obodas II (III), the predecessor of Aretas IV, we have few documents of certain date. The characters in these inscriptions are fairly broad and present few ligatures: the *aleph* (') is already closed, but there is still an X-shaped variant of it that tends to be specialized for use in final position.

The "classic" Nabatean script, which Starcky also calls "Nabatean calligraphy" because "with its many curves and ligatures, it is dependent on the scribe's cala-

1	2	3	4	5	6	7

Table of written characters illustrating the development of Nabatean script, which included a cursive variant.

Funerary inscription from Medain es-Saleh (formerly Hegra; JS, no. 7), incised into the facade of rock tomb no. 21 and dated to 27–28 C.E. Written forms at Hegra, like the tomb facades, remained true to the classical tradition as it had developed under the reign of Aretas IV.

Left: Facsimile of an inscription on a limestone slab fragment, datable to the second century C.E., found at Petra in a tomb at the exit from the Siq (Brünnow and Domaszewski, Petra, no. 64). It is the only known example of this type (Petra Museum).

Middle: Facsimile of an inscription on limestone found in 1982 in the east delta of the Nile, but originally from Tell esh-Shuqafiya, attributed to 34 B.C.E. It mentions Queen Cleopatra and a year, read as either the fourteenth or the eighteenth of her reign (Zagazig, Egypt: private collection).

Right: Facsimile of an inscription, in part fragmentary, found among reused materials in the zone of the Wadi Musa. It records the offering of a statue of a deified King Malichus I (56–29 B.C.E). It also mentions King Aretas IV, his wife Shaqilat, and various members of the royal family.

Drawing of pedestal altar of 29–30 C.E. found at Siʻ in the Hauran. The inscription records the erection of a statue.

Altar or cippus from Umm al-Jimal, in the Hauran, erected in honor of Dushara (*CIS* II, 190). On one side, a Greek version of the inscription names the god as "Dousarei Aarra."

mus" (*DBS*, col. 931), is, once again, a chancery script transposed onto stone with few alterations. This stage is well documented, but all examples are inscribed in stone or, in the case of coins, stamped into metal. We have a few papyri only at the end of the first century B.C.E. and the beginning of the following century. The earliest inscriptions in this writing style are dedications offered at Miletus and Delos for the health of Obodas. Another series of inscriptions dates from the reign of Aretas IV, during the final years of the first century B.C.E. and the early years of the first century C.E. These include the dedication of a statue of Aretas, found in the temenos of the Qasr el-Bint at Petra and attributed to the early years of that sovereign's reign; a fragmentary inscription found at Sabra, just south of Petra, which names Aretas and Queen Hagiru, attributed by Starcky to 9–10 C.E.; the dedication of the chapel of en-Numeir (ca. 20 C.E.); the inscription on a marble tablet of the Temple of the

Winged Lions (29 C.E.); and a reused tablet found on the right bank of the Wadi Musa that mentions the family of Aretas IV (between 25 and 35 C.E.). The long funerary epigraph on the tomb called Qabr at-Turkman, or Turkmaniya, must be nearly contemporary to or immediately posterior to the inscription on the Wadi Musa tablet.

Outside Petra, the Natirel dedication from Khirbet et-Tannur dates from the second year of Aretas IV's reign, that is, from 8–7 B.C.E.; the two oldest tombs in Hegra are from 1 B.C.E.–1 C.E., or the ninth year of Aretas's reign (JS, nos. 8, 16; *CIS* II, 197, 198). Scattered instances of other tombs with inscriptions continue to 74–75 C.E., which corresponds to the fifth year of the reign of Rabbel II (JS, no. 22), but the writing style varies little, except in the very latest texts. Among the inscriptions found outside Nabatean territory, the one at Cos dedicated by Syllaeus dates from 9 C.E., the eighteenth year of the reign of Aretas IV, while an inscription from Pozzuoli (*CIS* II, 157) dates from two years later.

At this point, Nabatean writing had vertical letters with more strongly elongated ascenders than previously, and many more ligatures appear. The base of some letters that had previously been formed by two almost parallel strokes tends to close with a loop, for example, in the signs *h* and *m*. The *aleph* (ʼ) became like an X in final position. That variant eventually disappeared, and the looped form was always used. This graphic style was maintained without notable changes (aside from greater or lesser degrees of accuracy) for the entire reign of Aretas IV and part of that of Malichus II. For example, the writing style of the fragmentary marble inscription found near the Monumental Arch at Petra (which has been dated between 40 and 70 C.E., during the reign of Malichus, to whom the ex-voto is offered) is still considered classical. Later inscriptions from the reign of Rabbel II seem to show a tendency toward a greater schematization in the individual characters and a more cursive hand. This is particularly true of the few inscriptions from Hegra dating from that era, as indicated by Starcky.

Especially in the oldest documents, the writing style attested in the Hauran shows some notable differences from Nabatean writing, properly speaking. The inscriptions that can be dated securely go back to the end of the first century B.C.E. These include the dedication of the Temple of Be'l Shamin in Si' (first century B.C.E.) and a few roughly contemporary funerary inscriptions. Generally speaking, individual letters seem to be broader here; some strokes are more angular, and the characters appear more detached from one another than in contemporary inscriptions from the south. The writing style of Petra penetrated the north in the following age, however: it is attested by an entire series of inscriptions dating to the reign of Rabbel II, in the first century C.E., when the region enjoyed particular prosperity. We might also cite the inscription on a stele from Dmer (70 C.E.) and the dedication in honor of Shai' al-Qaum of 96 C.E. Nonetheless, even in this period, the Hauran inscriptions seem to some extent detached from the written tradition of Petra and the southern zones in general, often continuing to show less elongated, more clearly separated signs. One good example of this tendency is the Salkhad inscription in the museum at Suweida (*CIS* II, 184, 183), which J. T. Milik has combined into one text and dated to 95 C.E. (*Syria* 35 [1958]: 227–228).

The last period of Nabatean script followed the establishment of the Roman province of Arabia in 106 C.E. Because Bosra had become the capital of the state, it is not surprising that many inscriptions from this period come from the Hauran rather than the region around Petra. One inscription from Bosra that honors Dushara-A'ra is of uncertain date, but may be from the forty-second year of the eparchy, or the year 148 C.E. A group of papyri from the same overall period (between 93–94 C.E. and 136 C.E.), found near the Dead Sea, consists of a collection of documents known as the Babatha archive. Some of these papyri are in Nabatean, and some documents in Judaic Aramaic have signatures or brief subscriptions in Nabatean. The most complete papyrus in Nabatean, which is legal in nature (and has been published by Starcky), displays a highly elegant, very elongated cursive hand and characters with simplified strokes that make the document particularly difficult to read. Starcky compares the writing style to that of some of the painted inscriptions in the sanctuary of Gebel Ramm.

There are attestations of the late writing style throughout Nabatean territory until the third and fourth centuries. One important and famous funerary inscription, written in Nabatean and Greek, comes from Umm al-Jimal, in the Hauran. It honors a certain Fehru, who is called "preceptor of Gadimat, king of Tanuḫ." King Gadimat is a person well known in the Arabian tradition, where he is recalled as the chief of the Tanikh tribe and

Inscription on a rock wall of the Wadi Ramm sanctuary, near the 'Ain Shalleleh spring, asking for remembrance and protection.

Inscription on a rock wall, al-Habis. The writing is classical Nabatean.

Inscription in ancient Syriac, attributed to the third century C.E, on the vault of an arcosolium in a tomb in the necropolis of Hilar, near Diyarbakir. Some have considered this script from Edessa, rather than Nabatean, to have been the model for Arabic writing. It is likely however, that Arabic, which in its earliest attestations shows the use of Nabatean script, was later strongly influenced by the Syriac cultural environment.

Block bearing a Nabatean inscription of the third century C.E. inserted into a wall in Umm al-Jimal, in the Hauran (*CIS* II, 192). This is one of the latest Nabatean inscriptions. It is the epitaph of Fehru, the preceptor of the Arabian king of Hira, who is a familiar figure in Arabian tradition, and it records a conflict with Queen Zenobia of Palmyra. The text serves as historical confirmation of the use of Nabatean by the first pre-Islamic Arabian sovereigns. A Greek version of the same inscription shows the long persistence of Greco-Hellenistic culture in the Near East.

Facsimile of the funerary inscription of Raqos (JS, no. 17), 267 C.E., from a rock wall at Hegra. The vertical line to the right is written in northern-Arabic characters. The text contains various Arabic lexical and morphological usages, and the signs even show some similarity to Arabic script.

Facsimile of a funerary inscription from en-Nemara, in Syria (Cantineau, *Nabatéen*, 2: 49–50) recording Mar al-Qais, "king of all the Arabs." The language used is exclusively Arabic.

one of the first kings of Hira. He lived in the mid-third century C.E., and tradition relates his conflicts with queen Zenobia of Palmyra. The latest inscription (328 C.E.) comes from en-Nemara, northwest of Bosra. It is the epitaph of an Arab king, Mar al-Qais, and is written wholly in Arabic.

In the southern region, there is a bilingual funerary inscription from Hegra honoring one Raqos, written in Nabatean and Tamud, a northern Arabic dialect, that can be dated to 267, or the year 162 of the constitution of the province of Arabia. The language used contains Arabisms, the tracing of the signs is somewhat sloppy (perhaps because the inscription is scratched into a rock wall), and, as John F. Healey has shown, it includes some diacritical marks.

It is commonly thought that the Arabic characters used today developed from Nabatean characters. The intermediate stage is considered to be a type of writing similar to that of a series of Nabatean graffiti in the Sinai, which have been dated, on the basis of internal

evidence, to between 105 and 300 C.E. The bilingual inscriptions in Nabatean and Arabic discussed above were considered, on the basis of the form of the characters, to be examples of the transition from Nabatean to Arabic. Jean Starcky was the first to propose that Arabic script derives instead from Syriac, also a script derived from Aramaic, and used to the northwest as a written form of the speech of the city of Edessa. This hypothesis is based on Arabic tradition, but also on the argument that both Arabic and Syriac characters are written on an ideal straight line, whereas Nabatean characters reach above and below such a line. The question is still in dispute, and both interpretations can be found in the literature. The fact that the Nabateans' spoken language shifted to Arabic but they continued to use the traditional Nabatean writing is obvious, as are the formal similarities between the two graphic styles. Ancient Syriac documents are also written in a form derived from a cursive Aramaic that also presents similarities with Arabic, in particular in the proportions of the letters. This has led to the notion that Syriac exerted a secondary influence as Edessa prospered and the dialect became increasingly widespread, circulating throughout the Near East as a cultivated, literary language when Nabatean and Palmyrene were no longer used.

Gods and Cults

The sources that enable us to reconstruct Nabatean religion are, once again, in large part epigraphic documents that furnish the names of the deities venerated. Personal onomastics, which in many cases includes elements connected with the sphere of the divine (compounds with the name of a god, who is expected to protect the newborn), contributes to what we know about the names of the gods and the sorts of actions attributed to them. For example, the god "gives," "protects," "restores," or the individual declares himself the "servant" of a certain deity. There is a gap, however, between the official cults and those attested by onomastics. The latter may be more familiar in character, and they may reflect older and more conservative traditions than the ones we learn of through dedicatory inscriptions. To cite only one example, the principal god of the Nabatean pantheon and the god of the reigning dynasty was clearly Dushara, but he seldom figures in theophoric names.

The authors of late antiquity or the classical period—Strabo in particular, but also Stephanus of Byzantium and the lexicon known as the *Suda*—tell us much about Nabatean gods and cults, but we can also learn a good deal from later Arabic literature when it conveys pre-Islamic beliefs and traditions. The typology of objects with inscriptions and the study of sacred sites add context to the bare epigraphic and literary data. A careful comparison of what is known of the cults of populations close to the Nabateans in time and space or of successive cultures in the region can also lend depth and definition to reconstructions, but vast lacunae remain, as is true of all ancient populations without a surviving mythological and cult tradition.

The pastoral and nomadic origins attributed to the Nabateans have led scholars to conclude that their religion was initially a cult of natural phenomena and tribal divinities that changed and grew in complexity with their contact with sedentary culture and evolved further with a more urban way of life. The truth is in fact more complex. We know the Nabateans to have been a sedentary and, above all, an ethnically mixed population, as reflected in onomastics, where names of varied origins coexist at any given time. Hence it is clear from even the earliest evidence that the Nabateans' religion was stratified, composite, and in part geographically diverse. The very elements that might seem typical of the religious expression of pastoral nomads—the cult of a nonanthropomorphic god, the protector of a specific group and connected with astral phenomena—had already been present for some time in the Near East, interwoven with other religious manifestations more characteristic of agricultural, sedentary, and urbanized cultures.

With these remarks as a preface, it should be noted that the names of some Nabatean divinities and certain features of their cults can be considered to pertain to populations generically defined as Arabic, and as such can be found among other pre-Islamic populations, in particular among the Arabs of the north—the Lihyanites, the Safaites, and the Thamuds—whereas other traits derive from the Aramaic sedentary populations. We can also draw a distinction between the region of the Hauran, which retained traditions that can be generically defined as Syrian and where not all the cults of the central portion of the Nabatean state penetrated to an equal degree, and the region around Petra, where religious thought was more closely tied to that of the northern-Arabian regions. Nor should we underesti-

Reproduction of a tracing published in the *Corpus inscriptionum semiticarum* (*CIS* II, 350) of the inscription on the facade of the anonymous tomb known as the Turkmaniya Tomb, circa mid-first century C.E. It is a typical example of Nabatean calligraphy.

The two obelisks of the high place on the Zibb 'Atuf.

mate the influence of Hellenistic Greek cults and, later, Roman practices. The discussion that follows will first present the principal deities, then what we know of practices that were specific to the Nabateans, in particular, their high places, betyls, and funerary monuments.

Male Deities

Dushara. The principal god of the Nabateans was Dushara (written *dwšr'* in Nabatean). He is named on many occasions at Petra, although we cannot be sure that any temple in that city is dedicated to him: the most likely candidate—the Qasr el-Bint Far'un—lacks dedicatory inscriptions. The name of this deity originates from an epithet, *dhu Šara*, "he of [the god of] Shara," which has been interpreted in several ways (see, in particular, Jean Starcky in *DBS*, cols. 986–987). It may be a common noun designating some sort of geographical feature, a territory, a road, or a mountain. Following this notion, the name may signify "[the god of] the mountain." The

sixth-century C.E. grammarian and lexicographer Stephanus of Byzantium is often cited in support of this interpretation. Under the heading "Dousares," he writes: "Belvedere and high summit of Arabia, so called after Dousares. That is a god venerated among the Arabs." Thus Dushara appears as a god who resides on the top of a mountain, as is true of many Near-Eastern divinities who govern natural phenomena, such as the so-called god of the storm. These divinities are often named "lord of the (mountain)," with a toponym, as is the case for Ba'l Ṣapon, a god attested from the second millennium B.C.E. and often mentioned in the Phoenician area, whose name means "lord of the (mountain) Ṣapon," a peak on the Syrian coast near today's Latakia.

The notion of a reference to a mountain peak suggests another, more likely interpretation of "Shara" as a toponym, the place of residence of the Nabatean god—specifically (although not without some difficulties of a phonetic nature; see *DBS*, col. 987), the mountainous area to the south of Petra. This area is still called "Shara," but spelled in Arabic as šarat^un. The term does not seem to be attested before the Islamic period, although in theory it could be older. Dushara, as his name indicates, would thus be a local deity who resides on the top of a mountain, the source of local rainfall, hence a being who presides over the seasonal cycle of vegetation and over fertility (the reason for identifying him with Dionysos).

Although venerated at Petra, Dushara may have had his first cult at Gaia (el-Ji), in the Wadi Musa (as Starcky has proposed). In several places, including Petra, he is called "god of Gaia," which may have been the first Nabatean capital. The oldest known sanctuary to Dushara in Petra is the triclinium situated at the eastern end of the Siq, near the entrance to the gorge leading to the city, where one Aṣlaḥ placed a dedication some time between the late second century and the early first century B.C.E. Not far from there, a graffito in a rupestrian chapel names Dushara as "god of Madrasa" (*CIS* II, 443), yet another toponym. Dushara is also invoked in the famous funerary inscription of the Turkmaniya monument at Petra.

Even if he was known by his epithet, Dushara must have had an actual name, just as the god Baʿl Ṣapon was named Hadad in an earlier age. The term "Aʿra" is often associated with the name Dushara in inscriptions, particularly from the Hauran. In one bilingual inscription in Nabatean and Greek from Umm al-Jimal (after 106 C.E.), the god is called "Dushara" in the Nabatean portion, but in the Greek inscription he is given as "Dousarei Aarra," in the dative (*RÉS*, no. 1096). On the basis of this inscription, Dominique Sourdel has posited that Aʿra was Dushara's real name. A number of inscriptions that name Dushara-Aʿra in Nabatean define him as "the god who is at Bosra" (for example, *RÉS*, no. 83, from Imtan), hence it is preferable to suppose that after Rabbell II had made Bosra the royal city of residence, the cult of Dushara was superimposed on that of the city's local god, who was called Aʿra, thus creating a dual or paired deity. The name "Aʿra" has in turn been explained as deriving from an Arabic verb meaning "to spread" or "to dip," which would connect it with cult practices owed to this deity (and perhaps to others) that involved smearing the stele or the stone sacred to the god with the blood of a sacrificial animal. This practice, however, has not been confirmed by other information from this region. Starcky has instead suggested (*DBS*, col. 991) that Dushara's real name may have been Ruḍa, an Arabic deity name found in

Rock graffito from the Shu'b Qes, Petra, commemorating a devotee of Dushara and invoking the god's "remembrance."

Marble base in the form of an altar with Latin dedication to Dushara, from Pozzuoli. This altar testifies to the continuity of the cult of Dushara among the Nabatean colony in that Italian city in spite of their adoption of Latin (Naples: Museo Archeologico Nazionale).

Palmyrene in the Aramaic variant ʾArṣu, where the ṣ of the Aramaic corresponds to the Arabic ḍ and the initial ʾa functions to facilitate the pronunciation of two contiguous consonants. The same god is called Ruldaiu in one Assyrian document, a name which may correspond to the Greek Orotal (or Orotalt), a god mentioned by Herodotus (3.8; 1.131) as the only male deity venerated by the Arabs and whom he identifies with Dionysos. Although a number of scholars accept the connection with Herodotus's Orotal, it remains on the level of hypothesis.

As we have seen, the cult of Dushara was tied to specific local sanctuaries, but because Dushara was also the god of the Nabateans as a group, he became the special protector of the royal house. At Petra he is called "the god of Manikatu" in the dedication in the Siq triclinium, a name that may be related to the dynastic name Maliku, or Malichus, one of the first Nabatean kings (see Starcky, *RB* [1957]: 208). The god is also called "the

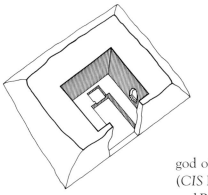

Axonometric projection and section of the Aṣlaḥ triclinium near Bab el-Siq (Brünnow and Domaszewski, Petra, no. 21). This is the site of one of the earliest Nabatean inscriptions preserved. The god Dushara was honored here.

Facsimile of an inscription from Imtan, in the Hauran (93 B.C.E.), carved on a stele, or cippus, in honor of Dushara-A'ra, "god of our lord" (Cantineau, *Nabatéen*, 2: 21–22). It is a typical example of the merging or superposition of two divinities of similar nature in one sanctuary.

Cubic votive cippus, by the side of the road bordering the Siq, showing in relief the facade of an aedicula containing two betyls.

god of Rabbel," and in royal inscriptions of Aretas IV (*CIS* II, 208, 209, 211), Malichus II (Qabr at-Turkman), and Rabbel II (Imtan, *RÉS*, no. 83), he is called "the god of our lord," an expression that refers to the reigning sovereign.

The cult of Dushara took hold in southern Hauran as well, as shown by the inclusion of his name in combination with that of A'ra at Imtan, in two dedications from Bosra, and in a bilingual dedication from Umm al-Jimal. There are also mentions of Dushara on coins from Adraa, in a sanctuary at Meshquq (between Bosra and Imtan), and in a temple at Suweida. "A priest of Dushara" is mentioned in a center not far from Salkhad. The cult of the god spread beyond the borders of the

Nabatean realm with the expansion of Nabatean trade, and there is evidence of his veneration at Sidon (*CIS* II, 160), Pozzuoli (*CIS* II, 157), and at both Miletus and Delos, where Syllaeus, the king's minister, left an inscription to Zeus-Dushara "for the health of his king." The identification with Zeus shows that Dushara was considered the major god in the pantheon. It is possible, although less sure, that the Greek dedication to Zeus Hagios on an altar, now lost, found at Petra facing the Qasr el-Bint contained the name "Dusarei" on the third line (*PEQ* [1957]: 13–14, pl. XV B).

Various epithets that occupy the normal place for a proper name may designate a specific divinity, as in the case of an inscription inside a tomb at Hegra that in-

View of the gorge that provides access to Petra. In Petra, sites connected with cult practices were on the tops of high places and were reached by narrow paths or steps. The rocks to either side of gorges and gullies often contain representations of altars or betyls incised in the rock or in relief and inscriptions commemorating devotees or requesting divine protection.

Relief representing the bust of a god, Zeus or Dionysos, but probably also identifiable as Dushara, the chief god of the Nabateans.

Facsimile of an inscription carved on a stele or cippus from Salkhad, in the Hauran, 70 B.C.E., dedicated to the Syrian god Be'l Shamin. A greater variety of cults is attested in the Hauran, the northernmost part of the Nabatean kingdom, than in Petra.

vokes a deity using the expression "he who divides the day from the night." Given that Dushara is named in the text inscribed on the facade of the same tomb, it is highly likely that the epithet refers to him, and that he was considered the supreme god, not, as has been suggested, a solar deity. Identifying Dushara with the sun, in particular *Sol invictus,* as some scholars have suggested, does not seem to be proved by any certain evidence. On the other hand, the epithet "lord of the world" (*mr' 'lm'*) attested at Hegra in the epitaph of Raqos (267 C.E., JS, no. 17) seems to refer not to Dushara but to the god Be'l Shamin, who is so denominated at Palmyra. Names compounded with that of the god, all of which are of the type, "servant of Dushara" (*'bddwšr'* and *tymdwšr'*) are attested in particular in the southern Hauran.

The earliest representation of Dushara was probably in the form of a betyl, a term that means "house of god." There is a likely reference to the Nabatean god in a passage from the *Suda Lexicon,* which links him with Ares, probably for reasons of assonance. It states, under the heading "Theus Ares" (perhaps a combination of *theos* and Ares): "The god Ares. . . . His cult statue is black stone, a square, unworked, in height four feet, in width two. It rests on a base of hammered gold. To him they sacrifice and make libations of the blood of sacrificial

victims. This is how they perform libations. And the whole temple is adorned with much gold and there are many votive offerings.

In the Roman period Dushara was identified with Dionysos and took on the latter's iconography, as evidenced by epigraphic and literary mentions in particular. We learn from a later text, by Hesychios of Alexandria (fifth century C.E.), who quotes Isidorus of Charax, that Dushara is "the Dionysos of the Nabateans." A head crowned with vine leaves found at Petra has thus been identified as a head of Dionysos. In coins of the Roman era, however, the god appears both as a long-haired young man, following the traditional iconography for Nabatean kings, and in the form of a betyl. For example, in a bronze minting die from the period of Commodus (177 C.E.), made in Bosra, the reverse of the coin shows a young man with long curls and the legend, *Bosrenon Dousares.* A coin from the reign of Caracalla (209–210 C.E.) shows instead three betyls on a platform preceded by steps; the same iconography appears on bronze coins under Elagabalus; one rounded betyl is shown on bronzes from Adraa. Another coin from the age of Elagabalus, from Kerak (the ancient Characmoba), shows a sacellum with betyls and a large seated human figure. G. W. Bowersock has interpreted this image as a statue connected with an anthropomorphic cult of Dushara in which the three betyls represent Dushara flanked by Ruḍa/'Arṣu and Theriandros, a term that signifies "god-man" and also appears on an inscribed gem. The two flanking figures can be considered manifestations of Dushara, thus the three betyls, still according to Bowersock, are not a triad of three distinct deities, but rather a genuine trinity, one god in three manifestations.

As was true of other populations in the regions of Syria and Palestine, until the beginning of the first millennium B.C.E., the Nabateans venerated a series of other male divinities as well as Dushara. These were variants of the national god or of the gods venerated by earlier local populations whose reciprocal connections with Dushara are not absolutely clear and whose names are usually given as an epithet. Moreover, as is often the case in the region, preexisting cults were absorbed and, at least beginning in the Hellenistic period, divine attributes such as the throne assumed a genuinely godlike nature.

Be'l Shamin. The name Be'l Shamin signifies "lord of the sky," originally the epithet of a fertility god. Adored from the beginning of the first millennium B.C.E. (for example, at Biblos), his cult was widespread in the Syrian area. Even before the Hellenistic period, he had become one of the supreme gods of the Aramaic-speaking populations and was identified with Olympian Zeus. In Nabatean territories Be'l Shamin was venerated near Petra at el-Ji (Gaia); at Wadi Musa, an inscription (18–40 C.E.) designates him as the "god of Malichus" (Malichus I). Farther to the south he is named in the sanctuary of Allat at Gebel Ramm (Iram). His cult probably came from the Hauran, where he had an important sanctuary at Si', built toward the end of the first century B.C.E. and later restored. The Nabatean inscription on the architrave of the sacred complex there states that "the inner temple, the outer temples, the portico, and its covering" were built in a period between 33–32 and 2–1 B.C.E.

Some dedications to Be'l Shamin come from Bosra itself and its environs, where he appears as the protector of the tribe of the Qasiu (*RÉS*, no. 2042; *CIS* II, 174) and as the "god of Sa'idu" (*CIS* II, 176); at Salkhad an inscription calls him "Be'l Shamin, god of Mattanu."

Qos. Qos, like Be'l Shamin, was well known in the first millennium B.C.E., but in southern Palestine. We know of him as the national god of the Edomites, whose kings often bore compound names including his: there is evi-

Male head in limestone, bought on the antiquities market but perhaps from Petra. It shows a bearded man with a highly stylized hairstyle of rows of spiral curls, wearing a Phrygian cap. The subject has been interpreted as a priest on the basis of comparison with a figure whose hairstyle is similar and whose hand is raised in adoration or blessing (Amman: Archaeological Museum, J 2022). A similar head was found in the Temple of the Winged Lions.

Limestone Victory found at Khirbet et-Tannur. It originally served as a base for a bust of Tyche, a protective deity or tutelary genius, and it was surrounded by the twelve signs of the zodiac (now in the Cincinnati Art Museum). Part of the sign of Pisces is visible at the top right; the figure is wearing a peplum, belted and pinned at the shoulders with two rosette-shaped pins. The head has been dated to the late first century B.C.E. (Amman: Archaeological Museum, J 13484).

dence from the eighth century B.C.E. of such names as Qos-malak (Qos reigns) and Qos-gabbar (Qos is strong). The principal god of a people, he had characteristics typical of a god of the storm, as demonstrated in the Nabatean era by his identification with Zeus and by a depiction at Khirbet et-Tannur in which he is shown seated on a throne holding a lightning bolt and flanked by two bulls. Even after the disappearance of the Edomite state, the cult of Qos is attested in the region by many compound proper nouns in Aramaic documents of the fourth century B.C.E. In the Nabatean era Qos not only continued to appear in proper names but was still the object of special veneration: during the reign of Aretas IV, a temple (excavated by Nelson Glueck) was dedicated to him at Khirbet et-Tannur, in the valley of the Wadi Hasa, southwest of the Dead Sea. Written documents include three dedicatory inscriptions to Qos with the epithet "god of Ḥwrw," very probably the name of the place at which the temple was located. His cult does not seem to have been very widespread, but it is attested in the Hauran, and at Bosra a basalt eagle from the second century C.E. bears a dedication to him with an inscription in Nabatean and in Greek, further proof of the god's celestial nature.

Al-Kutba. Al-Kutba was the "lord of the temple." At Petra and at other sites within the Nabatean state, both in the north and the south, but in particular at Tell esh-Shuqafiya, in Egypt, there is evidence of a god of Arab origin named al-Kutba, or "the scribe" ("al-" is the definite article in Arabic and *ktb* is the root of the verb "to write"). This deity is considered to have originated in the Dedan region (today's al-'Ula), where he is attested

in Lihyanite inscriptions in the spelling *hn'ktb* and *hktby* (*h(n)-* is the Lihyanite article that corresponds to the Arabic *'l*). Al-Kutba was venerated at Petra, as seen in an invocation carved in a triclinium in the Wadi Siyyagh, near the principal spring in Petra, where the donor declares himself "remembered before *kwtb'*, this god." The inscription permits a sure reconstruction of the vocalization of the god's name as "Kutba." Another dedication—where the god's name is written *'lktb'*—appears in a sanctuary near the spring of 'Ain Shallaleh, at the foot of the Gebel Ramm. He was also venerated in Egypt, both at Tell esh-Shuqafiya and in the smaller of the two temples of Qasr Gheit, near el-Qantara, where an altar is dedicated to him. The attestations in Nabatean are important, because they demonstrate that this deity was male, something that has recently been questioned because of Syriac texts that mention a goddess named Kutba who is qualified as "Arab" in the feminine. This was a later modification, however: Kutba "the scribe" can be equated to the Mesopotamian god Nabu, who was, among other things, the god of writing. Also like Nabu, al-Kutba can be seen as the celestial figure corresponding to Hermes/Mercury, and diffusion of his cult in Arabia has been connected with the long periods of residence in that area of the Babylonian king Nabonidus. Jean Starcky (*DBS,* cols. 995–996) has reopened the question of whether al-Kutba can be identified as Ruḍa, hence equated to Dushara.

The god al-Kutba seems to be paired with a female deity. In the inscription (no. 17) from Wadi Ramm (see page 72, above), "Kutba, who is at Gaia" is linked with al-'Uzza, a name that is, once again, an epithet and that signifies "the strong one" in the feminine. The names appear on two adjacent betyls carved into the rock wall. Al-'Uzza, coupled here with the god identified with Mercury, is also considered to have a connection with the planets as a representation of Venus. Starcky proposes that the couple formed by al-Kutba and al-'Uzza can be equated with the Orotal-Alilat pairing mentioned by Herodotus. Orotal, in turn, may have a phonetic relationship with Ruḍa/'Arṣu at Palmyra, a god who corresponds to Hermes/Mercury and forms a pair with 'Azizu, the god of the star Venus, who is in turn a male version of al-'Uzza. Hence we can conclude that al-Kutba is yet another manifestation of Dushara. Two other betyls at Wadi Ramm state: "This [in the feminine] is al-'Uzza, and this one [in the masculine] is the lord of the temple [or, of the house]." Al-'Uzza and the "lord of the temple" are also mentioned together in an inscription at Petra, and three attestations of the same expression occur at Hegra. The "lord of the temple" is, once again, Dushara, and, according to Starcky, the temple mentioned here can be identified as the Qasr el-Bint, the principle religious building of Petra.

Shai' al-Qaum and Lycurgus. Another deity of northern-Arabian origin, also known by his epithet, Shai' al-Qaum ("he who guides [protects] the group [the clan]"), is attested in many Safaitic sites and was venerated throughout the Nabatean area. This god is not known at Petra, but given the broad diffusion of attestations to him in both the northern and the southern portions of the Nabatean state, we can ascribe this absence to the hazards of discovery. The first mentions in Nabatean of Shai' al-Qaum appear in an inscription from Tell Ghariyeh, near Bosra, that can be dated to the year 26 of the reign of Rabbel II (96 C.E.) and in an inscription from Hegra. His cult was present at Palmyra as well: he is named on tesserae there, and in one instance he is represented wearing a helmet, which seems appropriate for a god who is the "guide of the group" or clan (*RTP*, p. 46, no. 332). At Palmyra itself the most important dedication to Shai' al-Qaum was made in 132 C.E. by a Nabatean soldier, who offered him two altars and invoked him as a "good and remunerating god, who drinks no wine" (*CIS* II, 3978). This expression has been connected with the abstemious habits that Diodorus Siculus attributes to the most ancient, non-wine-drinking Nabateans. It has also been noted that this characteristic is highly appropriate for a god who manifests himself as the antagonist of Dionysos. Shai' al-Qaum has in fact been identified as Lycurgus, Dionysos's adversary in Greek mythology, but in a version that differs from the

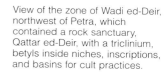

Facsimile of an inscription dated 96 C.E. carved on two basalt tablets at Tell Ghariyeh, near Bosra (Cantineau, *Nabatéen*, 2:20–21), honoring Shai' al-Qaum, the protector of the group or the clan. This was a deity of Arabian origin, identified with Lycurgus, venerated in the Hauran, in the southern sector of the Nabatean kingdom.

View of the zone of Wadi ed-Deir, northwest of Petra, which contained a rock sanctuary, Qattar ed-Deir, with a triclinium, betyls inside niches, inscriptions, and basins for cult practices.

Above, left: Wadi Ramm sanctuary. A betyl carved into the rock and an inscription naming al-'Uzza and the "lord of the temple," certainly an epithet of Dushara.

Above, right: Wadi Ramm sanctuary. Depiction in a betyl of the goddess Allat "who is at Bosra." In this case the cult from the Hauran had been transported to a sanctuary in the south. The figure is in poor condition, and scholars disagree about details (Is the figure posed on a crescent moon?).

Facsimile of a betyl with schematic eyes and nose. An inscription identifies it as Atargatis, the great Syrian goddess of fertility. The betyl is carved into a rock face of a high place in the gorge of the Wadi Siyyagh, at Ras Slaysil, to the northwest of Petra.

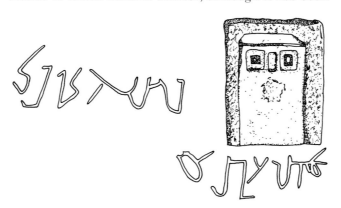

canonical one set in Thrace. The Arab variant of the myth of Lycurgus is reported by Nonnus of Panopolis in books 20–21 of his epic poem, the *Dionysiaca,* written at some point in the fifth century c.e. In this passage Dionysos combats Lycurgus, the son of Ares, who is described as a mythical king of the Arabs, later deified. After these events, the Arabs venerated Lycurgus, offering libations of blood and incense sacrifices. The cult of Lycurgus was in fact widespread in the Hauran, where a number of dedications to him in Greek have been discovered, thus leading to his identification with Shai' al-Qaum. One of the votive monuments to Lycurgus is an altar from Shobha that represents him holding a cylindrical object bearing two pinecones, the symbolic significance of which remains unclear, although it has been

seen as an attribute intended as a contrast with the grapevine of Dionysos/Dushara. The upper part of this altar shows five sculpted oil lamps, probably intended as receptacles for aromatics.

Other gods. Five dedications from Gerasa "to the Arabian god" or "to the sacred Arabian god" have been dated to the second century c.e.; two first-century c.e. inscriptions from the same site and the same sacred zone record the god Pakeidas (a name that must derive from the root *pqd,* "to govern"), in one instance associated with Hera. We know nothing certain about these gods, who are mentioned only in Greek inscriptions. Given that the dedications to Pakeidas are older, it is possible, as Starcky sustains, that the epithet of "Arabian god" was attributed to that deity, who might also be Shai' al-Qaum/Lycurgus, the "Arabian king-god."

A god named Hubalu is mentioned in the company of Dushara and Manawat in the Kamkam inscription from the Hauran (*CIS* II, 199). The same Hubalu may perhaps be the god mentioned in a dedication from Pozzuoli (*CIS* II, 158). His name also appears in compound names. According to the Arabian author Ibn al-Kalbi, the god Hubal was venerated at Mecca before Islam, when he was replaced by Allah.

Other gods named in Nabatean inscriptions are Du

Tada (or Du Tara), Asharu (known at Palmyra as well), and Gad, who was a protective deity like Tyche or Fortuna.

Goddesses

Allat. Allat was the Arabian deity identified with Athena. Her name is a contraction of *al-Illahat*, which means "the goddess," thus she corresponds to the Alilat mentioned by Herodotus as the companion of Orotal and the equivalent of the Greek Aphrodite. In Nabatean inscriptions her name can be simply Ilat; in the Safaitic inscriptions of northern Arabia it is Ilat or just Lat. Her cult seems to have been common throughout Nabatean territory, but the attestations are more concentrated in the north. She is never named in inscriptions from Petra, but a relief from the zone of the Qasr el-Bint of a bust of Athena is quite probably an image of her. One of her principal sanctuaries is that of the Gebel Ramm, mentioned several times, created during the reign of Rabbel II (Wenning, *Nabatäer*, pp. 101–104). This sanctuary contains important inscriptions and graffiti in which the goddess is called "the great goddess who is at Iram" or "Allat, the goddess who is at Iram." An inscription at 'Ain Shallaleh (Wenning, *Nabatäer*, no. 2) calls her instead "Allat, the goddess who is at Bosra." We can suppose that Rabbel II brought the cult of Allat from the capital of the Hauran to the sanctuary by the Wadi Ramm, although her cult is not documented at Bosra. That cult is amply documented, however, in other centers of the Bosra region. At Salkhad the reconstruction of a temple in her honor was completed by a certain Rawahu, in whose inscription the goddess appears as "Allat, their goddess [goddess of the dedicants], who is at Salhad." Among the inscriptions from the age of Rabbell II at the same site, one invokes "Allat and her *wagra*," a term Arabic in form that probably designates the cult chapel containing the image of the deity. Another inscription on an altar is dedicated to "Allat, lady [literally, "the one," in the feminine] of the place," which we can understand, like *wagra*, to denote the sacred site or the place of the diety's cult. In another inscription (*CIS* II, 185) she is called (if the interpretation given is accurate) "mother of the gods of our lord Rabbel." The cult of Allat is attested in the south as far as Hegra, where in a dedication of 1 C.E. she is called "Allat of 'Amnad," a term that probably refers to a locality or a sanctuary (*CIS* II, 198).

Ibn al-Kalbi (*The Book of Idols*, 10.3ff.) tells us that the nonfigurative representation of Allat was a "square rock" on top of which the clan that venerated her had

Alabaster bust of Isis of an iconography uncommon in the area, found in the ez-Zantur sector of Petra during the course of Swiss excavations under the direction of Rolf A. Stucky. The fact that alabaster is not present locally supports the notion that the statuette was an Egyptian import.

placed a structure. In the sanctuary of the Gebel Ramm, immediately to the right of the inscription that speaks of "Allat who is at Bosra," there is something resembling a figure with one arm raised that seems to depict a humanized betyl (*DBS*, fig. 705, detail no. 3), but the relief is in poor condition and the interpretation is contested. Allat is represented following the iconography typical of Athena on an altar from Hebran, in the Hauran, where Dushara may also be depicted as Dionysos. Still, even if Allat is represented here as the war-like Greek goddess, the notion of her that predominates in the texts is that of a tutelary goddess. In this role, she, like a local Tyche, is confused with Atargatis, the Syrian goddess who is mentioned once at Petra (*CIS* II, 423) and whose high place has been identified at Ras Slaysil, to the northwest of Petra.

Al-'Uzza. The goddess al-'Uzza, who is associated in the Gebel Ramm sanctuary with al-Kutba (the god identified with Hermes/Mercury), is first attested in Lihyanite graffiti, perhaps of the fourth–third century B.C.E., as "'Uzzay o han-'Uzzay." As we have seen, the goddess is equated with Aphrodite/Venus, and she corresponds to the Alilat mentioned by Herodotus but usually called Allat. This connection is demonstrated by a bilingual inscription from Cos of 9 B.C.E., dedi-

Facsimile of an altar with an inscription found near Salkhad, in the Hauran, that bears a dedication to Allat, called "the mistress of the place." The meaning of this epithet is unclear and may refer to either the sanctuary or a locality.

Facsimile of a group of Nabatean inscriptions from the valley of the Wadi Mugharah, in the Sinai, copied in 1850 by P.V. Lottin de Laval and reproduced in the *Corpus inscriptionum semiticarum*. There are a number of rock graffiti of recent origin in this same region that still reflect cult practices typical of the Nabateans and that mention Nabatean proper names along with more typically Arab ones.

Right: General view of the necropolis at the exit from the Siq.

cated to a goddess identified in the Nabatean text as al-'Uzza and in the Greek text as Aphrodite. Isaac of Antioch, a fifth-century author, calls the same goddess "Beltis" (the feminine form of Bel, meaning "the lady"), 'Uzzay, and Kaukabta ("the star"). It should be noted, however, that in some cases Allat and al-'Uzza tend to merge or share characteristics. In general, Allat tends to fade in favor of al-'Uzza, who eventually predominates. The pairing of al-Kutba and al-'Uzza found at Gebel Ramm came to correspond to Herodotus's Orotal and Alilat, while the personality of Allat came to be assimilated with that of Athena and Atargatis, moving away from that of al-'Uzza and Aphrodite. This process seems to have been complete by the first century C.E. Al-'Uzza is portrayed in the sanctuary of Iram as a squared idol with eyes. It is certain that there was a temple dedicated to her at Petra, as seen, in particular, in a document of 124 C.E. found at Nahal Hever, near the Dead Sea, which mentions an Aphrodiseion in that city. No temple of the sort can be securely identified among the religious edifices of Petra, though suggestions have included the Qasr el-Bint and the Temple of the Winged Lions (see Wenning, *Nabatäer*, 233).

Al-'Uzza was also venerated in the Sinai, where the only compound name including her name has been found (*CIS* II, 946) in the form of *'bd'l'zz*, or "servant of al-'Uzza," a name that later became common among pre-Islamic Arabs. Other inscriptions from the same region (*CSI* II, 611, 1236) name a priest of the goddess (*khn 'zy'*), thus showing that a sanctuary to al-'Uzza existed there. She was venerated at Ruwwafa in the form *'zzy*, or 'Uzzaya, as implied in a graffito cited by Starcky. Later her cult penetrated further to the south, where the planet Venus was represented by the god 'Athar and where a Sabaean inscription of the fourth century C.E. tells of a person who made a gold statue for 'Uzzayan (*CIS* IV, 558, 559). The goddess was still venerated in the Byzantine age: St. Jerome (*Vita Sancti Hilarionis, PL*, 23, col. 41) records the cult of Venus as the morning star (Lucifer) at Elusa (Khalasa). Ibn al-Kalbi reports that she was still venerated at Mecca in the ninth century C.E.

Manawat. Manawat was the goddess of fate. Her name, attested in inscriptions in various spellings, is derived from the Aramaic *menata*, a word meaning "part" or "portion," the root of which is *mnw*. Thus she represented the portion, or lot, that every individual receives, which is to say, Fate. Ibn al-Kalbi records her as Mana(t), the Arabic form of her name, and notes that she was the oldest goddess of a triad that she formed with Allat and

The principal high place of Petra, on the summit of Gebel el-Madhbah, a name that means "Mount of the Sacrifice." It is an open-air sanctuary with a temenos, or sacred precinct, at the highest point of which there are installations for cult practices. A series of platforms where idols may have been placed stands at the top of steps and faces a courtyard with a rectangular table at its center. To the left there was an altar. The complex also includes wells and basins. The name of the deity venerated here is unknown.

al-'Uzza. She seems to have been especially venerated near Medina by the Aus and Khazrag tribes. In the year 8 of the Hegira, the prophet Muhammed has 'Ali destroy an idol of her (*Book of the Idols*, 8.7ff.). In the Nabatean period the cult of Manawat is attested in Hegra in particular, where she is named immediately after Dushara in rupestrian tomb inscriptions. Two inscriptions (*CIS* II, 197, 198) mention her with "her Qaisha" (*mnwtw wqyšh*). This term has been connected with the element "al-Qais," which frequently appears as an epithet of divinity in Arabic personal names. It has prompted much discussion. Some scholars consider it the name of a deity. Jean Starcky (*DBS*, col. 1001) supposed, basing his argument on the Arabic *qa'is* (measure), that "Qaisha" is the cubit, a symbol of just measure, and is a deified attribute of Manawat in much the same way that the seat or *motab* is a deified attribute of Dushara.

Isis. The Egyptian cult of Isis, widespread in the Hellenistic and Roman eras in both the East and the West, is also well attested in the Nabatean area. At Petra a winged sun with horns and ears of wheat—the symbols of Isis—decorates the central acroterion of the Khazneh; a fine image of the goddess comes from the Temple of the Winged Lions; a statuette of Isis imported from Egypt was found in the ez-Zantur area. Two sanctuaries are also dedicated to the goddess, one at Wadi Abu-'Olleqa, north of Petra, and the other at the entrance to the Wadi Siyyagh.

Religion

The High Places and Other Outdoor Sanctuaries

As we have seen, the deity Dushara, from very ancient times and throughout the Near East, typically manifested itself and often resided on a mountain summit or

Steps leading from the Tomb of the Roman Soldier to the high place of the Zibb 'Atuf. The devotees who used this route have left traces of their passage in cult niches carved into the rock walls and graffiti bearing invocations.

other high elevation. This was where open-air sanctuaries were set up. They were of a very simple type and were usually called "high places," a term present in the Hebrew Bible. The high place was not connected to the veneration of one specific god, which means that unless dedicatory inscriptions or cult objects that can reliably be ascribed to a particular deity are found there, it is impossible to assign high places to one or another of the known gods. In the Nabatean sphere, the essential elements of a high place were a sacred space with an altar, a betyl, and a triclinium. A triclinium, generically speaking, is a room or an outdoor space for gatherings or communal meals, edged by benches for the participants. Although high places vary little in their essential elements, they show a certain variety according to the terrain on which they are installed—gullies, rocky heights, simple flat places—

and according to the size and complexity of the arrangements.

At Petra the principal summits dominating the city all have such sites. The main ones are on the Zibb 'Atuf and the Gebel Khubtha, but there are lesser installations on the al-Habis hill. The Zibb 'Atuf, also called Gebel el-Madhbah, or "hill of the sacrifice," overlooks the city to the east, and it may have been reached by means of a path leaving from the zone south of the theater, or else by a stepped path rising more to the north. According to Jean Starcky, it is likely that it could also have been reached, as is true today, from the Wadi Farasah, where one pilgrim left an invocation to Dushara (CIS II, 401). The sacred place itself consists of a platform that functioned as a courtyard measuring some 65 m × 20 m, flanked by cisterns. This space contained a triclinium approxi-

mately 14.5 m × 6.5 m, in front of which there was a base for betyls and an altar, perhaps for sacrifices, preceded by steps; next to it there was another round altar, perhaps for libations.

There must have been a second triclinium to the north of this and, somewhat more to the east, some 10 meters from the first triclinium, a square basin 1.25 m deep with sides 2.65 m long. The god to whom this high place was dedicated is not known, but many scholars suppose him to have been Dushara and take the site to be the oldest in Petra. Evidence is lacking, however. Not far from the summit there are two tall rock structures, usually called "obelisks" because they are roughly square and narrow from bottom to top. They have been assigned ritual significance and connected with Dushara and al-'Uzza. Not all scholars are in agreement with this interpretation: Philip C. Hammond thinks them simply pillars, remainders from an abandoned rock quarry, and Robert Wenning interprets them as funerary monuments (nefesh).

The other famous high place and the largest complex of installations of this type at Petra (in reality, more than one sacred space) lies across the Siq on the high plateau of el-Kubtha. In the northwest part of this zone, a certain number of other sacred places have been identified that include triclinia, water reservoirs, cisterns, and niches containing betyls or representations of betyls. These sites are not far from Dorotheos, and some of these installations may have been connected with houses. One of these sacred places consists of three courtyards with benches and a chapel measuring 2.20 m across, reached by means of a flight of stairs. A vast rock sanctuary, also reached by flights of stairs, lies at the summit. The long stepped path that leads to it begins near the tomb of Sextius Florentinus, and not far from the top there is a niche for two idols with a dedication to al-'Uzza and the "lord of the temple." Among the usual arrangements at the top there is a horseshoe-shaped triclinium known as the stibadium. Other features include a betyl represented in relief on the back wall of a chapel, basins, cisterns for rain water, and, more to the east, a long cistern that once had a vaulted roof. Two other sacred zones have been identified in the western part of al-Habis.

The entire area around Petra is literally constellated with sacred places of many sorts. To the northwest, the road that leads toward the plateau of ed-Deir has several triclinia, betyls, and, at the site known as Qattar ed-Deir, a genuine rupestrian sanctuary. Various installations for worship and gatherings have been found in the area of Wadi Numeir, and at en-Numeir a chapel of Obodas II (III) has an inscription of 20–21 C.E. commemorating the king-god Obodas I, who was buried at 'Avdat. There are two sanctuaries of Isis with cult images, as we have seen, at Wadi Siyyagh and Wadi Abu-'Olleqa, to the south, and there is a sanctuary of Dushara with an inscription to that god at Sadd el-Ma'agian.

Sanctuaries and cult sites have of course been documented throughout the Nabatean territory, and their typology is in part connected to the cultural history of the region in which they are located. This means that the situation in the Hauran differs from what is typical of the Negev, the Sinai, or the southern regions of the Hisma and the Hijaz. In the Hauran, the famous sanctuary of Si', which was dedicated, as an inscription tells us, to the Syrian god Be'l Shamin, deserves mention; the most important site in the Sinai is the sanctuary of 'Avdat; in the Hisma there is also the famous sanctuary of the Gebel Ramm (the ancient Iram), with the temple of Allat near the 'Ain Shallaleh spring, explored some thirty years ago by Raphaël Savignac, who identified several structures (excavated later), but also many inscriptions and betyls. The site of Ruwwafa has a temple similar to the one at Gebel Ramm and various inscriptions in Nabatean, Thamudic, and Greek. In the Hijaz, the site of Hegra has provided not only many tombs but a sanctuary known as Diwan, near the Gebel Ethlib, that includes betyls in niches and Nabatean inscriptions that mention Dushara, Allat, and other deities.

Betyls, Altars, and Other Cult Objects:
The Religious Vocabulary
The ancient authors who speak of Nabatean divinities often describe stones of various forms that they take as representations of those gods. As we have noted, such nonfigurative representations are called "betyls." This

Detail of the high place of the Gebel el-Madhbah, showing a part of the sector reserved for the altars and other cult objects. In the foreground is a portion of the courtyard, where the faithful gathered.

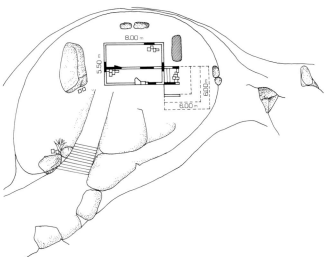

term derives from an expression that signifies "house of the divinity," which indicates that such stones were not precisely images of the gods, but rather were the place where the gods resided or manifested themselves. This belief had become attenuated in the Nabatean era, when the betyls, to which more or less schematic human features were often added, seem to indicate that the devotee venerated the stele as a representation of the deity itself. Moreover, when there is an inscription identifying the betyl, the phrase used is of the type, "this is al-'Uzza," or, more simply, "the lord of the temple."

The anthropomorphic images of Nabatean deities that we possess have been borrowed from classical iconography, but both sorts of figuration—the aniconic and the anthropomorphic—continued to be produced at the same time. As G. W. Bowersock has shown, coins from various Nabatean cities of the Roman age depict, at times on the two sides of the same coin, a triad of betyls and a humanized image of the god

Dushara. It has always been supposed, with a high degree of certainty, that the three betyls are cult images in the main sanctuary of the city, as is true, for example, of the depiction of enthroned betyls on the coins of certain Phoenician cities. These traditional images exist side by side with cult statues of the Hellenistic type (which were also reproduced on coins), but they did not replace the aniconic images.

The typology of betyls shows few variations: at Petra and at Hegra they are often carved in relief on a rock face; less frequently, they are carved into the rock or simply incised onto the surface. The most common form is a simple rectangle, but they can also be triangular, a truncated cone, or, more rarely, hemispherical. If the two obelisks—truncated pyramids 6.5 to 7 m high—of the Gebel el-Madhbah are indeed betyls, they are unique instances.

Betyls can appear in isolation, but they are often present in groups. Usually they are placed in a niche, which

Cult aedicula carved into a rock face in the Sadd el-Ma'agian gorge. A first facade flanked by attached columns stands within a deep cavity; it contains a second facade with an arched architrave between two engaged columns. The niche, which at one time must have contained the cult image, is now empty.

Left: View of the en-Numeir hill, where there was another important cult site. Petra and its environs contained many open-air sanctuaries other than the high place of the Gebel el-Madhbah, all on the summits of hills or at the heads of gullies cut by wadis.

Right: Gorge of Sadd el-Ma'agian, northeast of Petra, which contains a cult site. In the walls of the gully are niches with betyls, objects of veneration for those who visited the site.

View of the Wadi Ramm sanctuary, near the spring of 'Ain Shallaleh. Here and in many other cases the sacred place was centered around a spring, and the cult celebrated the virtues of water. The rock face over the spring contains many inscriptions and betyl figures.

probably represents a religious building. A niche or aedicula may contain as many as three betyls, often of different sizes, although the central one is usually the tallest. Most of the betyls in Petra are anonymous; only in a few cases can they be identified by a text or a schematic representation of a face. One striking example is the inscribed betyl from the Temple of the Winged Lions that represents a winged female deity.

Just as the betyl was sacred because, at least originally, it was the seat of the divine presence, other objects were sacred because of their connection to divinity. Altars were among these. They were often figured on the access ways to sanctuaries, where the deity resided; they provided the support for a betyl, when they might be shaped like a throne, a platform, or simply a base for the betyl, in which case it was known as a *motab*, a noun derived from the verb root *ybt*, which means "to be" or "to sit." In some inscriptions the name of the god Dushara is followed by "his [the god's] *motab*" or coupled with that phrase on the same level of importance. That the seat of the deity was sacred is confirmed (even outside the Nabatean sphere, in particular, in Phoenicia) by votive thrones, which may either be empty, bear a seated deity, or even be presented, in a more or less geometrical form, as a direct object of devotion. Like altars and seats, stelae and ex-voto images were also sacred objects.

We know some of the names for cult sites and their furnishings. The Nabatean language used the common Semitic term *bayta*, the same term used for a house, to refer to a temple (for *byt(')*, see *CIS* II, 182). The term *birta*, which originally designated a fortress, was used for the principal temple of Si' (for *brt(')*; see *CIS* II, 164). The term *mahramata*, from the root *ḥrm*, "to be sacred" or "consecrated," indicates a sanctuary in inscriptions from Pozzuoli and Dumah (*mhrmt(')*; *CIS* II, 158; *RB* 64 [1957]: 215). The meanings of the terms used in the inscriptions from Bosra (*RÉS*, nos. 2093, 2094) are still under discussion. One use of the term *theatron* (a transliteration from the Greek, transcribed as *tytr(')*) to designate a sacred space is attested (*CIS* II, 163; see also *RÉS*, nos. 803, 804, 2023), but its exact form and function are still not clear. The stele or votive cippus is *nisbeta* (*nṣbt(')*, from the root *nṣb*, "to erect"; *RB* 43 [1934]: n. 16; *RÉS*, no. 1088) or *maṣ ṣeba* (*mṣb(')*; *Syria* 35 [1958]: 246, etc.).

The human image—the statue—is called *salma*, a term that takes the masculine if the statue is of a male, the feminine if it is of a female (for example, the statue of the deified Obodas is called *slm(')*; *CIS* II, 354). In

Sadd el-Ma'agian. Cult niche with a stepped platform and, inside, a betyl in the form of a truncated column. The inscriptions point to veneration of Dushara and al-'Uzza, but they also mention "all the gods," without further specification.

Two cult niches with betyls (nos. 154, 170) carved into a rock face in the gorge of the Siq. Again, these anonymous representations indicate a divine presence but provide no precise identification.

the Hauran, an altar is *masghida* (*msḡd(')*, from the verb root *sgd*, "to adore"). Hence an altar is an object by means of which the deity is adored, a sense that is transferred to the sanctuary itself (see *RÉS*, no. 2024) and, in Islam, to the mosque.

Some terms are not found in the southern part of the Nabatean territory and may reflect a Syrian influence. One of these is *hmn(')*, or *hammana*, a term used at Palmyra to designate an altar for burning incense or the construction that contains it, also attested in Nabatean to indicate a sacred construction. The altar at Cos that bears the dedication of Syllaeus contains the term *rb't(')*, or *rabata*, which by its etymology indicates a squared object. The same term is found elsewhere with other meanings, a cult edifice for example: Sidon (*CIS* II, 160); environs of Bosra (*RÉS*, no. 482); Bosra (*RÉS*, no. 2092). A related and etymologically similar term is *'rb'n'* (*RÉS*, no. 2036). Jean Starcky has proposed that these terms can be understood as incense altars, and that later the meaning shifted to that of a temple honoring fire. The word *hmn*, a chapel, seems attested in Syria, however, as early as the latter third of the second millennium B.C.E.

Sacrifices and Offerings

We have little information regarding sacrifices. A pas-

Outline of feet carved into the rock of the sanctuary of en-Numeir. Such representations symbolizing the faithful are quite common. Another example is at the sanctuary of ed-Deir.

sage in Strabo, who cites Athenodorus as his source, refers to sacrifices in honor of the sun that supposedly took place on rooftops: "They worship the sun, building an altar on the top of the house, and pouring libations on it daily and burning frankincense" (16.4.26). Isaac of Antioch also reports that Arabian women went up to the rooftops to invoke al-'Uzza. No archaeological information confirms these traditions. In similar fashion, there is no concrete confirmation of a custom of spreading betyls with the blood of sacrificial victims. Certainly the Nabateans, like all ancient peoples, must have offered animals and edible plants as sacrifices and must have made libations. The small "horned" altars have been interpreted as incense altars or, at least, structures for burning substances presumed to have been aromatic. The offering of sacrificial animals, followed by a communal meal, is confirmed by the spaces or rooms with benches known as triclinia. Nabatean, like other Semitic languages, has a term for the communal ceremony with a banquet: *mrzḥ(')*, the vocalization of which is uncertain. There are many attestations of the term, which denotes either the festive gathering itself or a religious or festive confraternity that met periodically to honor a particular god. An inscription carved over a niche near the edifice of ed-Deir in Petra records the "confraternity" or "association" of Obodas, the god, indicating that a group met there periodically in celebration of the deified king.

Right and below, left: Group of cult niches in the form of aedicula facades, with pilasters surmounted by architraves and pediments, sculpted on the rock wall of the valley of the Siq. The aediculae may have been empty or may have contained one or more betyls.

Far right: Rectangular aedicula sculpted into the rock at the sanctuary of en-Numeir, showing a schematic throne. The "throne" of Dushara is mentioned in inscriptions and was in itself divine, along with the god who occupied it.

Right: Stairs carved into the rock, leading to a sacred site.

Below: Funerary triclinium and Garden Tomb, in the zone of Wadi Farasah. The triclinium was placed in front of the porticoed building that is visible; it was probably covered with a vault. In such halls the dead were remembered with banquets, perhaps on the anniversary of their death. No written texts remain to record these practices, but the funerary inscription of the Turkmaniya Tomb mentions such installations.

Funerary triclinium in front of the Tomb of the Roman Soldier, in the zone of Wadi Farasah. The hall is decorated with engaged columns and rectangular niches like large windows set in the intervals between the columns. The guests at funeral ceremonies would have sat on cushioned benches.

The question of whether the Nabateans practiced human sacrifice arises, as it does for many ancient peoples, but there is absolutely no confirmation of it. Jean Starcky records and discusses the evidence, which is scant and late. According to Porphyry, for example, "The Dumatii, a people of Arabia, annually sacrificed a boy, whom they buried under the altar, which was then used by them as a statue" (*De abstinentia*, 2.56). In this case, however, the practice is reported by a Christian, and child sacrifice was a cliché, a charge often leveled at pagans. Only for the fourth century c.e., when the Nabatean state had already disappeared, is there specific mention of a sacrifice, that of four hundred virgins in honor of al-'Uzza, but this event occurred in the city of Hira and, if there is any truth in the story, the slaughter may have been an exceptional, war-related event.

The Priesthood

As is the case with ritual, some terms regarding the priesthood have come down to us, but we know nothing about the actual functions of priestly personnel. The word that indicates a priest in Aramaic, *kumra*, *kmr(')*, occurs only rarely in Nabatean, in the singular or in the plural, although there are instances of it in one inscription from Petra, another from the Hauran, and one from Egypt. Elsewhere the more frequent term is *kahin*, *khn(')*, which comes from Arabic but was used

both *kahin* and *afkal* (CIS II, 506, 1748). Another function for which we have evidence is *petora*, or *ptwr(')*, probably an interpreter of dreams or a seer.

Petra furnishes particularly few attestations of priestly titles, although there is documentation of confraternities or cult societies, for which the noun *mrzh* is used, as we have seen. The *mrzh* of Dushara, "god of Gaia," who must certainly have been present at Petra, is instead attested by an inscription from Oboda ('Avdat) incised on a basin that served as a krater for banquets. The heads of the confraternities must have had notable social prominence; we know that at Palmyra the head of the confraternity of Bel was one of the most influential men in the city.

The Cult of the Dead

Despite Strabo's assertion that the Nabateans displayed such extreme scorn for the dead that they buried their kings with no special honors, the Nabatean dead must have been honored with ceremonies similar to those that paid homage to the gods. This is demonstrated not only by the sumptuous rock tombs of Petra and Hegra, but also by installations of a religious nature connected with tombs and by epigraphic evidence. At Petra the inscription in the en-Numeir chapel, already mentioned (*CIS* II, 354), is proof of the cult of the deified King Obodas, and the cult of a less well known god, Du-Tada (or Du-Tara), must have involved ceremonies that were both religious and funerary. The inscription of the tomb known as Qabr at-Turkman lists an entire series of installations—rooms, a courtyard, and wells—that undoubtedly functioned in the service of a cult of the dead. Triclinia carved into the rock, either inside funerary buildings or in the open air in front of the tomb, were certainly made with funerary ritual in mind. Funerary monuments, often with inscriptions, are scattered throughout Petra. These stones, which are similar to betyls (for which they are in fact easily confused), are known as *nefesh*, an Aramaic term that means "vital breath," although later the word came to indicate the funerary monument itself.

Just as the betyl was the dwelling place of the sacred, the *nefesh* monument generally represents and commemorates the dead person; it does not necessarily indicate the place of burial, however. For example, two identical funerary inscriptions from Medaba state: "This is the tomb and the two *nefesh* which are above it," thus clearly distinguishing between the tomb itself and the *nefesh* and emphasizing the symbolic character of the latter. Still more characteristic is the inscription on a *nefesh* at Petra that commemorates a person born

in other Semitic languages close to Aramaic, the so-called Canaanite languages, Hebrew and Phoenician in particular. This means that it is impossible to tell whether there was any difference in function between the priest—*kmr*—of Allat named in one text (*CIS* II, 170) and the priest—*khn*—of Allat recorded in the sanctuary at Iram (*RB* 41 [1932]: 591). There is ample testimony to the title *afkal* (*'pkl(')*), and the term "servants of *afkal*" is recorded at Gebel Ramm (*RB* 43 [1933]: 411). This ancient term of Sumerian origin, also attested in Palmyra and Hatra, probably penetrated into northern Arabia in the neo-Babylonian period. Here, too, the specific functions that the term implies are unclear, but it does seem that the same person could be

in that city (given in Nabatean as Reqem) but who died and was buried in Gerasa. Thus the monument in Petra commemorates the deceased in his home city.

The religious life of the Nabateans, like that of all ancient peoples, seems indissolubly mingled with their daily life. Sanctuaries and tombs are present everywhere in Petra, and they are much more in evidence than dwellings. Inscriptions always contain a religious element. Despite the fairly high number of Nabatean deities, scholars have often considered the religious beliefs and practices of the Nabateans to have been fairly simple, although Dominique Sourdel's reconstruction of the various cults of the Hauran offers an exception to this rule. There does not seem to have been a complex, hierarchi-cally organized pantheon. In spite of the diversity in their names, the Nabatean gods had similar characteristics, and in fact their names may have varied because they emerged from cults in different regions and at different times. Scholars have often stressed the tendency of the Nabatean gods to merge, but these notions need to be corrected, at least in part, because they seem to be based on ideas or ideals that have not always been clearly demonstrated. One such idea is the hypothesis of a simple religion of nomadic peoples; another, a tendency to suppose that a faith in an essentially unique god was inherent in this people and all other "pagan" peoples. Without completely rejecting these general reconstructions, and acknowledging that many phenomena of syncretism have been observed, it nonetheless seems opportune to emphasize the fact that the documentation exhibits immense lacunae that can falsify the hypothetical reconstructions. Almost nothing survives of Nabatean mythology, although the Lycurgan tradition permits a hint of it. Nabatean religious belief and practice are still attested, for the most part, by archaeological remains and laconic inscriptions as yet unsubjected to in-depth interpretation. The long history of the region in which the Nabateans settled and the diversity of the traditions attested in that area point to a complexity of beliefs and traditions that still needs to be brought into focus.

Political and Public Functions; Trades and Occupations

Almost all that we know about Nabatean society consists in some political and military titles and the names of functions and occupations. Indirectly, however, we can reconstruct the lifestyle of the population during certain periods. The diversity of the territories that were included within the Nabatean state, combined with changes over time, invite us to be sensitive to differences in the daily customs of its inhabitants, in particular, to differences between north and south and between urban and rural areas.

Much of our information derives from the well-known passages in the works of Diodorus Siculus and Strabo that have already been mentioned, in which Diodorus provides information on the Nabateans beginning in the late fourth century B.C.E. and Strabo reports on the situation in the first century B.C.E., when the Nabateans were a sedentary population and had formed an urbanized state. The two authors give opposing images of Nabatean social organization, but both accounts are highly valuable to the historian. Diodorus reports: "For the sake of those who do not know, it will be useful to state in some detail the customs of these Arabs, by following which, it

is believed, they preserve their liberty. They live in the open air, claiming as native land a wilderness that has neither rivers nor abundant springs. . . . It is their custom neither to plant grain, set out any fruit-bearing tree, use wine, nor construct any house. . . . Some of them raise camels, others sheep, pasturing them in the desert. While there are many Arabian tribes who use the desert as pasture, the Nabataeans far surpass the others in wealth although they are not much more than ten thousand in number; for not a few of them are accustomed to bring down to the sea frankincense and myrrh and the most valuable kinds of spices, which they procure from those who convey them from what is called Arabia Eudaemon [Arabia Felix]. They are exceptionally fond of freedom; and, whenever a strong force of enemies comes near, they take refuge in the desert, using this as a fortress; for it lacks water and cannot be crossed by others, but to them alone, since they have prepared subterranean reservoirs lined with stucco, it furnishes safety (Diodorus, 19.94.2–6)." Diodorus goes on to narrate the events of the war against Antigonus, speaking of the "rock" where the Nabateans customarily took refuge.

Strabo (16.4.21, 26) instead describes a sedentary society and a monarchical and democratic state in which the king is one citizen among many and Petra is a large, peaceful, cosmopolitan city. Both descriptions have been considered trustworthy, because they both are

View of the plateau surrounding Petra. We know from Diodorus Siculus that the Nabateans had their impenetrable refuge in this zone as early as the late fourth century B.C.E. Petra was not a real city at that time, however, and contemporary Nabateans are described as essentially nomadic.

Entrance to Petra through the valley of the Siq. The landscape agrees with Diodorus's description of it: he reports that the Nabateans "live in the open air, claiming as native land a wilderness that has neither rivers nor abundant springs," and he adds: "It is their custom neither to plant grain, set out any fruit-bearing tree, use wine, nor construct any house. . . . Some of them raise camels, others sheep, pasturing them in the desert" (19.94.3–4).

based on sources contemporary to the events they narrate; thus the two authors' accounts are often compared to demonstrate that the Nabateans passed from a semi-nomadic stage to a type of sedentary life still marked, however, by its origins as a tribal society. The concepts of nomadism, pastoralism, and bedouin society have been examined on several occasions, even fairly recently by Ernst Axel Knauf, who judges the Nabatean state to have been one of the rare examples of what might be called a fully realized bedouin state. Bedouins are, by definition, nomadic pastoralists who live by raising camels, as Diodorus related, and who, thanks to the camel's ability to travel long distances in the desert (but also thanks to the nourishment and material for tents that the camel provides) are completely free of any reliance on sedentary agriculturalists. Yet the camel's capabilities for

transport rendered the bedouins indispensable to the sedentary populations, a situation that offered notable opportunities for enrichment, as Diodorus points out, which in turn led to social stratification and the emergence of a chief. Gain, or the need for gain, leads this sort of society to predatory activities, which further increase the bedouins' skills as warriors and their ability to assume power and form a state. According to Knauf's reconstruction, among the Nabateans, military power was in the hands of one tribe, the Nabaṭu. Their leader was a king, and their economic center was a city—Petra—the wealth of which was founded on long-distance commerce, which meant that it was based on the camel as a means of transport. The royal family held the wealth and controlled the rest of the tribe largely through religion. This reconstruction has been subjected to detailed

Zibb 'Atuf, slope facing the theater.

criticism by M. C. A. Macdonald, and the passage from Diodorus and the accuracy of his sources have been questioned by David F. Graf, according to whom Diodorus was delivering a stereotyped, literary description of only limited value as a historical account.

In contrast to the bedouin state reconstructed by Knauf and the literary nomadism that Diodorus describes, Nabatean society appears to have been, from the very beginning, a stratified society, only one part of which was a Nabatean nomadic element that merged with a population of sedentary agriculturalists (still present in the Persian era), whose language the nomads adopted. Even religious cults were varied and often local: Dushara, the principal Nabatean god, appears to have been tied to a specific place from the start: he was "the god of Shara" rather than the god of a tribal group.

Finally, even if the wealth of the kingdom was in large part based on revenues from commercial activities (unlike nearby states, Judea in particular), the organization of the state did not differ in its essence from that of the sedentary states that surrounded it. At the head of that state there was a monarch, about whose functions and prerogatives we have little information.

Even considering all the reservations necessary when little data is at hand, the Nabatean monarchy seems to have been relatively stable and not specifically linked to religion, unlike the neighboring state of Judea, which was conditioned by the cult of *yahwe* and by a rivalry among classes and priestly groups. The titularies that some of the Nabatean sovereigns chose for themselves hint at influences from the eastern Hellenistic modes for conceiving of royalty. Aretas III appears as "Philhellene,"

Nabatean coin with a profile of Aretas IV crowned with laurel. The legend gives his title, "King of Nabaṭu, who loves his people" (Paris: Bibliothèque nationale).

Fragment of a bilingual inscription on marble in Nabatean and Latin, found in Rome in the sanctuary of the Magna Mater on the Palatine. The overall data show that between the late first century B.C.E. and the early years of the first century C.E., Nabatean society was expanding, thanks to trade revenues, and its structure was hierarchical.

Above: Coin with the heads of Obodas II (III) and his wife.

Right: Coin of Tigranes of Armenia (95–54 B.C.E.), a contemporary of Obodas I and Aretas III.

written in Greek, on coins minted at Damascus. Malichus II picked the title "who loves his people," which corresponds to the Greek Philopatris or Philodemos; Aretas IV was "he who has made [his people] prosper," or, more literally, "has made [them] live," "has made [them] healthy," or "has delivered his people," phrases that can be assimilated to the Greek Sosipatros. Such titularies are unknown in earlier epigraphic formulas in the Near East, even if the concept of the king who brings prosperity and showers benefits on his people is traditional in the ancient Near East.

Some queens are also known from inscriptions and coins. Shaqilat, the mother of Rabbel II, acted as regent for a number of years at the beginning of her son's reign; she was served by a minister named 'Unaishu, whose name survives on a tomb inscription where the queen is called the sister of the king and the minister is given the title of brother. This is probably a way of expressing equal rank rather than a reference to dynastic marriage between siblings. The terms occur in the Near East from very ancient times; and the notion of rank is particularly clear in documents of the last phase of the Bronze Age, around the fourteenth century B.C.E. There is evidence, however, that Shaqilat, the wife of Malichus II, was the daughter of Aretas IV and thus Malichus's sister (*PEQ*

113 [1981]: 24). That king may have had more than one wife, given that we know Aretas IV had wives named Haldu and Shaqilat, and Rabbel II had wives named Gamilath and Hagiru. The wife of the king was undoubtedly an important figure: not only did she have the title of queen, but at times her effigy appears on coins coupled with that of the king.

Some inscriptions name not only the king and the queen but the king's children and grandchildren: one inscription from Petra commemorates Obodas the king-god (*CIS* II, 354) and names King Aretas IV, his wife Shaqilat, and their children Malichus, Obodas, Rabbel, Fasael, Sha'udat, and Hagiru, plus a son of Hagiru, also named Aretas. A fragmentary inscription, also from Petra but of unknown origin, names the three sons of Aretas given above plus one daughter named Shaqilat, called "queen of the Nabateans," and another, Gamilath, also given the title of queen. The family of Aretas IV is named in another inscription from 'Avdat as well.

Succession to the throne was hereditary, as we can see from inscriptions that show, for example, that Malichus II, the son of Aretas IV, was the father of Rabbel II. Aretas IV, on the other hand, seems to have been a usurper, but Jean Starcky has shown, on the basis of an inscription found near Petra, that he must have been a member of the royal family, either the nephew or the grandchild of Malichus I. The text of this inscription also names a certain Hagiru, calling her "the queen," who must have been the connection between Malichus I and Aretas IV. The latter king was flanked by a minister at his side who, as Strabo tells us (16.4.21), was called the "brother" of the king. This bit of information from a literary source is confirmed by epigraphy: a bilingual Greek and Nabatean

Great stepped tomb at the exit from the Siq.

Steps carved into the rock on the path up to Gebel ed-Deir.

inscription in Miletus names Syllaeus, referring to him as the king's brother, but the title on the Greek portion of the inscription gives him as the *epitropos*—administrator, or minister—of the king. The Petra funerary inscription of 'Unaishu, mentioned above (*CIS* II, 351), calls him the "brother of Shaqilat, queen of the Nabateans." The functions of minister or *epitropos* were broadly defined—at least where Syllaeus was concerned. From the information we have about him, he appears to have had some diplomatic as well as administrative functions, given that he was sent to the courts of neighboring states (to Herod, for example) and even to Augustus in Rome. Thus he must have been a genuine representative of the king on a high level.

We know something about certain other civil and military posts within the organism of the state. St. Paul tells us (2 Corinthians 11.32) that an ethnarch of Aretas IV operated at Damascus, although his exact functions are still a matter of debate. It is generally supposed that he was the government functionary at the head of the Nabatean colony at Damascus rather than an actual gov-ernor, in particular because in that period Aretas does not appear to have been the ruler of that Syrian city.

There are also a few known terms for local functions or functionaries. The dedicatory inscription from Petra that gives the names of the royal family of Aretas IV was offered by one Diodoros who is called "the head of the horsemen" (*rb pršy'*), which corresponds to the Greek title of hipparch. An inscription in two copies found at Medaba (*CIS* II, 196) mentions a chief of the encampment (*rb mšrt'*), a title that may correspond to the Greek *stratopedarcha* or the Latin *praefectus castrorum*. The fact that these responsibilities are given in Nabatean leads to the thought that the corresponding functions preexisted their Greek or Latin counterparts in the area, because other terms for functions, presumably borrowed, are direct adaptations into Nabatean from Greek or Latin. This is true, in particular, of the title "strategus," which appears several times—in two inscriptions from Medaba, for instance—in the spelling *'srtg'*. The exact responsibilities of this high official are, once again, unclear from the inscriptions. The title

View of the facade of the Lion Triclinium situated on the road to ed-Deir. The facade has pilasters, with capitals decorated with vegetal motifs, and a Doric frieze of alternating triglyphs and paterae, with Medusa heads at either end. The two lion figures from which the tomb gets its name flank the doorway. The hall inside has benches for the faithful, thus classifying the monument as a triclinium rather than a tomb. It is attributed to the reign of Aretas IV (9-8 B.C.E.–40-41 C.E.).

may designate the prefect or governor of a province. The local term *ršy* seems to apply generically to someone in authority.

We do not know how the population of the cities was organized, but we do have some information regarding the existence of tribes. We know, for example, of a tribe called *šlmw* (spelled "Salamioi" by Stephanus of Byzantium), while another tribe cited at Hegra is probably named Mazin (the group is cited with the ethnic term "the mazinita," spelled *mznyt'*). The term *šrkt*, attested at Ruwwafa, is used in connection with a Thamud northern-Arabian population, though it is unclear whether the term implies a confederation or a federation. The word used corresponds to the Greek *ethnos*, but the reading of the final letter is uncertain.

Where other functions and occupations are concerned (aside from the names for priests or seers, discussed above), there are only scattered mentions of the artisans who made some of the monuments. Frequently, in fact, the person who designed or made the inscription is mentioned at the end, thus indicating that such persons enjoyed a certain status in Nabatean society. In the Hauran, the term *'mn'* is used to designate the person who executed a monument; at Hegra *psl'* seems to fulfill the same function. At Hegra we can trace genuine families of sculptors who evidently passed on their craft from father to son.

The way the Nabateans lived can be reconstructed in part from archaeological evidence. We know about their careers as merchants thanks to data on the caravan routes and to information on the expedition guided by Syllaeus. Where festivities are concerned, we know something about the symposia and about the *actia Dusaria*, Greek-style artistic and athletic competitions instituted at Bosra by Septimus Severus.

Codified laws must have regulated relations among Nabatean subjects and their contacts with state and religious authorities. No codes of law are known to exist, but the papyri of the Babatha archive, which relate litigations about property and succession and are redacted in a precise, legal style, imply the existence of an elaborate body of law. The papyrus of Nahal Hever, published by Joseph Naveh, provides an example of a contract. An inscription from the Temple of the Winged Lions demonstrates the existence of laws connected with religious practices. We have information on property rights from inscriptions carved on the rupestrian tombs, nearly all of them from Hegra, that cite detailed rules governing the ownership and the use of the tombs, adding specific injunctions to prohibit persons not

hprk', attested in several documents, probably indicates a governor or prefect. According to Starcky, this term corresponds to the Greek *heparchos*: before the area became a province in 106 C.E. it was an eparchy, *hprky'* in Nabatean. Other scholars consider the title equivalent to the Greek *hyparchos* (hipparch), originally a general of horsemen. The term *kylyrk'* is a Nabatean transformation of the Greek title usually rendered as chiliarch, the leader of a unit of one thousand soldiers. To end the list, there is a probable mention of a centurion at Hegra in a term adapted in the spelling *qntryn*.

Two inscriptions from Ruwwafa offer the term *hgmwn'* for a function that can be defined as administrative since it corresponds to the Greek *hegemon*. It

specifically authorized to do so from changing the structures or making use of them. These inscriptions place the property under the protection of deities—almost always Dushara and Manawat—and enjoin them to lay a curse on violators of the norms listed. At times, fines are specified, to be paid either to the god (or to the priest, called *afkal*) or to the king, in which case they usually consist of "one thousand silver drachmas of Aretas"—that is, official coinage. Documents regarding funerary properties were placed in an edifice called *byt qyš'*, a term that has been interpreted (after rejecting several other suggestions) as the temple of a deity whose name must have had a special significance that we cannot grasp, or else as a "house of measure," a sort of archive (a measuring device—*qyš'*—was the attribute of Manawat, the goddess of fate or destiny).

To conclude, written documents tell us little about the life and social organization of the Nabateans. The data that have been preserved show the Nabateans to have been a relatively simple society, even though they drew from a variety of traditions, as is clear, in particular, in their cults and in their terms for priestly functions. It is worth noting that the direct, written sources tell us nothing about the commercial activities to which the Nabateans owed their wealth; instead, they show religious piety, construction skills, a talent for administrative and military organization, and precision in their juridical norms.

The City of Petra

The Rediscovery

The Western world "rediscovered" Petra in 1812, when the Swiss explorer Johann Ludwig Burckhardt, the first traveler to arrive since the age of the Crusaders and the voyage of Sultan Baibars in 1276, visited the city.

The son of a Swiss colonel in the French army, Burckhardt spent his first twenty years at Neuchâtel, Leipzig, and Göttingen; from there he left for London in 1806 with a letter of presentation to Sir Joseph Banks, the founder of the Association for Promoting the Discovery of the Interior Parts of Africa. The Association found in the young Swiss the ideal person to carry out its cultural aims. After beginning the study of Arabic at Cambridge, Burckhardt left for Syria, where he stayed at Aleppo, studying Arabic and Islamic and Koranic law, and during his sojourn he had occasion, although with notable difficulties and many vicissitudes, to visit the ruins of Baalbek, Palmyra, and the city of Damascus.

In 1812, at the request of the Association, he went first to Cairo, then to Tripoli, then back to Syria. He then set out southward through the lands of biblical tradition, passing through Philadelphia and crossing the hills of the ancient territories of Moab and Edom, to arrive at the village of el-Ji, close to Petra. On 21 August 1812 Burckhardt and his Arab guide, following the bed of the Wadi Musa, entered into the narrow tunnel of the Siq and reached the valley with its rock walls. The next day the explorer noted in his travel diary: "It appears very probable that the ruins in Wadi Musa are those of the ancient Petra." His discovery remained wrapped in silence, however; when Burckhardt arrived at Cairo in September of the same year, he left again immediately for Central Africa, where, after some adventures, he died of malaria in 1817. His *Travels in Syria*, the diary of his first trip from Damascus to Cairo, was not published until 1822; it was followed in 1823 by *Travels in Nubia* and in 1829 by *Travels in Arabia*. News of the discovery of Petra had already been circulated long before then, however, thanks to two officers of the Royal Navy, Charles Leonard Irby and James Mangles, who had traveled to the region in May 1818 and spent several days in the ancient city. Their *Travels in Egypt and Nubia, Syria and Asia Minor*, self-published in London in 1823, contains a number of amusing evaluations of Nabatean architecture, which they judged to be "loaded with ornaments in the Roman manner, but in a bad taste, with an infinity of broken lines and unnecessary angles and projections, and multiplied pediments and half pediments, and pedestals set upon columns that support nothing" (405–406).

During the course of the nineteenth century at least two hundred other travelers described the city,

Facing page: The theater, seen from el-Khubtha.

Right: Marquis Léon de Laborde, who visited Petra in 1826, in Arabian dress.

Khazneh el-Far'un. Lithograph from a watercolor by David Roberts, from *The Holy Land, Syria, Idumea, Arabia, Egypt, and Nubia* (London: F. G. Moon, 1842–1849).

among them Léon de Laborde in 1826 (*Voyage de l'Arabie Pétrée*, Paris, 1830); ten years later, the Reverend Edward Robinson, an American biblical scholar who drew a connection between the rock facades of Petra and Assyrian art; and David Roberts, a member of the Royal Academy, who, along with Edward Lear, was responsible for some of the finest drawings of the monuments of the city. In 1865 scientific study of Palestine and the Bible lands was advanced by the founding of the Palestine Exploration Fund, followed five years later by that of the American Palestine Exploration Society.

The creation of these cultural societies provided a base for launching archaeological research in the Near East. Nearly everywhere in the mid-nineteenth century, a new phase of militant archaeology began as an outgrowth of a newly established insistence on historical method in the study of ancient culture and art. As more and more explorations were launched, their focus shifted from a search for art objects and individual bits of information to controlled investigations of the monuments in their setting. A growing number of scientific institutions established missions, and these and state archaeological services replaced the dilettantes. The epicenter of this shift to scholarship was precisely the eastern Mediterranean.

The years between 1880 and 1914 were what might be called the golden age of these archaeological endeavors; these were dominated by German scholars, and thanks to generous funding, they realized surveys and regular campaigns of excavation and study. In this manner, a historical picture of the eastern territories in the Hellenistic age and under Roman domination began to take shape.

The first genuinely scientific explorations of Petra were carried out by Aloïs Musil and, above all, by Rudolf-Ernst Brünnow and Alfred von Domaszewski, who published a detailed report on the rupestrian fa-

cades of Petra in 1898, cataloguing more than eight hundred monuments and elaborating a system for numbering the tombs on the basis of their location that is still in use today. Their treatise, *Die Provincia Arabia,* which included photographs and drawings, was a major work of documentation, and it was enriched some years later by Gustaf Dalman, whose primary interests were religious sites and monuments, triclinia, and cult niches.

In 1916–1917, during the First World War, scholars connected with the Turkish and German armed forces worked at Petra, and we owe to the scholarship of Theodor Wiegand, Walter Bachmann, and Carl Watzinger the first hypothetical identification of the civic buildings, preliminary ground plans of their sites, and a map of the city. That map, combined with the aerial photographs of Sir Alexander Kennedy and enhanced by additions and modifications from excavation data and later studies, still provides the basic scheme for a reconstruction of the urban plan of Petra.

The final two decades of the Ottoman Empire were thus determinant for productive archaeology and studies on Petra, and they witnessed the creation and diffusion of a corpus of data that provided a basis for more recent studies and a growing store of information. After the First World War, a new chapter in the study of Nabatean culture proved highly productive, though in a different way and for a number of reasons. First, the increased level of security that followed the constitution of the Emirate of Transjordan in 1921 facilitated access to the Nabatean territory of Petra, which began to attract tourists, albeit on a limited scale. At the same time, the creation of departments of antiquities on both banks of the Jordan River and the establishment at Jerusalem of British and American schools of archaeology created conditions favorable for archaeological research.

The first excavation campaigns at Petra were undertaken in 1929 by an English mission under the direction of George Horsfield. From that day on, research and excavation, followed by restoration operations, have continued in the city thanks to the Jordanian Service of Antiquities and to American, German, English, and Swiss missions.

Much has been elucidated, but much remains to be done.

The Layout of the City

Petra is situated on a plateau surrounded by towering mountains with rocky peaks—the Gebel al-Habis to the west and el-Khubtha and Zibb 'Atuf to the east—that create a natural barrier against the desert. Three gorges have been cut through the friable sedimentary rock by streams or wadis (Arabic for a streambed) to the east, the north, and the south. In the dry season, these provide the Petra basin with communication routes to the plains to the north and the desert to the east. The spring from which the Wadi Musa originates and the streambed that traverses the ancient city were probably what induced the Nabateans to choose the site as their main place of settlement.

The city's principal lines of development are not yet completely clear, although many studies devoted to various aspects of the problem and archaeological investigations conducted in recent years have undeniably enriched (and in part changed) knowledge and scientific information about Petra.

For some time after their arrival, the Nabateans do not seem to have created a genuine city or made monumental structures. Rather, early Petra was a settlement of a semi-nomadic sort, with small, modest habitations built of river stones and clay mortar, which we can date by means of ceramic finds to roughly the beginning of the third century B.C.E.

That situation, although hypothetical, is confirmed by the lack of significant archaeological documentation for the Hellenistic age, hence it does not contradict what Diodorus Siculus tells us in his long dissertation on the Nabateans (2.48), whom he calls nomads without permanent habitations. Diodorus also speaks of a "rock" that was "extremely strong" and secure, although unfortified. It was accessible by "but one approach, and using this ascent they mount it, a few at a time, and thus store their possessions in safety." This description fits Petra admirably well: the city is naturally protected by heights, and its fortifications, constructed later on its north and south slopes, date to the first century B.C.E. at the earliest.

Strabo and Pliny the Elder give us further information. Strabo speaks of the city as the metropolis of the Nabateans, a center that had already been developed and that enjoyed a geographical position at the heart of a profitable commerce in perfumes and spices. He states: "It lies on a site which is otherwise smooth and level, but it is fortified all round by a rock, the outside parts of the site being precipitous and sheer, and the inside parts having springs in abundance, both for domestic purposes and for watering gardens." Moreover, "Petra is always ruled by some king from the royal family," and as for the inhabitants, "their homes, through the use of stone, are costly" (Strabo, 16.4.21, 26). Pliny provides a similar description of the city and its involvement in international trade. He states of Petra: "It lies in a deep valley a little less than two miles wide, and is surrounded by inaccessible mountains with a river flowing between them. . . . At Petra two roads meet, one leading from Syria [through] Palmyra, and the other coming from Gaza" (*Natural History*, 6.32.144).

Thus the ancient sources insist on the fact that Petra was an extremely secure site: indeed, the only easy access was to the east and, then as now, it consisted of a narrow streambed closed in between rock cliffs at times eighty meters high. This passage, called the Siq, is about two kilometers long. Its breadth

A portion of the Siq, the streambed that provided the only access road to Petra. Traces of the channels used to bring the water of the wadi to the city are clearly visible on the rock walls. In the foreground: remains of stone paving, probably from the late first century C.E.

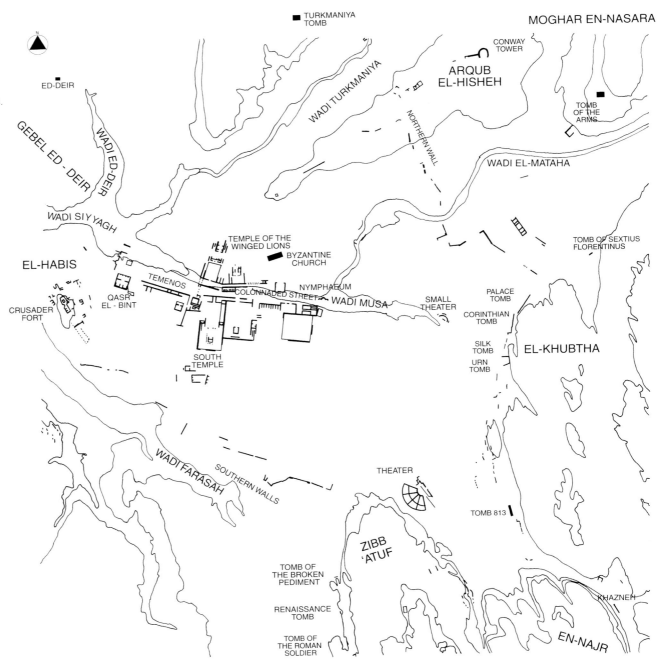

The valley of Petra, showing the city and the surrounding heights.

varies, and in some points, where the rock walls are sufficiently far apart to create an open space, there may have been caravansaries, or camping grounds for caravan trains. A succession of inscriptions, betyls, niches, and votive altars carved into the rock walls that line the passage attest to the long frequentation of this road, which played a role of major importance in the commercial and military development of the Nabatean center up to the third century c.e.

In order to guarantee a permanent water supply to the population and the convoys that traversed the area, the Nabateans dammed the water of the Wadi Musa at the eastern, or outer, end of the Siq, a move that was necessary not only in order to manage the water supply but also to contain winter floods. They then brought the water into the city by means of a channel tunneled into the rock. In the first part of its course this channel followed the slope of the rocky terrain, and where bedrock was lacking, the Nabateans constructed an artificial waterway made of closely fitted stones and clay pipes, a mixed construction of stone fragments, clay mortar, and plaster, some traces of which remain today. When the city reached its maximum size, this ingenious channel system and the presence of a large number of cisterns excavated into the rock permitted the Nabateans—just as Strabo says—to provide the city with gardens and sizable public fountains.

The dam and the hydraulic installations must have been constructed at roughly the same time as an elevated passage that led into the Siq over a bridge, thus facilitating access to the road from the east and into Petra. This project was in fact intended to make the Siq, which was paved with cobble stones, the normal access route into the city, and the raised roadbed ended at the western end of the Siq with a monumental arched gateway. The arch collapsed in 1896, but traces of its decoration with niches bordered by engaged columns can still be seen on the rock face.

The realization of these works projects cannot be dated with certainty, but the presence of inscriptions on the rock surfaces datable to the second half of the first century C.E.—which were certainly made before the paved road—suggests that the construction was carried out during the reign of Malichus II or that of his successor, Rabbel II.

At its western end, the Siq opens out into the valley that contains the city. The Petra basin is shaped something like an amphitheater: the rock cliffs surrounding it were used for tombs and habitations excavated into the rock; the highest peaks were cult sites. A crown of elaborate rock facades, lined up next to one another or stacked one above the other, borders the edge of the basin that formerly was the heart of city life.

The timing and characteristics of the various phases of the city's development are not yet completely understood, given that only a limited amount of investigation has taken place in the urban area and little has yet been published. The monuments that have been excavated and documented are few in relation to the urban area that remains to be explored. The city seems in fact to have been extensive in Nabatean times, although the identification of many civic edifices and residential quarters is still in doubt, as is the chronology of many structures.

As the narrow passageway through the Siq opens out into the valley, the city plan gradually takes shape along the Wadi Musa, the main axis, which lies almost exactly east-west, dividing the city in two. In Roman times the Colonnaded Street, a monumental thoroughfare built on the traces of an older Nabatean road, paralleled the Wadi Musa. Public and religious buildings lined either side of this main street. At the western end of the street, a monumental gateway with three bays opened into a sacred area that now contains what remains of the principal temple of Petra, the Qasr el-Bint Far'un, an Arabic expression that means "the castle of the daughter of the pharaoh."

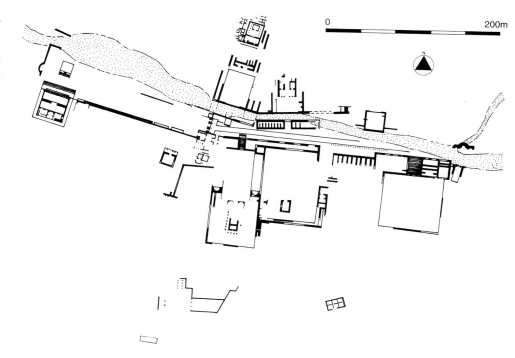

Plan of the central area of Petra (from Iain Browning, *Petra*, 3d ed. [London: Chatto and Windus, 1989], p. 144, with additions and modifications from recent excavations).

A theater, almost entirely carved out of the rock, was constructed at the southern edge of the valley, along the northeast slope of the massive Zibb 'Atuf, a project that involved the destruction of a number of rupestrian tomb facades that had been part of a preexistent necropolis. The theater was constructed on a typical Roman plan, faithfully following the Vitruvian model, although many elements—the drainage system for rain water, for example, and details of the architectural decoration such as floral capitals of the Nabatean type—were certainly of local inspiration.

The cavea, cut into the rock cliff and divided into forty-five rows of seats, separated horizontally into three levels (*moeniana* in Latin) and vertically into six wedge-shaped sections (*cunei* in Latin) marked off by stairs, was capable of holding some 7,000 to 8,500 spectators. The semicircular orchestra, cut from an outcropping of bedrock, was thirty-eight meters across, extending along the entire stage. The original *pulpitum* was decorated with the customary niches, but they were filled with plaster in a restoration still in ancient times, during the last phase of the theater's use. Unlike the cavea, the *frons scaenae* was built entirely of local stone, originally faced with marble or plaster. It very probably had a double, perhaps even a triple, order of columns, the lowest of which is still in situ. At both sides of the stage, barrel-vaulted corridors led through passageways and down steps to the orchestra and the cavea.

Because of the completely Roman character of the

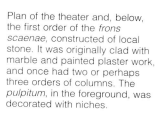

Facing page: The monumental facade of the Khazneh as it appears to a visitor emerging from the Siq.

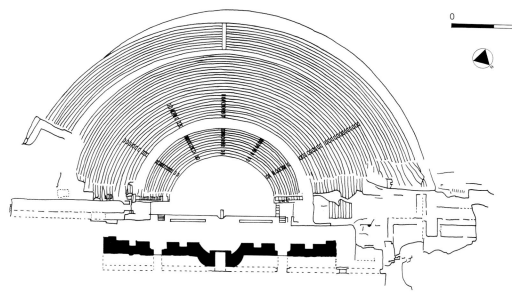

0   50m

Plan of the theater and, below, the first order of the *frons scaenae*, constructed of local stone. It was originally clad with marble and painted plaster work, and once had two or perhaps three orders of columns. The *pulpitum*, in the foreground, was decorated with niches.

theater's architecture, scholars long held it to be one of the civic improvements made after the Nabatean territories had become a Roman province in 106 C.E., but excavations in the early 1970s seem to indicate instead a date in the first century C.E., perhaps during the reign of Aretas IV or Malichus II. What is certain is that as time passed, the construction underwent restorations and modifications until it was destroyed in an earthquake in 363 C.E.

Traces of pavement found in front of the theater reveal that the major thoroughfare leading from the Siq across the city to the temple complex of Qasr el-Bint also served buildings located outside of the central city.

According to the stratigraphic data that has emerged from excavations conducted in the 1950s, the paving of the principal street—if not the erection of its monumental decor—must have occurred between the end of the first and the beginning of the second centuries C.E. The terminus post quem is determined by two coins of Aretas IV and one of Rabbel II found on an archaeological level that was cut by the foundation trench of the paved way, and by the existence, in the northern sector of the street, of four rooms stratigraphically older than the paved street, which are datable, on the basis of many sherds of Nabatean painted ceramic ware, to the first century C.E.

An earlier version of the central, east-west artery of Petra, probably constructed in the first century B.C.E., was paved with stones from the streambed, thus obliterating the earliest Nabatean habitations. The later great street was nearly three hundred meters long and as much as six meters wide, and it was bordered by two ample sidewalks separated from it by two steps topped by sandstone columns. The street was paved with slabs of limestone and marble, and the absence of vehicle tracks indicates that it was not a traffic artery but a ceremonial way.

The layout of the Colonnaded Street faithfully imitates a model that is fairly frequently seen in the Roman East, the earliest example of which seems to be the great colonnaded way in Antioch in Syria, which Flavius Josephus attributes to the generous patronage of Herod the Great. Similar urban constructions of roughly the same period as the Colonnaded Street in Petra include a street in Gerasa, where Ionic columns were added to the first part of the *cardo* at the end of the first century C.E., and the *decumanus* of Bosra, the ancient, pre-Roman main street of that Nabatean city, which was edged with columns in the age of Trajan.

At the eastern end of the Colonnaded Street, to the right as one exited the Siq, there was a large public fountain known as the Nymphaeum that marked the juncture of the Wadi Musa and a secondary stream, the Wadi el-Mataha, which must have been one of the terminal points in the system for delivering water from the aqueduct to the citizenry, the specifics of which are not known.

Only the masonry base of the walls of the Nymphaeum remain, but the original plan of the structure must have been triangular, a shape determined by the nature of the terrain, and it must have faced the street with a rectilinear facade broken by a central exedra flanked by niches containing water spouts. A precise date cannot be assigned to its construction, but it was probably begun soon after the reconstruction of the Colonnaded Street, in the early decades of the second century C.E.

On the opposite, or southern, side of the street the remains of a small building are still visible—two pilasters flanked by a wall ending in a small niche—which has been identified as originally having been a nymphaeum. It is more probable, however, that it was a votive chapel or small temple.

None of the structures aligned along the low rise overlooking the southern side of the street have as yet been explored systematically, and the ground plan that derives from Walter Bachmann's reconstruction of 1921 has to be taken as only indicative. This vast complex of ruins is commonly interpreted as a series of commercial buildings, and their typical layout seems to be an ample courtyard surrounded by rooms that may have been for storage or spaces for selling merchandise. The side of this complex that faces the street is broken up into a tight row of shops, all belonging to a later phase (the fourth century C.E.), when they probably replaced constructions of a similar nature. The existence of these large public spaces at the center of the city seems closely connected to Petra's growing needs as a center of caravan trade and to its heavy commercial traffic.

Access to this area from the Colonnaded Street was probably marked by an archway, two monumental molded plinths from which have been found. An inscription in Greek honoring the emperor Trajan and dating to 114 C.E., recovered in the immediate vicinity, may have pertained to the same archway. A good-sized stairway leads up from street level to the so-called upper market, beyond which there are areas identified as the central, or middle, market and the lower market.

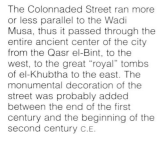

The Colonnaded Street ran more or less parallel to the Wadi Musa, thus it passed through the entire ancient center of the city from the Qasr el-Bint, to the west, to the great "royal" tombs of el-Khubtha to the east. The monumental decoration of the street was probably added between the end of the first century and the beginning of the second century C.E.

The lower market connects with the terrace of the temenos—the sacred precincts—of a tetrastyle temple *in antis* commonly known as the South Temple, which is also accessible from the Colonnaded Street by a flight of stairs and an entrance in the form of a monumental propylon leading to a large courtyard, probably once surrounded by colonnaded porticoes. The entire southern edge of the courtyard was at one time occupied by a second monumental stairway, flanked by two exedrae, that led to a second large courtyard, at the center of which the sacred edifice was placed on a high podium. With its succession of courtyards at various levels, the imposing mass of this temple must have made a striking scenic effect, dominating the valley and the street.

Recent investigation, still ongoing, has revealed that this sanctuary remained in use until the mid-sixth century and underwent at least three phases of construction. An earthquake that occurred in the middle of that century undoubtedly caused the complete destruction of the temple, but the extensive materials found on the site, fragments of architectural decoration, and Nabatean capitals with floral motifs all point to a date in the first century C.E., a dating that seems confirmed by the nature of the plan. The overall conception of the temple in fact recalls a model widespread in other regions of the Near East in which a great sacred area with a regular geometric plan is dominated by a temple in the Greek style. In Palestine, for example, the temple constructed by Herod in honor of Augustus at Samaria (Sabastiyah)—a temple rising on top of a hill at the end of a double-colonnaded courtyard—has a similar plan, as does the great temple complex of Bel at Palmyra, in Syria, built in 32 C.E.

As is true of the other temple buildings in Petra, archaeological data throw no light on the identity of the deity venerated in the South Temple. Some have claimed that it was Tyche (who was indeed venerated locally) on the basis of a head of that goddess that obviously was part of a larger-than-life statue, but the identification is uncertain. The notion that the sacred precincts were dedicated to the goddess al-'Uzza is just as hypothetical, as is the idea that the temple can be identified as the Aphrodiseion, a temple dedicated to Aphrodite that is recorded as having existed at Petra in a papyrus of 124 C.E.

To the north of the Colonnaded Street—still in the eastern sector and nearly facing the great South Temple—are the monumental remains of the so-called

Remains of the Nymphaeum, a great public fountain built at the northeast end of the Colonnaded Street. The original construction, conceived as a terminal point for the city aqueduct, had a roughly triangular plan that masked the point where a secondary watercourse joined the Wadi Musa.

The western sector of the Colonnaded Street, showing the stairs leading up to the great South Temple, currently being excavated by an American mission.

Temple of the Winged Lions. In the past this temple was usually identified as a gymnasium, but its real purpose was made clear as a result of excavations under the direction of Philip C. Hammond in the 1970s. The name by which the building is currently known comes from the unusual decoration of some capitals, which show crouching winged lions in the place of the volutes more typical of the Corinthian style.

Access to the temple from the Colonnaded Street could be had from a bridge that crossed the Wadi Musa, beyond which was an area bordered by columns, a courtyard, and finally a temple, which had a square ground plan divided into a portico *in antis* and a cella. Although a fragmentary inscription of 27–28 C.E. has suggested that moment as the date of construction of this temple, the matter is still under discussion (as is the deity to which the temple was dedicated). Scholars do agree that the temple was not restored after a fire, probably in the final years of the reign of Rabbel II, that destroyed the roof and irremediably damaged the internal furnishings, and that much of its construction material and its architectural and sculptural decoration was reused elsewhere. The temple complex is of notable importance for an un-

The Temple of the Winged Lions follows a typically Nabatean plan. It lies along the northwestern side of the Colonnaded Street, on the far side of the Wadi Musa, and was reached by a bridge across the wadi. A group of artisans' workshops was clustered around the temple.

The Great Temple, or South Temple, rose to the south of the Colonnaded Street. It was preceded by a propylon and porticoed courtyards.

Nabatean capital with a vine and floral decoration, from the Temple of the Winged Lions.

derstanding of the religious architecture of Petra for a number of reasons: the richness of the findings, the way the various buildings are articulated, the various building phases, the eclecticism of details that show typically Nabatean elements overlaid by details and motifs from the Greco-Roman tradition, and the presence of annexed workshops.

Immediately to the east of the Temple of the Winged Lions, a series of fairly monumental ruins—a great courtyard and other architectonic structures accessible from the street by means of a bridge over the Wadi Musa and a stairway—occupy the terrace overlooking the southern side of the Colonnaded Street. This complex is usually designated as the Royal

Palace, but both this identification and the conjectured ground plan are unreliable, as they are based on minimal and uncertain data.

At the western end of the Colonnaded Street a triple-arched gateway provided a monumental propylon leading into the temenos, the vast sacred enclosure of the Qasr el-Bint Far'un. This arched gateway is a large structure made of blocks of rose-colored sandstone that originally bore a wealth of architectural and sculpted decoration. The three bays, a large central entry and two smaller, lateral ones, are framed by pilasters decorated with a floral frieze, but the middle arch contains alternating panels with busts of deities and round floral motifs. In front of the east face of the gate there are four columns with individual square plinths that once projected out from the face; the west face is simpler and arranged in a manner seen in many other Nabatean monuments. At either end there are pilasters doubled by quarter-columns with Nabatean capitals, while two engaged columns divide the architectonic space occupied by the three arches. The north and south entrances were flanked by tower-like constructions: today only a part of the outer wall of the northern one remains. The southern tower served as a vestibule to a complex of buildings immediately to the south.

In the ancient world, the importance of moving from the realm of the profane into sacred space was always signaled, and very often access to the sanctuary was given monumental form by a propylon. On the one hand, the triple-arched gate of Petra recalls the Eastern tradition of the fortified gate, alluded to here by the lateral towers almost integrated into the main body of the structure; on the other hand, it displays architectonic forms, applied orders, and decorative motifs such as the floral frieze that clearly reflect Hellenistic and Roman influences.

The date of this propylon, although still uncertain, seems strictly linked to that of the Qasr el-Bint and its temenos and, above all, to the construction of the Colonnaded Street. The chronologies that have been proposed, which are based on architectonic and stylistic analysis of the monument and consideration of its function within the layout of the city, range from the late first century B.C.E. to the late second century C.E.

The most likely hypothesis, which derives from stratigraphic investigations of areas near the gateway, is that the triple-arched construction is more recent than the Colonnaded Street and probably replaced an older structure that was contemporary to the temple,

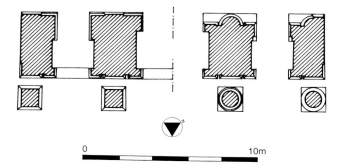

Plan of the three-part monumental gateway to the temenos.

Eastern face of the gateway to the temenos. Detail of the pilaster of the central portal showing vegetal motifs alternating with busts of deities.

its sacred precincts, or both. It can perhaps be compared to the "Nabatean" gate at Bosra, which is formed of one large vaulted passageway set between two towered structures and has very sober decoration. For urbanistic reasons, the Bosra gateway is thought to predate Trajan, which would mean that the Petra gateway is of a later (though still unspecified) date.

Beyond the propylon, or entrance area, the paved street broadens into the large paved courtyard of the sanctuary and continues from there, without a break, into the courtyard containing the altar, in front of the temple. As is true of many of the monuments in Petra, the location of the Qasr el-Bint Far'un was determined by the terrain. The large open space is an irregular rec-

tangle with a southeast-northwest orientation that diverges from the line of street, following a slight bend in the bed of the Wadi Musa. The great arched gateway thus functions to link the center of the city and the temple and to mask the difference in alignment.

From the earliest settlement at Petra, the area of the Qasr el-Bint must have been an established place of veneration. As recent excavations have revealed, a monument of some size probably preceded the current temple, a notion that seems to be confirmed by the difference in alignment between the north-south orientation of the temple itself and the propylon. The new urban layout dictated by the Colonnaded Street thus had to adapt to the preexisting temple complex and respect its orientation.

The building itself is probably the earliest example of monumental architecture at Petra. Its square ground plan is divided, in a manner conventional in the Eastern tradition and common to many temple buildings of Moab and southern Syria, into a pronaos, a cella, and a tripartite adyton. It still displays consistent traces of rich decoration in stone and stucco on its outside and inside walls.

The terminus ante quem for the construction of the temple is provided by an inscription in Nabatean, the dedication of a statue to King Aretas IV from the early years of the first century C.E. carved into a stone block in a bench running along the southern wall of the sacred precincts. The bench formed a base for votive offerings and is stratigraphically later in date than the walls surrounding the temenos. This chronological information and many details of the architectural decoration and the stucco ornamental motifs lead to a proposed date for the temple itself of the second half of the

Qasr el-Bint. The temenos and the great South Temple. On the left-hand side, remains of the altar. Along the wall south of the temenos there were benches reserved for the faithful and, above them, a base for statues and ex-votos.

Facing page: The great gateway with three arched portals, at the western end of the Colonnaded Street. This was the monumental entrance to the vast area of the Qasr el-Bint, and it separated the temple precincts from the area of ordinary life. It was constructed (in its final phases at least) after the Colonnaded Street, probably in the mid-second century C.E.

119

The rear wall and east wall of the Qasr el-Bint, showing well-conserved segments of a Doric frieze of triglyphs and metopes.

first century B.C.E., even though the sanctuary and its ornamentation must have been restored in later ages.

It is commonly accepted that the temple was dedicated to Dushara, the primary deity of the Nabatean pantheon, but recently discovered figurative representations and fragmentary inscriptions suggest that al-'Uzza, the female deity, was associated with the cult as well.

The complex of rooms accessible from the tower flanking the southern door of the triple-arched gateway to the temenos presents another problem of identification, largely because excavation is as yet incomplete and later walls superimposed on the site complicate interpretation. From the tower-vestibule, which opened onto the precincts of the Qasr el-Bint through an impressive entrance placed not far from the monumental gateway, the way led to a quadrangular space, originally a hall open to the west and bordered by columns. This space is followed, immediately to the south, by at least three other rooms, now underground. These are generally considered to be part of a baths complex, and they consist, in order, of a stairway turning around a central pillar decorated with panels in red and yellow stucco, a domed circular room with walls containing arched niches flanked by engaged half-columns, and a rectangular room with a domed

ceiling on pendentives, also decorated with colored stucco work.

The circular room has been thought to be a caldarium, but excavations have found no hypocaust, flues, water channels, or other hydraulic equipment that might support that interpretation of its function. An alternative hypothesis has been advanced, which supposes that the circular room and the adjoining rooms were part of a palatial residence. There are, in fact, points of comparison between these structures and the monumental complex of the fortress-palace of Herodium built by Herod the Great around 23 B.C.E. This and other elements (floral capitals in a semi-Corinthian style and some details of the architectural decoration close in style and motifs to those in the Qasr el-Bint and in the Khazneh) have suggested a date between the end of the first century B.C.E. and the beginning of the first century C.E. It has been objected that this early date would imply a very precocious use of domed vaulting on pendentives; moreover, the precise function of the building and its relationship to the temple wall have yet to be clarified. A small temple on a podium, fronted by six freestanding columns and preceded by stairs, stood on a terrace dominating the temenos of the Qasr el-Bint from the south, sharing its orientation. This structure

120

Plan of the buildings to the south of the temenos gateway. Formerly thought to be part of a baths complex, the constructions are now considered to pertain to a building, perhaps a palace.

The narrow opening cut between high rock walls that leads to the Siq.

Aqueduct excavated along the
face of el-Khubtha; below it,
cisterns and cult installations.

has not yet been studied, and its relationship to the adjoining structures has not been defined.

During the course of the first century B.C.E., Petra erected a system of fortifications to the north and to the south of the city. These were in reality isolated fortified points, constructed where the natural protection of the rocks was least, and were flanked by a discontinuous line of masonry curtain walls and bastions. The placement of these walls is not easy to reconstruct, and only some elements have been identified—for example, the so-called Conway Tower, a circular construction made of large irregular stone blocks that stands on the northeast crest of Arqub el-Hisheh, a point of great strategic importance because it controlled all the access routes to the city from the north.

A few centuries later, when the city had contracted, a second series of walls was constructed, still to the north of the city but closer to the center. This system, which has been dated to the fourth century by column drums and other reused materials in its con-

struction, is much more regular in design than the segmented outer fortifications, and it is the only continuous portion of city wall recognizable today.

The visitor's first impression of Petra has always been that of a valley richly endowed with rupestrian facades. Visitors never remark on the presence of residential quarters, to the point that in the past it was often thought that there were none.

Even archaeological investigation has concentrated above all on rupestrian architecture and religious edifices, only recently raising the problem of residential quarters and the typology and layout of houses. Petra was a city of the living, however, and all the archaeologists who have excavated there have encountered remains of habitations, even elaborate ones, constructed of stone or excavated into the rock.

As we have already seen, domestic installations found in the area of the Colonnaded Street—a series of simple structures with clay walls and floors, but with a floor plan that is difficult to establish—reveal a long, ongoing occupation in constructions of almost unvaried form, ranging from the late third century to the first century B.C.E.

The earliest known houses, carved into rock faces and, for the most part, concentrated along the hills overlooking the central area of Petra, are usually considered to have been constructed during that same time span. These housing complexes, aligned along rock terraces or grouped in what seem to be genuine neighborhoods, are often difficult to interpret. In plan they are typically divided into a series of intercommunicating rooms, at times arranged around a central chamber. In some cases, masonry structures complement rooms excavated into the rock. Unlike the tombs, these habitations have no exterior architectonic decoration, but their interior walls reveal an extensive use of painted stucco that attests to the care that the inhabitants of Petra took to beautify spaces devoted to daily living.

One of the larger housing complexes opens along the eastern slope of the massif of al-Habis, to the west of the Qasr el-Bint. The remains of two houses that must have been part of an extensive rock-cut construction several stories high are visible here, rather high up. They contain evidence of particularly elaborate wall decorations, including a series of niches, small fluted columns, and small pilasters surmounted by a frieze of metopes and triglyphs, all skillfully worked in stucco. In some sites, stucco work is replaced or accompanied by painted polychrome geometrical and figurative motifs. This is the case in one ornately decorated habitation, part of a group of rupestrian houses along the Wadi Siyyagh, on the northern slope of al-Habis, and in the Painted House of Siq el-Bared, at el-Beida, a bit to the north of the city.

The residential nature of el-Beida, a suburb of Petra, is attested by a rock house with a triclinium, the walls of which are completely covered with frescoes. The vaulted ceiling has a particularly vivacious painted design of vines and medallions populated by exotic animals and winged hunting putti. Comparison with models in Pompei, Alexandria, and Rome suggests a date of the first century C.E. for this fresco, and its high artistic level betrays the hand of an artisan trained in a workshop in some great Hellenistic center. All of the motifs of the painted stucco decoration in these houses reflect a strong Hellenistic influence, in particular, cultural links between Nabatean art and the Alexandrian artistic tradition.

Another group of rupestrian houses lies at the foot

Top: Open faces of rock dwellings on the north slope of al-Habis, near the Wadi Siyyagh.

Bottom, left: Nabatean painted ceramics with vegetal decoration, Petra, first century C.E. (Amman: Archaeological Museum).

Bottom, right: A ceiling in el-Beida, at Siq el-Bared, north of Petra, painted with floral motifs in a chamber of a rock-cut complex (Brünnow and Domaszewski, *Petra*, no. 849).

of the massif of el-Khubtha, in the cliffs across from the theater. Between the late second century and the first century B.C.E., a necropolis occupied the upper level of the rise. When the city grew, the zone changed use and was transformed into a quarter of private houses. This was not an isolated instance of changing land use: in Petra, the close proximity of houses and tombs makes it particularly difficult to distinguish between urban space and funerary space, even though, as a general rule, necropolises were located outside inhabited areas.

A large but only partially excavated building in the zone of el-Katute, in the southern part of the city, illustrates the characteristics of domestic architecture in the first century C.E. It has been identified as a large habitation and is carefully constructed, with regular courses of cut stone and notable traces of interior decoration in painted stucco. The plan of the house, which is not easy to discern, is divided into a series of rooms that seem not to communicate with one another. The building also has a courtyard that connects with the interior through a door. This house, if that is what it is, was continuously inhabited from the first half of the first century C.E., perhaps around 25 C.E., as attested by sherds of Aretine pottery ware and a coin of Aretas IV, until the late Nabatean age.

Excavations recently completed by the University of Basel along a broad natural terrace that extends along the base of the ez-Zantur hill seem to attest to an early extension of settlement along the southern

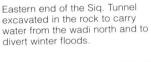

Eastern end of the Siq. Tunnel excavated in the rock to carry water from the wadi north and to divert winter floods.

slopes of the valley, as documented by ceramic fragments from the second and first centuries B.C.E. and by evidence of a genuine residential quarter immediately after that period. A large Nabatean stone house built between the first century B.C.E. and the first century C.E. occupies the site of an earlier, more modest habitation. The basic plan of the house is Greco-Hellenistic, with a peristyle surrounded by receiving rooms and an area set aside for private quarters. Local variants of this model include an off-center courtyard and a large paved courtyard that closes the house plan to the south and cuts off the view. This rich habitation was destroyed in the second century C.E., and the entire area seems to have remained unused until the early fourth century, when two separate two-story houses with external staircases were built on the site. This entire edifice was devastated by the earthquake of 363. In one of the rooms, in fact, skeletons of a woman and a child who lost their lives in the cataclysm were discovered, along with a small hoard of coins, some dated the year of the earthquake, which the woman was probably attempting to carry to safety. A partial reoccupation of the complex is attested, however, up to the early fifth century.

The entire eastern end of the Petra valley and the area along the banks of the Wadi el-Mataha are to date completely unexplored. Only one building, the so-called small theater, of which no visible trace remains on the terrain today, was studied in some detail during the early 1900s, but its date and function are unknown.

To conclude: the archaeological data available on the formation and the development of the city are not particularly exhaustive. They certainly merit thorough study, accompanied by extensive on-site investigation. We can, however, reconstruct the general lines of the urban plan of Petra (albeit with some approximation), and we can state that Petra shared some of the characteristics of other caravan cities (Gerasa, Palmyra, and, in particular, Philadelphia). In other ways, however, Petra's organization seems noticeably different from the plan typical of the cities of the Hellenized Near East.

What is unique to the irregular organization of the vestiges of Petra's urban space and their seeming distribution over a fairly large area may perhaps be explained by a settlement phase that preceded all encounters with Hellenistic and Roman formulas of urban planning. Analysis of the documentation in fact shows almost no evidence of a Hellenistic phase

in Petra; construction seems instead to have been concentrated in the first century B.C.E. It thus seems possible to suggest that, like Gerasa, Petra initially consisted of small, diversified nuclei of habitation, separated from one another and scattered through the territory of the future city according to a tribal logic, that only later joined to form a genuine *polis*.

Around the middle of the first century B.C.E. the central portion of the Petra basin shifted from being primarily for domestic use to include areas set aside for public use. At that time, the simple structures of the preceding era were covered over with a broad artificial terrace created to support the road that crossed the basin from east to west, following the direction of the stream that, then as always, served as the main route, and moving toward the zone occupied by the principal cult center. The sanctuary of Qasr el-Bint rose in a privileged part of the basin, at the place where roads within the valley met in a natural exten-

sion of the trails leading to the city. Like the great sanctuaries of Baalbek and Palmyra, the temple must have fulfilled a social and political function as well as a religious one, serving to unite not only the inhabitants of Petra, but also the population of the farmsteads and caravansaries grouped around the city and the fluctuating and numerous populations of the caravan trains. The extension of the temple courtyard can also be explained by its function as a gathering place, a place for exchanges, encounters, and contacts among Nabatean subjects from different areas.

The zone reserved for religious edifices apparently continued to be concentrated in the western sector of the city. It was there, perhaps in the early years of the first century C.E., that the Temple of the Winged Lions was erected, on the opposite side of the Wadi Musa from the Qasr, but sharing its orientation. The great South Temple was built during the course of the same century, perfectly aligned on an east-west axis.

House cut into the cliff across from the theater. A series of rooms was arranged around a central hall. A sober exterior contrasted with the rich stucco and painted decoration of the interior walls of these habitations.

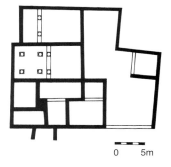

0   5m

Ez-Zantur. Schematic plan of a Nabatean house of the early first century C.E.

125

El-Beida, Siq el-Bared. Monumental facade in the form of a temple with portico *in antis* over a system of small rooms.

The nearly contemporaneous dates for three temples with notably different ground plans and the eclecticism of religious architecture in Petra reflect the Nabateans' intense contact with other cultures and the new cosmopolitan character of the city.

As urban improvements launched during the final decades of the first century B.C.E. continued throughout the following century and beyond, the city's monumental decor was enriched with new monuments added on either side of its ancient axis. Petra's commercial activities must have taken place in the southern sector, the part of the city closest to the access route through the Siq. This was where the agora must have been located (perhaps at the so-called upper market), and the commercial and administrative spaces connected with it. In other words, this was the civic area. Those who were passing through the city could also make use of the buildings, such as the theater, built at the edge of the urban area.

Unlike the nearby cities of Gerasa, Philadelphia, and even Bosra, Petra seems to have seen a sharp decline in construction activities during the course of the third century C.E., although excavation findings pertaining to daily life show that the standard of living remained quite high. After a catastrophic earthquake in the mid-fourth century, the occupied por-

tions of the city must have shrunk still further, to become concentrated in only a few parts of the urban area. The theater ceased operations even before it was destroyed by the earthquake. Shops built along the southern edge of the Colonnaded Street during the course of the fourth century, constructed in part with stones from collapsed columns, occupied a good part of the former pavement area, thus indicating that the street must have been at least in part unused, and that it certainly had lost its original function as a monumental processional way.

In the sector stretching from the Nymphaeum to the so-called Royal Palace, north of the Colonnaded Street, stratigraphic evidence from the late-Roman and Byzantine ages is still under analysis. Indisputably, northwest of that area, a necropolis was created on top of earlier city buildings. All the data signal a progressive decline of the municipal organization and of economic conditions in the city.

Nonetheless, Petra lived on, and at the end of the fourth century it was the seat of a diocese. In 446–447, the building known as the Urn Tomb was transformed into a church; in roughly the same period, a Byzantine basilica with a nave, two side aisles, and fine mosaics with human figures and vegetal motifs was constructed along a slope north of the Colonnaded Street, to the east of the Temple of the Winged Lions. The variety of decorative styles used in the capitals of columns in the basilica (excavated only recently) points to the reuse of materials from previous structures. The Byzantine occupation of the Qasr el-Bint is attested by a burial found along the southern wall of the building.

Earthquakes in 551 and 747 brought on the definitive destruction of the city, and afterward only the temporary presence of the Crusader fort on al-Habis left any sign of occupation.

Detail of a floor mosaic with figures and vegetal motifs, which decorates the side aisles of the great Byzantine basilica.

127

Rupestrian Funerary Architecture

From the moment of the rediscovery of Petra, the extraordinary testimony of the monumental rock facades has captured the attention of scholars, and many have worked to provide a typological and chronological framework. These monuments, which remain the most characteristic expression of Nabatean art, offer a unique opportunity to follow the development of absolutely original architectonic forms and to understand the many external influences affecting the artistic panorama of Petra. The major hindrance to discerning a line of development in these facades is the paucity of surviving dedicatory inscriptions. Two things contribute to this lack: the tombs in question were frequently stuccoed or painted; moreover, as attested in some instances, Nabateans preferred to leave their epitaphs on the stone that closed the burial loculus inside the funerary structure.

The typological sequence that Alfred von Domaszewski established for Petran tombs is still a point of departure for classification of the facades, even though his scheme has been modified and improved more than once, and as time passed analyses of the topographic distribution of the funerary buildings, studies of their reutilization at various points in time, and more in-depth studies of individual decorative elements were added to it. Scholars now distinguish several well-defined tomb types, ranging from the simplest forms to the most complex and architectonically most elaborate, but they note that Petran tomb styles show a surprising longevity and that different styles coexisted at any given time.

The most elementary—one even might say primitive—burials are pit graves, individual rectangular cavities excavated into the rock, which are attested at higher altitudes throughout the city, but in particular

Right: Bab el-Siq, the Tomb of the Obelisks. The monumental facade has four pyramidal obelisks, sculpted on all sides, that symbolize the dead buried inside the funerary edifice.

Facing page: The Urn Tomb stands, like the great "royal" tombs, on the slopes of el-Khubtha. It is a monumental edifice with a pediment and a central acroterion in the form of an urn. Its tetrastyle facade is preceded by a spacious courtyard bordered by Doric columns.

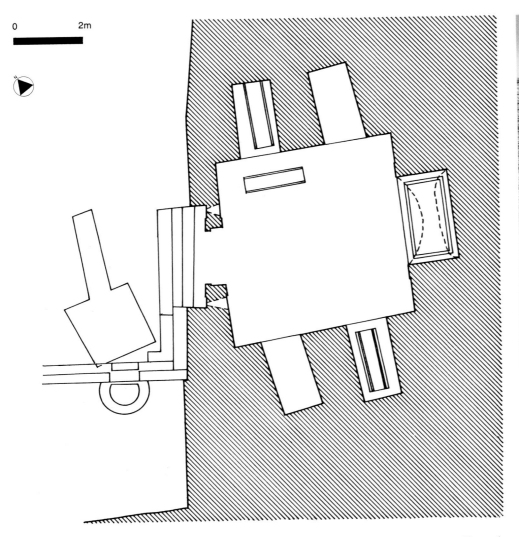

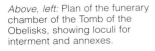

Above, left: Plan of the funerary chamber of the Tomb of the Obelisks, showing loculi for interment and annexes.

Above, right: Rock wall south of the theater, showing tombs topped with crenelations, double crenelations, and an arch motif.

in the zone of Bab el-Siq. The use of this type of burial, which is certainly very old, seems to have continued, though with varying intensity, until the fourth century C.E. Almost as simple is the type of tomb known as a "shaft grave." These were underground funerary chambers reached by means of a well-like shaft dug into a rock bench and containing a variable number of pit graves, closed with slabs, excavated into the chamber floor. This burial arrangement, which is widespread in the Hellenistic necropolises of Sidon in Phoenicia and 'Athlit in Palestine, was probably the most frequent type at the beginning of the Nabatean occupation of Petra. Pottery fragments datable to the third and second centuries B.C.E. permit us to place these collective chambers at the beginning of the settlement's development, but tombs of this type continued to be used, as some objects found among the grave goods testify—for example, a silver drachma datable to the reign of King Obodas II (III).

A slightly more complex variant of the shaft grave is the dromos tomb. Here access to the funerary chamber,

in which loculi for the deposition of the dead were hollowed out of the walls, was through a horizontal passageway rather than a vertical shaft.

Near these tombs or above them, there are at times monuments carved in relief from the rock wall in the forms of obelisks, pyramidal stelae, or miniature towers. According to an ancient Eastern funerary custom amply attested at Petra and widespread in the Semitic area, these low reliefs, which on occasion are simple graffiti on the rock, symbolize the *nefesh*.

It is not an easy task to trace the origins of the Nabatean *nefesh*. Some have connected it with the tower-shaped funerary monuments of Palestine; others, because of its pyramidal top, have likened it to certain tombs of the Middle and New Kingdom in Egypt, in particular, to the pyramidal funerary chapels of the necropolis of Thebes. Another possible origin that has been considered is a direct influence from Ptolemaic Egypt, especially in the third century B.C.E., when Egypt's influence extended as far as southern Syria. In that age, the city of Alexandria was a veritable melting

pot of artistic ideas, and we know from a passage in Lucan (*Pharsalia*, 8.296) that the Ptolemies were buried in pyramidal mausoleums.

The *nefesh* can appear in different forms, however, and through time it underwent transformations that reflect outside influences and bring it closer, architectonically, to the Western stele. Its significance apparently did not change: as a personal monument to honor the deceased, it was more properly commemorative than funerary and was often independent of the place of burial or the tomb.

The contrary case of a *nefesh* inserted into a funerary edifice is exemplified in a totally original manner at Petra by the Tomb of the Obelisks, whose imposing facade stands on the left bank of the Wadi Musa, outside the entrance to the Siq. The upper part of this monument is crowned by four obelisks in high relief, placed originally on a square base. A niche in the rock wall behind, between the two central obelisks, contains the statue of a standing male figure, dressed in the Greek manner. Inside the funerary chamber, which is accessi-

ble through a doorway framed by pilasters and surmounted by a Doric frieze, five loculi have been excavated, the largest of which, in the back wall, is in the shape of an arcosolium.

A Nabatean epitaph found at Medaba helps to clarify the particular disposition and significance of the Petra tomb, which bears no inscription. The Medaba inscription states: "This is the sepulcher and the two monuments [*nefesh*] placed above it which 'Abd'obodat, *strategus*, made for Aitibel, *strategus*, his father, and for Aitibel, leader of the camps [*stratopedarchus*,]. . . . The above work was made in the 46th year of his [Aretas IV, 37–38 c.e.] rule" (*CIS* II, 196). The four obelisks and the Greco-Roman statue thus symbolize the five persons buried in the tomb, and they attest to the persistence of ancestral funerary customs along with the reception of decorative and sculptural motifs of the Western tradition.

The rupestrian tombs most commonly found at Petra are clearly of Eastern derivation (Assyrian and Persian). They are structures in the form of a tower topped by

131

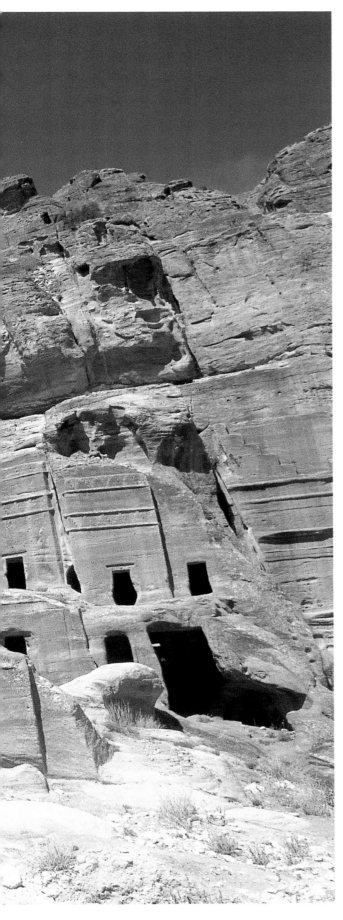

jagged, stepped crenelations, present in particularly large numbers aligned (at times on several levels) along the eastern end of the Siq, in the necropolis of the theater, and on the southern slopes of the hills behind the enclosure of the Qasr el-Bint. The facades of these structures characteristically include a frieze of one or two rows of stepped crenelations. The face of the monument, carved out of the rock, narrows slightly from bottom to top and is usually smooth. In the simplest examples, the door that gives access to the funerary chamber is a rectangular opening, at times surmounted (as in some tower tombs of the theater necropolis) by a horizontal groove that once held a stucco cornice. Other holes or horizontal grooves that appear in the walls above the door must have been used for decorative elements made of perishable materials or as supports for preparatory structures to aid whitewashing. We know that the facades were, at least in part, whitewashed, plastered, or painted because in some cases visible signs remain of plaster or painting, mostly in yellow, red, and blue.

The interiors of the tombs are arranged in a relatively common, uniform manner. The walls of the funerary chamber or chambers are broken up by loculi of various forms, set perpendicular to the wall or parallel to it, sometimes are large enough to contain one or more sarcophagi. Burial pits might also be dug in the floor of the chamber in a manner similar to that of the shaft graves.

In some of these tower-like constructions, not only the face, but also the sides have been excavated to make them protrude from the cliff face, forming a three-dimensional structure. This is a typically Nabatean adaptation of a type of burial tower found in the Syro-Phoenician environment until the late Hellenistic and Roman ages—for example, in the cylindrical constructions decorated with rows of crenelation in the necropolis of Marathus ('Amrit), which date from between the sixth century B.C.E. and the second century C.E. The basic innovation at Petra was to reduce to a facade a structure that had originally been an architectonic whole.

Even the crenelation motif was not originally Nabatean. It can be documented in the protohistorical architecture of the ancient Near East, and it was perpetuated in Persian art of the Achaemenid age in Persepolis and Susa during the sixth and fifth centuries B.C.E. It then spread throughout the Syro-Phoenician area, where it is amply attested even in the imperial age, when it is at times combined with Greco-Roman

Southern sector of the theater necropolis, general view.

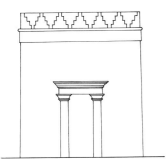

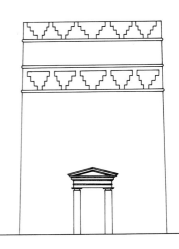

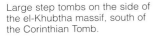

Schematic drawings of facades showing a single band of crenelations, a double cornice surmounted by crenelations, a double cornice with a single-divide crow-step crenelation, and a double band of crenelations.

elements, as in the temple of Bel or the sanctuary of Be'l Shamin at Palmyra.

In the crenelated funerary structures of Petra, the Hellenistic elements are limited to a richer decoration of the entrance, which may have a cornice and doorposts sculpted into the rock surface or may be surmounted by a genuine tympanum supported by small pilasters.

Another form of funerary architecture common in Petra is known as a stepped tomb. In this variant of the tower monument, a facade topped by a series of jagged crenelations is replaced by two large half-crenelations, angled to face one another, thus resembling five steps of a stair rising on either side toward the rock cliff. A further innovation was the addition of a quarter-circle

molding running under the top portion of the facade.

Often these tomb facades include rather elaborate architectonic embellishments. The tomb front may be bracketed by engaged columns or by pilasters surmounted with horned Nabatean capitals; the access door to the interior chamber may be bordered by double doorposts and topped by an architrave. In the most complex examples, an attic—either smooth or decorated with a series of dwarf pilasters or semi-pilasters—is inserted between the trabeation below and the molding above.

For this type of tomb top as well, the Nabateans adopted and fused elements that were common in the East. The motif of the stepped half-crenelation had already been used in Assyrian and Achaemenid architec-

Large step tombs on the side of the el-Khubtha massif, south of the Corinthian Tomb.

Tomb southeast of the theater (Brünnow and Domaszewski, Petra, no. 70). The tomb projects strongly from the rock wall behind it. Its architectonic design is identical on all three sides, with the exception of an access door to the funerary chamber on the east face.

ture, and the quarter-circle molding is a variant and a geometrization of the Egyptian cyma recta. What made this type of architectonic decoration innovative lay in the Nabatean architects' transformation of the older prototype when they placed traditionally Hellenistic elements (double doorposts, for example, or engaged columns and pilasters) next to typically local themes such as the horned Nabatean capital. That particular form of capital, which probably derived from the large voluted Palestinian capitals, was the result of a mediated evolution and a transformation of classical orders, Corinthian in particular. The result was a roughly hewn capital, with angles that took the form of a horn and a base at times draped with a leaf, while a central flower became so stylized as to be barely sketched. Some scholars consider the articulation of the tombs' attic in small engaged columns and dwarf pilasters to be a characteristic from ancient Iranian architecture, but it seems more plausible that this style derived from Hellenistic two-storied halls, with the Nabateans transforming the Greek structural elements into ornamental motifs.

Rock tombs in the theater wall (Brünnow and Domaszewski, Petra, nos. 113–115), with double crenelations and stepped crenelations. Beneath them, remains of funerary buildings, now destroyed.

Monumental stepped facade of the Silk Tomb, showing the veining in the rock that creates a striking chromatic effect. Engaged columns span the face of the tomb, and the high attic has decorative dwarf pilasters.

The Silk Tomb—so called because of the extraordinarily vivid veining in the rock out of which it is sculpted—displays one of the most monumental facades of the stepped type. It is situated at the base of el-Khubtha, on the slope facing the city center. Four engaged columns surmounted by Nabatean capitals line the lower part of the facade; the central area, between the second and third columns, has been widened slightly to frame the door leading to the funerary chamber; each of the intercolumnar areas to either side contains a niche with an image in relief, unfortunately illegible today. Four dwarf pilasters on a podium, aligned with the engaged columns of the lower order, decorate the attic.

A tomb at Moghar en-Nasara (Brünnow and Domaszewski, Petra, no. 649), situated along the rocky slope of the hill that dominates the city from the north, is a particularly significant example of the multiple motifs and complex influences to be found in Nabatean art after contact had been established with the Hellenistic world. The facade of this tomb is of the traditional stepped variety. It has pilasters with Nabatean capitals at the corners and a very elaborate entrance framed by small pilasters coupled with a quarter-column and surmounted by an architrave and a pediment. Between each pair of the four small pilasters that decorate the attic, however, there is a frieze of shields and trophies alternating with medallions bearing a Medusa head. This theme may have originated in Pergamum, where a frieze of arms decorates the balustrade of the propylons of the sanctuary of Athena Polias. The theme became common in the decorative art of the Hellenistic age and up to the Roman empire, and in fact it appears elsewhere at Petra, in a series of panels found in the temenos of the Qasr el-Bint. The details of the relief in Petra show a certain stylistic flair, but the way the continuity of the original design of heaped weapons is broken up into isolated images is far from typical of Western sensitivity.

In the past, scholars have mistakenly attempted to impose a chronological sequence on the rupestrian tombs capped with crenelations, double crenelations, and steps, assigning dates to the various types of eleva-

Two stepped tombs cut out of the summit of Moghar en-Nasara. The tomb on the left (Brünnow and Domaszewski, Petra, no. 649) is known as the Tomb of the Arms because of the frieze of arms set between small pilasters that decorates its attic.

tion and to decorative details. The simplest facades, those topped with only one row of crenelation, were supposed to be the oldest, followed in turn by those with double rows of crenelation, then those with stepped crenelation, which were considered more recent because architectonically richer and more complex. This relative chronology, elaborated by Alfred von Domaszewski, seemed confirmed by the topographic disposition of the tombs and was followed by other scholars until the rock tombs of Medain es-Saleh, the ancient Hegra, became known to the scholarly world.

Medain es-Saleh, today in Saudi Arabia, is located about 160 kilometers from the coast of the Red Sea and some 400 kilometers southeast of Petra. In ancient times, as we have seen, the site formed the southern border of the Nabatean kingdom, and it was both a center where caravans could replenish their water supply and, as many funerary inscriptions attest, a Nabatean military outpost and later a Roman outpost. The cultural environment, as can be seen from both the rock tombs and the Nabatean ceramic ware found there, seems to have been totally homogenous with that of the capital of the kingdom. Twenty-eight of the approximately eighty rock facades—tombs with

crenelations, double crenelations, and stepped crenelations—have been securely dated from inscriptions, and it is precisely from a study of the texts of those inscriptions that we know that the various types of funerary edifice do not correspond to a specific chronological sequence. Simple types and more complex, more elaborate facades were built contemporaneously, and all types were used throughout the period covered by the epigraphs, which is the first three-quarters of the first century C.E.

The oldest tomb at Hegra can be dated to the year 1 B.C.E.; the most recent one to 75 C.E. Whereas the first has one of the most elaborate facades of the entire necropolis, both in type and in style, others built many years later are capped with simple crenelations and have an unadorned facade. Because the texts of the inscriptions often give the name of the artisan who made the sepulcher, we know of two different workshops operating at Hegra and of three generations of builders who were responsible for various types of tombs that are undistinguishable chronologically.

At Petra, the necropolis near the theater provides further proof that facades with crenelations and with steps were built at the same time and that all the various types persisted for some time. Here some of the old-

Above, left and center: Hegra (now Medain es-Saleh, in Saudi Arabia), necropolis. Monumental stepped tombs F3 and D, constructed in 75 C.E. by the workshop of 'Abd'obodat, son of Wahballahi.

Above right, top: Hegra, tomb A5, constructed in 31 C.E. by Ruma and 'Abd'obodat. *Above right, bottom:* Funerary building A3, dated in an inscription to 5 C.E.

Facing page: Stepped tomb on the western slope of el-Khubtha identified as the burial place of 'Unaishu (Brünnow and Domaszewski, Petra, no. 813). The tomb's proprietor was minister at the Nabatean court during the first century C.E.

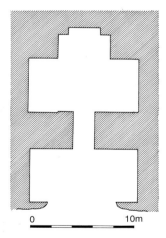

0   10m

and a small pediment; above it is an attic with a prominent molding, topped by a half-step crenelation. This is a particularly elaborate sepulcher, as it is preceded by a two-sided courtyard that must originally have been enclosed by a portico opening onto a funerary triclinium to the north. The interior consists of a nearly square chamber with three loculi in the rear wall and four in each of the two lateral walls. An inscription carved into the slab that closes one of the loculi, found elsewhere during the late nineteenth century but considered today to pertain to the tomb, gives the epitaph of 'Unaishu, "brother of Shaqilat, queen of the Nabateans." The epigraph names the owner of the sepulcher, who is the "brother" (that is, the minister) of Queen Shaqilat, a person of elevated rank with a prominent role at the royal court. Two other fragmentary inscriptions, recently found inside the tomb, bear a reference to "Malichus, king of the Nabateans," and a repeat of the phrase, "queen of the Nabateans." These are clearly formulas that indicate a date, as is customary in Nabatean inscribed texts.

These few epigraphic fragments enable us to set an approximative chronology for the tomb. Shaqilat is known in Nabatean coinage in three different roles: the spouse of Aretas IV, the sister of Malichus II, and the mother of Rabbel II, in whose name she reigned for six years, from 70 to 76 C.E. This means that the monument must date from the reign of Malichus II, somewhere between 40–44 and 70 C.E.

Another, longer epigraph is carved on the partially destroyed facade of the step tomb known as the Turkmaniya Tomb. The facade is divided in the usual way by a double pilaster with a quarter-column at either edge framing two engaged columns, all of these surmounted by Nabatean capitals. The tetrastyle lower order is extended into the attic by four semi-pilasters. The inscription is placed on five lines of the central intercolumnar space. Contrary to expectations, it does not give the name of the owner or the date of construction of the sepulcher; rather, it enumerates all the structures connected to the monument. Exactly as the epigraphic text states, the interior includes a vestibule and a funerary chamber with loculi for burials, and the facade was originally preceded by a courtyard with benches and a funerary triclinium.

The entire layout of this sepulchral complex, as it is described in the inscription, reveals a surprising similarity to the funerary monument of 'Unaishu, which must have been roughly contemporary. The paleography of the inscription and stylistic comparisons have in

est tombs, probably built during the second half of the first century B.C.E., were destroyed in the first century C.E. to create the upper gallery of the cavea of the theater. It follows that, at Petra and at Hegra, rock facades of these sorts must have been constructed, without particular variation in their structure, for more than a century. What is more, the necropolis does not seem to have been completely abandoned after the construction of the theater, which means that new tombs with crenelations must have been built after that date.

Although the traditional chronology has to be abandoned, the inscriptions we have available (though relatively few) and newly gathered data from excavation campaigns allow us to suggest hypothetical dates for some monuments.

On the western slopes of the Gebel el-Khubtha, almost directly across from the theater, a stepped tomb (Brünnow and Domaszewski, Petra, no. 813) stands out from a line of crenelated funerary monuments by virtue of a portal that provides an elegant decoration to its facade. Over the door there is a double cornice

The imposing facade known as ed-Deir, sometimes called "the Monastery," on the promontory of ed-Deir, north of Petra. The building's function was religious, not funerary. Built on two levels, it reiterates the architectonic motifs of the Khazneh, here on one plane rather than projecting, as in its prototype.

fact suggested a date for the Turkmaniya Tomb during the first half of the first century C.E., more precisely, between 30 and 50 C.E. Chronological data are too scarce and too uncertain to draw any final conclusion, but they seem sufficient to establish that this type of facade continued to be built at least until the mid-first century C.E., along with the funerary monuments with facades imitating Greco-Roman temples that were unique to the rupestrian architecture of Petra.

Tombs of the Greco-Roman type are usually capped with a pediment, less often, with an arch. They have engaged columns and quarter-columns—on occasion, freestanding columns crowned with Doric, Ionic, or Corinthian capitals—surmounted by a typically classic

trabeation, a Doric frieze of triglyphs and metopes with disks, or an Ionic frieze with an ovolo motif. Occasionally reliefs or figured sculptures decorate the faces of the tombs. In the more monumental examples, the tomb faces occupy two stories and have projecting architectonic elements. These constructional features, linked to Western traditions of temple architecture, led early scholars to consider these tombs posterior to Roman annexation. According to this view, these motifs were adopted at Petra after 106 C.E., hence after the Nabatean kingdom had come to an end and after the creation of the province of Arabia, a thesis that seemed confirmed by the absence of monuments of this type in the necropolis of Hegra and that still has some propo-

nents today. An examination of the funerary inscriptions at Hegra, however, has revealed a relationship between characteristics of tomb construction and the social class of the person for whom the sepulcher was made: the higher the rank and the greater the wealth of the tomb's proprietor, the greater the complexity and elaboration of the tomb, a rule that obviously affects the type of tomb chosen as well.

A focus on the strict relationship between architecture and society in the working out of rupestrian tomb facades permits us to explain not only why simple and more complex types should be built contemporaneously (reflecting differences in the social status of their proprietors), but also the diffusion throughout Nabatean terri-

tories of temple facades for tombs—something originally found only at Petra—during the course of the first century B.C.E. and in the following century. It seems plausible, in fact, that the most elaborate, and surely the most costly, tombs of this sort were destined for the royal family and the court entourage. This would explain the presence of such temple tombs in the capital of the kingdom at the moment of its greatest development and the absence of such structures in peripheral centers like Hegra, where Hellenization had little visible effect on funerary architecture.

The concentration of the more monumental forms of tomb architecture on the hillsides facing the center of the city seems to confirm the lofty status of their

Detail of the trabeation over one of the entrances to the Palace Tomb. The portal, bordered on either side by pilasters with Nabatean capitals and surmounted by a double molding with a smooth frieze, is framed by protruding pilasters with quarter-columns. The upper portion has a dentiled double cornice and a pediment.

Facing page: The Palace Tomb, so called because its exterior is thought to resemble what must have been the architecture of the great Hellenistic palaces. The architectural decoration of the facade is indeed extremely rich, and is articulated in a multiplication of juxtaposed elements that cover the rock face so completely as to suggest a *horror vacui.*

owners, even when no other element for identification exists. Until excavations that are still in the planning stage bring us more exhaustive conclusions, a relative chronology of pediment facades and temple facades can be elaborated only through an architectonic and stylistic analysis of the monuments and their decorative motifs, with all the limitations that such a method implies.

In this regard, the most studied and most discussed monument is the Khazneh el-Far'un, a structure with a two-story facade, a tholos motif, a broken pediment, and an extremely rich architectural and sculptural decorative scheme. The date proposed for the construction of this tomb oscillates between the first half of the first century B.C.E. and the second half of the second century C.E. The historical considerations and the architectonic and stylistic analyses supporting these estimates are so heterogeneous that they have led, during the course of years and scholarly studies, to support varied chronologies. For its subtle architectonic equilibrium, for the knowing play and illusionism of its perspectives, and for the rare elegance of its ornamentation, this construction has no equal in the architecture of Petra. Even its function—funerary monument, temple, or *heroon* (mausoleum)—has long been a matter of

controversy. Scholars today tend to date the Khazneh, the only rupestrian construction in Petra that includes no strictly Nabatean element, to the first century C.E., citing the exclusive use of late-Hellenistic Alexandrian components in its architectonic decoration and relying on stylistic comparisons between some of its ornamental motifs—capitals with floral decoration, for example—and their counterparts in the Qasr el-Bint.

It is not an easy task to evaluate how much the architectural motifs of this facade—the broken pediment, the tholos, the recessed niches in the upper story, the play of the projecting columns—owe to late-Alexandrian architectural models or to "real" Hellenistic palaces. The monuments of Ptolemaic Alexandria, like those of Seleucid Antioch, have not survived. The date of the Palace of the Columns at Ptolemaïs, to which the Khazneh at Petra has been likened, in particular for its architectonic affinity to the north and south faces of that great peristyle, is still under discussion, but it is certain that both the general layout and the decoration of the Petran palace reflect late-Hellenistic models. It is undeniable, however, that the Greco-Hellenistic tradition had a vast diffusion throughout the Near East, even if it was received in different ways, and that there must have been other constructions like the Khazneh: one such may have been the Qasr el-'Abd at Iraq el-Amir, a fortified palace not far from Philadelphia, built by order of Hyrcanus the Tobiad in the second century B.C.E.

We know the name of the constructor of this palace and its date of construction (182–175 B.C.E.) thanks to Flavius Josephus, who writes: "Hyrcanus . . . settled in the country across the Jordan, where . . . he built a strong fortress, which was constructed entirely of white marble up to the very roof. . . . He made chambers in it, some for banqueting and others for sleeping and living, and he let into it an abundance of running water, which was both a delight and an ornament to his country-estate" (*Jewish Antiquities,* 12.230–231). The building, which is relatively well preserved and is the only one of its sort that has come down to us, has two stories of roughly the same height; its facade is divided into three parts; the lower and upper tetrastyle orders have columns with Corinthian capitals; and over the upper trabeation there is a Doric frieze of metopes and triglyphs. The use of huge stones recalls techniques in the Syro-Phoenician tradition, but the Greek-Eastern style of architectural decoration is evident in sculptural reliefs: eagles at either end of the upper order of columns and a frieze with lions derive

144

Tomb in the form of a temple, known as the Tomb of the Roman Soldier. The central niche contains a sculpted male figure with a cuirass, the funerary statue of a high-ranking officer. The antiquarian details of the sculpture would seem to suggest a date toward the end of the first century C.E.

from a long Eastern tradition, but reveal the presence of Greek artists. Although little is yet known about the organization of Hellenistic workshops or relations between the commissioner and the executor of such projects, sources and inscriptions document a notable degree of mobility among the artisans of the various Hellenistic centers.

The facade of the Khazneh should be evaluated in the context of such considerations. It has often been stressed that there is an extraordinary affinity between the overall composition of the Petra monument and some depictions of buildings in the second style of wall paintings at Pompei. If it is true that the architectonic combinations pictured at Pompei reflect the actual architecture of villas and palaces of the late Hellenistic age, then we can read the facade of the Khazneh in the

same context. Moreover, it seems possible to document models common to the two artistic environments in the sphere of Alexandrian artistic culture.

The extent to which the Khazneh partakes of the Hellenistic tradition seems clear when we compare it with the facades of ed-Deir and the Corinthian Tomb. The imposing facade of ed-Deir rises to the west of Petra on the promontory, the Gebel ed-Deir, from which the monument takes its name. In structure, the edifice is nearly identical to the Khazneh, but the facade of ed-Deir, although architecturally even richer, lacks the spacial illusionism and the depth of planes that make the Khazneh unique. The lower half of the ed-Deir facade is divided by engaged columns rather than projecting, freestanding columns, and the upper story contains purely decorative empty niches with no receding second plane instead of the Khazneh's nine bas-relief sculptures.

In spite of the overall exaggeration of its architectonic motifs, the facade of ed-Deir creates a flatter effect; it seems a reduction "in relief" of the *frontes scaenae* of Asia Minor in the Roman imperial age. There is an even more obvious difference between the two monuments in the treatment of the trabeation. Where the Khazneh has delicate floral capitals and an admirable frieze of vine tendrils and volutes, ed-Deir's decoration is heavier and more rigid, with a massive use of local ornamental motifs such as Nabatean horned capitals and a Doric frieze of a stylized geometric design, with triglyphs and metopes in the form of disks.

The Corinthian Tomb, which lies on the slope of el-Khubtha facing the valley and the city, repeats some of the architectonic motifs of the Khazneh and ed-Deir in its upper story. The building takes its name from Corinthian floral capitals that are similar in design, but not in execution, to the ones in the Khazneh. It differs from the latter monument, however, in the exclusively decorative architecture of its facade, which has no projecting elements with structural function. Here the equilibrium of the Khazneh has disappeared, and the architectural scheme combines two different styles. The Hellenistic style of the upper story contrasts with the strongly eclectic taste and density of composition of the lower order, with its multiplication of horizontal lines and its protrusions, and with the repetition of architectonic elements in the attic. Such details relate this monument to other, more classically Nabatean structures such as the Renaissance Tomb or the Tomb of the Broken Pediment. The Corinthian Tomb is a nonorganic transcription of the original model in provincial taste.

The Corinthian Tomb is a collective sepulcher, with four separate entrances opening onto as many funerary chambers, a layout it shares with the Palace Tomb immediately to its left, the lower level of which is in the form of four juxtaposed temple tombs. Each of the four entrances to the Palace Tomb, richly decorated with double moldings and trabeations, pediments over the two central doors and arches over the lateral ones, opens into an individual funerary chamber. The decoration of the upper story imitates, on one plane, the architecture of a portico, with an alignment of nine pairs of engaged columns with Ionic capitals surmounted by a short trabeation. The construction is prolonged vertically by a sort of attic, divided into various registers by dwarf pilasters. A third level, also marked off by engaged columns and slightly set back, was completed only in part.

The facade of the Palace Tomb is the most monu-

The north wall of the funerary chamber of the Tomb of the Roman Soldier, with arcosolia for deposition.

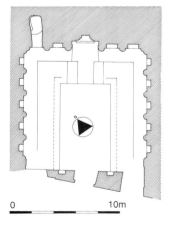

Plan and interior view of the triclinium adjacent to the Tomb of the Roman Soldier (Brünnow and Domaszewski, Petra, no. 235), also called the "Polychrome Room" because of the red, white, grey, and blue marbleized sandstone of the walls. This is the only triclinium hall in Petra that is decorated with engaged columns and niches.

mental and most imposing of all the tombs in Petra. Its complicated structural rhythms and its broader use of architectonic elements for purely ornamental purposes (with a determination that betrays an incomprehension of their true nature) denote a growing detachment from Hellenistic sensibility.

In conclusion, if the architectonic type of the rupestrian tomb is linked to the commissioner—hence to the desires and tastes of determinate social groups—the thirty-four pediment tombs and temple tombs at Petra can be attributed to persons of high rank, while the more than six hundred crenelated or stepped tombs can be assigned to persons of a middle level of the dominant class. Following this logic, we can conclude that the middle class in Petra, more conservative in its tastes, preferred Eastern forms, whereas the royal house and the court entourage turned instead toward Western models—Hellenistic-Alexandrian and Roman— that were amply represented in the first century B.C.E. throughout the Hellenized Near East. Those models, as

we have seen, might undergo a process of stylization in their forms, and the various modules of the classical orders might be altered or juxtaposed with no particular architectonic aim in mind, but the end result was not without elegance and monumentality.

The text of the inscription from the Turkmaniya Tomb, with its detailed description of the annexes to the tomb, confirms what has emerged from archaeological investigations: funerary monuments were in some instances part of a more ample sepulchral complex in which other constructions were added to the tomb itself, either for ceremonial purposes or to increase its monumental aspect.

A porticoed courtyard with a colonnade might precede the building, as is the case for the Urn Tomb (one of the best-conserved examples of this ground plan), or a funerary triclinium might be added to it. There are many examples of this custom in Petra. A triclinium is a rock chamber of varying size and aspect, the purpose of which, as attested in several Nabatean inscriptions, was to provide a space for annual banquets in commemoration of the anniversary of the death of the person honored by the tomb. Thus a triclinium is by definition situated near a tomb. Its interior usually has seats in the form of simple benches carved out of the rock; like the interiors of the tombs themselves, triclinia usually have no architectural ornamentation.

The triclinium of the Tomb of the Roman Soldier is a special case. Its facade, in the form of a small temple, which includes a statue in a central niche portraying the deceased wearing a cuirass, repeats some of the favorite motifs of Greco-Roman funerary architecture. The sculpture suggests a construction date toward the end of the first century C.E. Facing the tomb, and separated from it by a large courtyard, a vast chamber excavated out of the rock is preceded by an unornamented facade with three doors, each surmounted by a window. The interior is arranged as a funerary triclinium, with benches running along the lateral walls and (except for the central portion) along the rear wall. The entire chamber—a unique instance in Petra—is richly decorated. The walls are marked off by fluted engaged columns that alternate with rectangular niches imitating windows, which are themselves framed by pilasters with pseudo-Ionic capitals. The row of columns and niches is surmounted by a double trabeation with molded cornices. The entire decorative scheme reflects a generic Greco-Hellenistic influence.

The triclinium of Bab el-Siq, located beneath the Tomb of the Obelisks, has an elaborate architectural facade that makes use of motifs typical of pedimented tombs. The lower level of the two-part facade has pilasters at either end and engaged columns; the spaces between the lateral columns are crowned with a segmental pediment, while the somewhat broader central space is crowned by a large arch. The attic has dwarf pilasters divided into several horizontal registers, and the upper order terminates in a broken pediment. The interior of this building is completely unadorned and consists of a rectangular hall containing a *stibadion*, or horseshoe-shaped bench.

The connection between this large triclinium and the Tomb of the Obelisks is unclear. It has been proposed that a bilingual inscription carved into the rock wall along the opposing side of the Wadi Musa should be attributed to one or both of these monuments. This is a fragmentary dedication, in Nabatean and in Greek, commemorating the construction of an unidentified funerary monument "in the year . . . of Malichus." The lacuna in the text would have contained the date,

The Tomb of Sextius Florentinus, legate of the province of Arabia in 127 C.E., who died in 129. This is the only funerary edifice in Petra that can be dated with relative certainty.

which means that the inscription should be ascribed, chronologically, either to the reign of Malichus I (58?–30 B.C.E.) or to that of Malichus II (mid-first century C.E.). Paleographic indices seem to support the first hypothesis, but the archaeological evidence is too fleeting and too uncertain (the inscription might have pertained to a monument that was never completed) to permit any valid chronological conclusion.

The only certain chronological attestation that we possess for a funerary monument at Petra applies to the pedimented tomb of Sextius Florentinus, who was governor of the province of Arabia in 127 C.E. and whose funerary inscription in Latin is carved into the architrave of the lower order of the facade of his tomb. Although this tomb has been placed as the most recent example in conjectural reconstructions of the evolution of rupestrian architecture in Petra, its composite style—a tripartite facade containing a monumental entrance surmounted first by a trabeation and a broad arch, then by an attic divided into various registers decorated with

149

The great triclinium of Bab el-Siq, beneath the Tomb of the Obelisks. The interior chamber is plain, unlike the elaborate facade, except for a horseshoe-shaped bench for funeral ceremonies. The functional relationship that must have existed between the two monuments has not yet been sufficiently clarified.

The Gebel el-Khubtha, with the Tomb of Sextius Florentinus at its extreme northernmost point, viewed from the slopes of Moghar en-Nasara.

architectonic elements and topped with a pediment—does not differ in any way from the usual repertory and does not reveal any details specific to the Roman architectonic tradition.

For this reason the suggested dates for the Sextius Florentinus tomb range from the Augustan age to the mid-first century C.E. Some have even advanced the unconvincing hypothesis that the funerary edifice had been constructed previously and was given over to the service of the Roman governor by a wealthy family in Petra. The very position of the tomb at the extreme northern point of the Gebel el-Khubtha, a rock face that was already thickly occupied by other funerary ed-

ifices, lends support to its actual chronology, and the "traditional" decoration of its facade attests to the continuity and repetition of forms and the eclecticism of motifs that was characteristic of the great rupestrian monuments of Petra from their inception.

What we see in Nabatean architecture is one of the most interesting phenomena in the transplantation and transformation of Hellenistic and Roman culture in the Near East. The Nabateans, like other nomadic populations of Semitic origin, had no artistic tradition of their own, and they settled in a territory that has revealed no trace of a preceding figurative culture of any consistency. The Nabateans initially became part of

Once Petra entered the Hellenistic cultural sphere, the city became a center of reception for a vast artistic repertory, a process that was abetted by a wide circulation of project sketches, works of art, and artisans. The city of Alexandria, which at one time had close commercial relations with the Nabateans, clearly played a preeminent role in the development of the artistic culture of Petra, but it is equally clear that Alexandria was not the sole source of inspiration, and that other Hellenistic centers in Asia Minor (Pergamum) and Syria (Antioch) must also have played roles of primary importance in the transmission of fashions and models. Both the Nabatean royal house and the upper levels of society drew on these models for inspiration, which led to the rise of specialized workshops catering to commissioners' tastes.

Some scholars have suggested that in the final phase of Petran architecture, in the mid-first century c.e. or the second half of that century, there was a conscious and deliberate anti-classical reaction linked with the nationalistic politics of the last Nabatean sovereigns, and that the reaction translated into architectural terms as a decline in the use of formal motifs from the Western tradition. This thesis is contradicted, however, by the extensive use of Hellenistic motifs found in rupestrian facades throughout the first century of the Roman empire. Rather than reflecting an anti-Western reaction or any deliberate return "to the origins" (and one might ask: Which origins?), the persistence of local elements and elements from the Eastern tradition in both styles and iconography and the use of those elements along with Western themes, at the same time and in the same places, reveal instead that Hellenistic culture penetrated the Nabatean environment only externally or superficially and failed to be deeply internalized.

Whether the Nabateans imitated the forms of their architectonic models or translated them into the local idiom, they only partially understood the nature of those models, which became interchangeable as they were used in various combinations, alterations, and substitutions. Like the Doric frieze, they lost their structural value in a process of formal stylization, becoming purely ornamental.

In a process of cultural fusion typical of cultures on the margins of the Roman empire, Nabatean art used motifs from different traditions—Eastern, Greek, and Roman—to create a synthesis of a rich eclecticism and a clear originality and artistic sensibility.

the Syro-Phoenician artistic environment, which was already partially Hellenized but still retained many Eastern elements. The Nabateans' commercial relations put them in direct contact not only with Arabia, Egypt, and Syria, but also with Asia Minor and Greece, and eventually with Rome.

The large-scale adoption of Hellenistic (in particular, Alexandrian) motifs is manifest in Nabatean architecture and applied stucco decoration as early as the first century b.c.e., and it is likely that this process of Hellenization had something to do with the political attitudes of King Aretas III, who called himself "Philhellene."

Sculpture

What has just been said regarding rupestrian architecture in Petra is only minimally applicable to sculptural monuments. The overwhelming majority of the figurative sculptural pieces found at Petra are in fact of Greco-Hellenistic inspiration, and even those made locally recall the Western tradition in their iconography and style. The few reliefs that can be attributed to local tastes are cult idols and a few poorly conserved sculptures carved into rock faces.

The traditions of the figured relief and the freestanding statue are fundamentally incompatible with the nonrepresentational nature of Nabatean culture. This means that works of art were imported, as Strabo rightly remarked (16.4.26) in his enumeration of the goods that the Nabateans produced locally and those they im-

ported: "Embossed works, paintings, and moulded works are not produced in their country."

As early as the first century B.C.E., however, direct contact with Hellenized centers in Egypt and Syria not only made a noticeable impact on Nabatean architecture, but, thanks to itinerant artisans, must also have encouraged the importation and adoption of Hellenistic iconographic models as well, a process that probably was ongoing in roughly the same era as the construction of the earliest monumental rupestrian facades. This continual influx of men and ideas was responsible for the use of high relief sculpture, often of a notable quality, in the architectonic decoration of Petra's religious and civil monuments that made the city unique in the cultural panorama of the Nabatean kingdom.

The fortuitous nature of most of the findings that have been made, in particular, in the operations to clear and clean up the area at the foot of the triple-arched gateway and within the temenos of the Qasr el-Bint, makes it difficult to attribute a precise monumental context to the various reliefs and, consequently, to date them.

Panels with busts in relief found in the area around the triple-arched gateway to the temenos. They represent deities of the Greco-Roman pantheon: Athena, Hermes, Dionysos, and Melpomene, the muse of tragedy, holding a mask of Pan.

154

Relief of a veiled female deity with a diadem, probably Aphrodite. In type and style these sculptures suggest the presence at Petra of highly skilled artists, trained in a Hellenistic workshop.

Top: Winged head in sandstone of Eastern make and style, perhaps a local interpretation of Hermes.

Bottom: Winged Tyche holding a palm branch and a cornucopia sculpted in high relief on a block of limestone.

One series of sculpted panels with busts of deities found at the base of the gateway itself, near the south tower-vestibule, has been attributed to the decoration of the gateway (portions of which remain) or to a preceding structure. The entire Greco-Roman pantheon appears here: there is an Aphrodite, an Athena, an Ares, a bust of Hermes, an Apollo, an image of Dionysos, and one of Melpomene, the muse of tragedy.

These are painstaking portrayals in which not only the iconography but also the modeling is in Western taste, suggesting the presence of refined artisans. The execution and style of these works are not uniform, and next to more academic works—faithful but me-chanical transcriptions of the model, as in the bust of Melpomene, which reflects an obvious "neoclassical" taste—there are pieces of the highest quality. The fragmentary panel that contains the bust of Dionysos, in particular, is a work that springs from the best Hellenistic artistic experience: the god's abundant and wavy hair, held by a *taenia* and crowned with vine leaves, has fine movement; his fleshy face and half-closed lips are rich in chiaroscuro. The heightened pathos of the image recalls sculptural models of the school of Pergamum.

Although in their general adherence to Western types these reliefs reveal the presence of a variety of hands or of

155

Left: Bearded deity with a veiled headdress.

Right and below: Fragments of a relief showing gorgon heads, the lower portion of a cuirass, and an oval shield, parts of a frieze of arms and armor of Pergamene taste that must have been part of the decoration of either the triple-arched gateway to the temenos or the altar of the Qasr el-Bint, perhaps made to commemorate a royal victory.

project designs of varied provenance, in certain cases the iconography seems mediated, marking a distance from the Hellenistic repertory and displaying a different stylistic idiom. In the high relief bust that represents a male deity, perhaps Serapis, the Western tradition may be responsible for the general iconography, but details of its execution show a clear Eastern influence. The stylized treatment of the hair and beard, for example, reflects an artistic convention common in the Near East from ancient times. An image of a winged Tyche holding a cornucopia and a palm branch creates a composite iconography that likens that goddess to Nike and reflects a combinatory process characteristic of Nabatean art. On the other hand, the representation of a winged head with typically Eastern

formal characteristics represents a decisive departure from the motifs of the Western tradition and seems to derive from a local tradition of the Hermes type.

These relief panels, which are of different provenances, cannot be said to form a homogeneous group. Because some are worked in sandstone and others in limestone, it has been supposed that the latter were part of a portal constructed at the site of the great tripartite gateway and contemporary to the construction of the Qasr itself. What is certain is that there were local sculpture workshops, where artisans operated at the sides of artists trained in Hellenistic schools. Local masters very probably were responsible for another group of highly fragmentary reliefs, similar in style, found during exca-

Facing page: Bust of a male god, perhaps Serapis, sculpted from a limestone block. The upper part of the head is carved in the round; the rest is in high relief.

vations to clear the temenos. None of the deities represented in these fragments seems to belong to the Greco-Roman pantheon, and the stylistic details are quite unlike the more sophisticated sculptures found in Petra. Clearly, the decorative motif of the sculpted panel was repeated on many occasions, but it was executed by artisans of varied extraction.

The complex of the Qasr el-Bint was quite probably the original site of a series of some seventeen stone blocks bearing fragments of a frieze of arms found near the gateway to the sacred precincts. These panels depict shields, helmets, cuirasses, and other typical war trophies; the design so closely resembles the decorations that appear on the face of the Moghar en-Nasara tomb that the two schemes may, in fact, derive from a common design. As we have already seen, this theme comes from the Hellenistic tradition via Pergamum, and it became a part of the iconographic repertory of commemorative monuments of the Roman age. The original location of these panels is still a matter of heated debate. The sculptures may have come from a frieze on the propylon to the sacred enclosure; they may have been part of the decoration of the altar preceding the temple itself; they could have been placed inside the courtyard, perhaps as

part of the transenna or balustrade between the columns that formed part of the facade of the sacred edifice.

The influence of models from Pergamum can be found not only in a faithful transcription of motifs, but also in the style of execution characteristic of some figures. There is an extraordinarily expressive gorgon's head that probably decorated the central portion of a large shield in which the radial disposition of the hair, the strongly dramatic face, and an interest in coloristic effect reflect traits characteristic of the taste of Pergamum. From a stylistic point of view, this bust is comparable to a bust of Helios that is the only remaining part of the sculptural decoration of the metopes in the Doric frieze that topped the portico of the Qasr. One portion of this frieze is still in place on the eastern side of the temple, but the medallions bearing sculpted figures that alternated with rosettes at the center of the metopes were destroyed by iconoclasts. According to the date established for the temple, this relief must have been one of the oldest in Petra. The presence of a diadem with rays emerging from it clearly indicates that the bust represents an astral divinity—hence the conjecture that it was Helios—while the expressive facial features and animated glance recall heads from the altar of Zeus at Pergamum.

Fragments with festoons and garlands held by putti, found in the temenos of the Qasr el-Bint and certainly a part of that architectonic complex, also belong within the cultural context of the Hellenistic tradition. The style and refined workmanship of these decorative elements betray the presence of skilled artists capable of a high level of formal achievement.

The artistic panorama that emerges from these brief considerations confirms what has already been said about the construction and architectural and sculptural decoration of the Khazneh and regarding ornamentation in stucco in the Qasr and in the houses of Petra: the great Hellenistic schools had a determinant and very forceful influence at Petra as early as the first century B.C.E., conditioning all or almost all that was produced in the plastic arts in that city into the following period.

This is also true of freestanding statues, only a few sporadic fragments of which remain. It is possible that the scarcity of findings can be attributed to the Nabateans' lack of interest in works in the round and the rendering of whole figures. It is certain, however, that in Petra, as in all the other Hellenized cities of the Near East, there must have been votive and honorary sculptures in the Greek and Roman traditions, as is

clearly attested by dedicatory inscriptions from the temenos of the Qasr that explicitly allude to the presence of such images. This custom must have encouraged a thriving trade in imported models and works in marble, and especially in bronze, destined for an aristocratic minority open to "foreign" influences and fashions.

A bronze statue of a deity from the Wadi Siyyagh is perhaps a unique instance. This work, which may portray an Artemis hunting or a fighting Amazon, is a Roman copy datable to the second century C.E. presumed to have been imported rather than locally produced. How prevalent such works may have been is impossible to say in the current state of scholarship. An overall view of sculptural production in Petra shows that, in general and at the moment of its greatest political and economic expansion, the city was a major center for the diffusion of Hellenism in the East.

Limestone panel showing Cupid with a winged lion, perhaps part of the decoration of a balustrade.

Fragment from a metope from the Doric frieze of the Qasr el-Bint. The bust portrays an astral deity, probably Helios, wearing a diadem surrounded with rays (Amman: Archaeological Museum).

Monuments and Written Documents

The Qasr el-Bint Far'un and Its Temenos

The great temple emerges from within a vast semi-rectangular paved plaza at the western end of the Colonnaded Street. Excavations have completely freed the temple interior of rubble, and restoration of the elevation and the architectural decoration is in progress. The temple is oriented on a north-south axis; its square plan measures thirty-two meters to a side; and, with the podium, it is twenty-three meters high. Its layout includes an ample pronaos, a cella, and a tripartite adyton. It is built of blocks of rose sandstone laid down in regular courses, with an inner fill of smaller stone blocks and mortar. The temple proper is preceded by a facade *in antis* with four columns aligned between antae; the facade is set above a flight of steps, originally faced with marble, that runs along its entire width. A balustrade placed between the columns limited access to the portico. The pronaos, which was also at one time paved with marble, had in its western wall a niche probably intended to contain an inscription or a decorative element of some sort. From the pronaos, a large arched doorway, once preceded by three steps, leads into the cella, which, like the pronaos, is wider than it is long.

The rear part of the cella is occupied by the adyton, a sanctum sanctorum where the image of

the deity was kept, to either side of which there are secondary spaces. Today the structure of the eastern rear space has been elucidated satisfactorily, and the one on the other side must have mirrored it. These two rooms had two stories: a ground floor with two columns set between pilasters originally supported a sort of mezzanine or balcony that rested on three arches masked by a wooden structure. A staircase hollowed out of the thick outer wall and placed in the outside corners of the two rooms led to an upper story and the roof. The space on the eastern side contains evidence of a large window as well, probably closed with metal bars. Small marble reliefs of lions' heads and paws that may have served to decorate beds or tables have prompted the hypothesis that sacred symposia in honor of the deity were held in this room. We know in fact from Strabo (16.4.26) that thirteen adepts of the cult presided over sacred banquets, the banquet participants were entertained by two girl singers, and the king himself served the guests at the sacred table, probably acting as symposiarch.

The central room, the adyton proper, was raised approximately 1.40 m above the level of

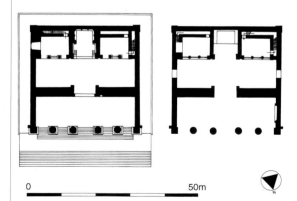

Plan of the ground floor and the upper story of the temple. The basic features of the ground plan are characteristic of southern-Syrian and Nabatean religious architecture.

Top: The front of the Qasr el-Bint Far'un. The temple, originally tetrastyle, was preceded by marble-clad stairs. The portico led through to the cella, at the rear of which there was a tripartite adyton, a space reserved for safekeeping of the image of the god and probably for sacred banquets.

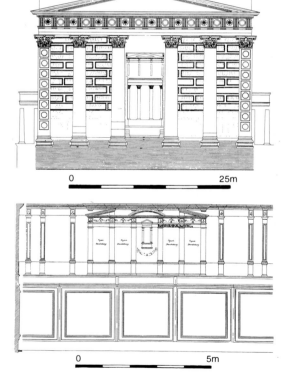

Elevations reconstructing the decorations on the face of the temple and on the outer rear wall, both originally completely covered with ornamental motifs in painted or gilded stucco (after François Larché).

the pavement. A double flight of seven steps led up to a sort of platform-altar, on top of which we may suppose the cult idol to have been placed. The walls of the adyton were decorated with engaged columns with double quarter-columns in the corners, while the front was flanked by two pilasters that probably supported an arch.

The original roof of the temple and its various adjuncts have long been a matter of discussion. Certainly the lateral rooms of the adyton had a flat roof, as indicated by holes in the walls for wooden joists. The cella, which would have been higher than its flanking spaces, probably had a double-sloped roof; the pronaos would have had a flat terrace roof; while the edifice itself was covered by a tympanum roof.

Single-story porticos reaching about halfway up the walls were subsequently added to both the eastern and western sides of the temple.

The architectural and sculptural decoration of the temple must have been extremely ornate, and stucco was widely used. The trabeation, which is still in place along the eastern wall, consisted of a double-banded architrave and a Doric frieze of metopes and triglyphs in which the metopes held, alternately, large double-petaled rosettes and busts of deities. These figured reliefs, like those of the triple-arched gateway to the temenos, were mutilated by later iconoclasts, and it is impossible to reconstruct their iconographic program, although it certainly must have been connected with the deity or deities to whom the sanctuary was dedicated. The one bust that remains (a representation of Helios) bears eloquent witness to the extraordinarily high quality of the workmanship of the reliefs and to their derivation from Hellenistic models.

The walls of the temple were completely covered, inside and out, with ornamental and architectural decoration in painted and gilded stucco. The pilasters that form the antae of the portico have a paneled design on three sides consisting of alternating squares, octagons, and circles, a design repeated in the frieze. The face of the pronaos and the external walls on either side were decorated with pilasters crowned by a dentiled cornice. The decoration of the rear outside wall was just as rich, with a series of engaged columns that left room at the center, at a spot

corresponding to the adyton inside, for a temple facade of six columns surmounted by an architrave and a frieze of putti carrying garlands and, above it, a broken pediment with a central arch.

The building interior was stuccoed as well, as clearly revealed by holes for affixing the stucco decorations and by the many fragments of applied decoration that have been found. The original decorative scheme for the central niche of the adyton has been reconstructed, demonstrating that it featured a two-level tetrastyle facade.

It seems completely plausible that the great temple was consecrated to Dushara, who was venerated at Petra in aniconic form as a betyl. New information on the cult has emerged from more recent excavations, however—in particular, a sandstone idol found on the pavement of the adyton that has been interpreted as an image of the goddess al-'Uzza and a fragmentary dedication in Greek to Aphrodite. We know that the dedication dates from the third century C.E., because it refers to Petra with the honorific title of *metro-*

Top: Pilaster of the northeast anta, showing traces of decorative stucco panels with geometric motifs.

Bottom: Trabeation of the eastern wall of the temple, showing a Doric frieze of metopes and triglyphs. The metopes have large stylized rosettes alternating with busts of gods.

colonia, attributed to it by the emperor Elagabalus. The existence of an Aphrodiseion in the second century C.E. is documented in a passage in the Babatha archive, while St. Epiphanius, writing in the fourth century, describes the cult that the Arabs of Petra still rendered to the god "Dusares" and his mother, "Chaamu." This name may be a corruption of the Aramaic *Almou* or *Chalmou,* which means "young girl or virgin." It is thus possible that the principal temple of Petra, the Qasr el-Bint, or "castle of the maiden," was the center of a joint cult of Dushara and al-'Uzza. In both its architectural layout and its decorative scheme, the temple is one of the most original monuments of the Hellenized Near East. The tradition indigenous to southern-Syrian and Nabatean religious architecture is incontestably manifest in the use of a square cella opening onto a vestibule, in the layout of the tripartite adyton, and in the use of a platform altar that follows the Eastern formula of the *motab*, but the temple is unique in having had a dual-sloped roof, a characteristic of classical temples, rather than a terrace roof. The nature

and the choice of the decorative motifs reveal the hand of artisans trained in workshops that respected the best Hellenistic tradition.

A large, roughly square altar some three meters high, accessible by means of steps and made of sizeable, irregularly hewn blocks of marble, stands in front of the temple.

The southern portion of the wall that surrounds the great paved plaza is well conserved, but on the northern side, toward the Wadi Musa, the wall is so badly damaged that only a few segments of the original construction are recognizable. The south wall was lined by a double row of benches that formed a sort of *theatron*, or forecourt, reserved for the faithful during sacred ceremonies that took place in the courtyard, near the altar, or in front of the temple facade. The same term appears in an inscription from the sanctuary of Be'l Shamin at Si' in the Hauran, which has a similar layout, thus confirming the architectonic link between the Qasr and the temples of southern Syria. A ledge, above the two benches, probably served as a base or stand for statues and ex-votos, as attested by the many inscriptions found there. The overall arrangement was created in two successive phases, certainly after the construction of the temple precinct and the temple itself.

The oldest epigraph found on the premises, a dedication of a statue to King Aretas IV on the part of a priest of the temple, has been dated on the basis of its paleographic characteristics to the early first century C.E. It suggests a possible date for the construction of the Qasr to the reign of Obodas II (III), that is, between 28 and 9 B.C.E.

Another dedication, inscribed on a marble plaque and probably also referring to Aretas IV, was found recently in the temenos (although not in situ), and yet another inscription found in pieces on the temple steps records "Sha'udat daughter of Malichus." This text refers to Malichus II, who had a daughter by that name. In any event, the presence of these dedications suggests that at various points in time, the temenos of the temple must have received statues and images of the royal family as well as rich votive offerings. It is known that the entire complex underwent various reconstructions and that the stucco decoration was redone on several occasions.

An imperial Roman phase is confirmed by fragmentary inscriptions in Greek. The first is a votive inscription to Zeus Hypsistos, the equivalent of Be'l Shamin or Dushara; the second is a dedication to an emperor whose name is not conserved but whom scholars tend to identify as Hadrian or Antoninus Pius.

A great marble hand found on the podium of the temple probably belongs to the category of imperial images, rather than cult statues.

The partial destruction of the temple building by fire is clear from coins of Gallienus and from pottery fragments. A burial along the southern wall offers evidence of the Byzantine occupation of the structure, as does a coin of Arcadius (382–408 C.E.), which provides the terminus ante quem for that occupation.

The earthquake of 19 May 363 irreparably damaged the Qasr, and another earthquake in the sixth century C.E. caused further damage and rendered the structure completely unusable.

Qasr el-Bint. Detail of the tripartite adyton in the rear portion of the cella. The central space, the sanctum sanctorum, contained the betyl that represented the deity venerated in the temple, Dushara, the supreme god of the Nabatean pantheon.

Qasr el-Bint. The eastern room of the adyton. The two central columns, set between pilasters, were built to support a mezzanine that could be reached by means of a stairway in the corner, set into the thick walls. The space on the western side was probably similar.

The Inscriptions

A certain number of Nabatean inscriptions have been found in the zone of the temple, and their importance for dating the sanctuary has been stressed. The following list gives the principal texts, emphasizing their special characteristics and their contributions to knowledge about Nabatean culture.

Base of the Statue of Rabbel I

In 1897, an inscription was discovered on a statue base (now lost) in the temple area. It was one of the oldest texts in Petra and one of the first Nabatean inscriptions. When it was discovered, the surface of the stone presented abrasions and lacunae on the right-hand portion. This base measured 76 cm × 52.5 cm.

Bibliography: *CIS* II, 349; Cantineau, *Nabatéen*, 2:1–2, no. 1.

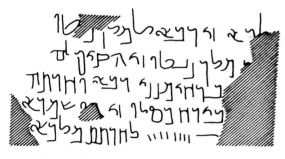

1. [DNH Ṣ]LM' ZY RB'L MLK N[B]ṬW
2. [BR . . .]T MLK NBṬW ZY HQYM LH
3. . . . BR ḤYMNNY RB' WḤDTH
4. . . . BYRḤ KSLW ZY HW ŠMR/D'
5. [ŠNT] 18 LḤ RTT MLK'

1. [This is the sta]tue of Rabbel, king of Nabaṭu,
2. [son of . . .]t, king of Nabaṭu, who has erected to him
3. . . . . Hayamnanai (?), the leader (the elder?) and has restored it
4. . . . . in the month of Kislew, which is Shamra (or Shamda)
5. [the year] 18 of Aretas, the king.

The antiquity of the inscription is apparent in the still-archaic tracing of the characters and in the use of grammatical forms typical of imperial Aramaic but which are no longer attested as such in middle Aramaic languages or in later

Nabatean. These are the relative pronoun *zy* in line 3, which later becomes *dy* (the two forms are present in the inscription of Aṣlaḥ), and the form *hqym*, "has erected" (or "caused to be erected") with the prefix *h-*, indicating the factive, which later became '-. On the basis of the shapes of the characters, Jean Starcky attributes this inscription to about 67 B.C.E., which means that the King Aretas cited can be identified as Aretas III Philhellene, whose reign can be set between 88–85 and 59–58 B.C.E.

The name of the dedicant's father is attested in Nabatean only here; it is considered a compound including the name of the Babylonian goddess Nanai. The epithet applied to him (literally, "the great") is ambiguous because it is not followed by a complement of specification. Although the phrase translated as "the leader" may indeed be a formal title, it could also be rendered as "the greater" or "the elder," simply indicating that there was another, less important or younger person of the same name.

The month of Kislew, which comes from the Babylonian calendar, corresponds to December; the second name given to the same month is unknown, an additional reason for the dedication's uncertain reading, especially because, as shown in the transcription "R/D'" at the end of line 4, the characters *r* and *d* were the same in Nabatean and can be distinguished only by context.

Inscription of Aretas IV

The inscription of Aretas IV, found in the temenos and still in situ, is carved into a sandstone block, now rather worn, and measures 50.70 cm × 27 cm.

Bibliography: Jean Starcky and John Strugnell, "Pétra: Deux nouvelles inscriptions nabatéennes," *RB* 73 (1966): 236–243.

1. DNH ṢLM' ḤRTT
2. RḤM 'MH MLK
3. NBṬW DY 'QYM
4. LH 'BDW PTWR'

1. This statue is (?) Ḥaritat,
2. who loves his people, king
3. of Nabaṭu, which has erected
4. for him 'Abdu, the seer.

Jean Starcky and John Strugnell, who published this inscription, date it to the first part of the long reign of Aretas IV (9-8 B.C.E.–40-41 C.E.), that is, to 9–8 B.C.E., on the basis of a careful analysis of the form of the letters. They also point out the still-archaic tracing of some characters, while others (in particular, *p* and *q*) are given in typical "calligraphic" Nabatean script.

As for the content of the inscription, the initial formula, *dn' ṣlm' ḥrtt*, is ambiguous. It cannot be translated, "This is the statue of Aretas," because the form used for "statue" or "image" has the ending -', which indicates determination, something impossible for a noun that governs a complement of specification. This means that we have to translate, "This [gift] is the statue of Aretas," or "This statue is Aretas." The term *ṣlm'* indicates an image, thus a statue, representing a specific person. The term is masculine in gender if the person depicted is male and feminine (*ṣlmt'*) if a female is depicted. Choosing the interpretation, "This statue is Aretas," as the publishers of the inscription have done, presupposes a conceptual equivalence between the statue and what the statue represents: its collocation within the sacred precinct thus puts the sovereign under the protection of the deity.

Aretas IV is presented here with his full title, but the titulary and the kingly title are given in an order that reverses common practice. Inscriptions usually designate this king as *ḥrtt mlk nbṭw rḥm 'mh*, or, "Aretas, the king of Nabaṭu, who loves his people." According to the publishers of the inscription, the order attested here is modeled on the usual title as given in Greek, where the epithet immediately follows the name of the sovereign, as in coins of Aretas III in which the legend in Greek reads *basileos Aretou Philellonos*, "of the king Aretas Philhellene." The Greek titles to which the Nabatean "who loves his people" might correspond are *Philodemos* or *Philopatris*, expressions not attested, however. Aretas IV is given in Nabatean as "who loves his people" in all the inscriptions that mention him by name, with the exception of one inscription from the first year of his reign, where he is simply, "Aretas, king of Nabaṭu" (*CIS* II, 332).

The name of the dedicant, 'Abdu, is an abbreviation that signifies "servant of [a specific

Facsimile of the inscription (first half of the first century B.C.E.) on the base of a statue of Rabbel I, erected in the time of Aretas III (ca. 88-85 B.C.E.–55-58 B.C.E.). Both the form of the characters and the language present characteristics that are still archaic and that Nabatean shared with imperial Aramaic.

Sandstone base incorporated into the south wall of the temenos of the Qasr. The inscription, which is still in situ, identifies the statue that it supported as King Aretas IV (9-8 B.C.E.–40-41 C.E.). The formula that is given here differs slightly from the usual wording.

god]." The ending in -w is typical of Nabatean proper nouns; the term 'bd, on the other hand, is frequent in all western and southern Semitic languages, in which it expresses the devotion of the person who bears the name for a specific deity, although it has no specific connotation of subjection. The specific vocation of the dedicant, here translated as "seer," is still disputed. According to one probable explanation, he may have been a soothsayer or an interpreter of dreams.

The Malichus Inscription

The second inscription found in the temenos of the Qasr el-Bint, near the monumental arch, is unfortunately fragmentary, but it is nonetheless valuable because it names the king, Malichus II, and his wife Shaqilat. It is drilled into a marble plaque now measuring 19 cm × 11.5 cm, 4 cm in

thickness. The right-hand portion of the plaque is broken, leaving only three lines, all fragmentary. The entire text must have occupied at least two slabs. The inscription bears the inventory number J 9531 in the Amman Archaeological Museum catalogue.

Bibliography: Jean Starcky and John Strugnell, "Pétra: Deux nouvelles inscriptions nabatéennes," RB 73 (1966): 243–247; Jean Starcky and Fawzi Zayadine, in Der Königsweg: 9000 Jahre Kunst und Kultur in Jordanien und Palästina (Mainz: Philipp von Zabern, 1987), 248, no. 245.

   1.]' WTRY KMY DHB' WK[SP'(?)
   2.]ṬBQR 'L ḤYY MNKW[
   3.]W̊ŠQYLT MLKY NBI[ṬW
   1.] and the two sheets (?) of gold and sil[ver (?)
   2.] . . . for the life of Malichus[
   3. and of Shaqilat, sovereigns of Naba[ṭu

The attribution of the inscription to the reign of Malichus II (40–70 C.E.) is confirmed by the publishing scholars' examination of the shapes of the characters. The inscription would have begun with a demonstrative pronoun designating the donated object, perhaps followed by the term ṣlm "the statue," to make a phrase such as "This is the statue and the two . . ." or "These are the statue and the two. . . ." The name of the dedicant would normally follow, along with a verb of dedication. The length of the lacunae cannot be reconstructed. Moreover, because the plaque seems to be intact on its left-hand side but the word "Nabaṭu" in the last line is not complete, we can posit that there was at least one other plaque, placed to the left of the one that has been conserved, on which the lines of the inscription would have continued. This supposition is based on the fact that, in Nabatean, words are not usually divided between one row and the next.

The object being dedicated, kmy, is a plural noun of uncertain meaning, attested only in this inscription. These objects were defined as being of gold, which is the reason for the totally hypothetical reading of wk[sp'] as "and of silver." The translation of kmy as a sheet, plate, or plaque is merely indicative, and is based on an uncertain comparison with an Akkadian word. There is confirmation of the presence of gold objects in cult sites in the Suda Lexicon, which states that an idol of Theusares (Theus Ares, or Dushara) was placed on a gold base. Offerings made of silver and gold are also cited in an inscription found in the Temple of the Winged Lions.

Nor is there a satisfactory interpretation for the first four letters of the second line of this inscription. The context suggests a proper name, that of the donor or his father, but there are no persuasive onomastic comparisons. What follows is a phrase frequent in dedicatory inscriptions: the objects given are offered "for the life" of someone, in this instance, as is often the case, the reigning sovereign and his family. The term "life" equates, essentially, to the health of the person, a concept that includes prosperity.

The name of the king, Malichus, is almost always written mnkw in Nabatean, with an exchange between l and n that is not uncommon in Semitic languages. The name is an abbreviated compound (displaying the customary termination in -w) derived from malik, which means "king," but also denotes a god and was originally an epithet.

The name Shaqilat, here probably the wife of Malichus, was also the name of a wife of Aretas IV and the mother of Rabbel II, for whom she acted as regent with the title of queen, as attested in two inscriptions from Petra (CIS II, 351, 354). The significance of this name is disputed.

The term that designates the two rulers is also unusual. The plural title of mlky nbṭw, rendered above as "sovereigns of Nabaṭu," would place the king and the queen on an equal plane. More often, the king is listed with his own title, mlk' mlk nbṭw, "the king, king of Nabaṭu," and his wife's name is followed by the title of queen (mlkt nbṭw), or else she is called "sister of the king," an epithet that at times follows that of "queen of Nabaṭu." Another inscription found in the temenos states, "Sha'udat, daughter of Malichus" (see Fawzi Zayadine, "Recent Excavations," ADAJ 25 [1981]: 355).

The Aretas Inscription

A block of sandstone measuring 61 cm × 59 cm, found during the operations in the northwest corner of the Qasr el-Bint enclosure carried out by the Jordanian Department of Antiquities, has affixed to it a marble plaque 30 cm × 25 cm. It bears an inscription of at least three lines, only one of which is legible today, and uncertainly at that.

Bibliography: Fawzi Zayadine and Suleiman Farajat, "The Petra National Trust Site Projects: Excavation and Clearance at Petra and Beiḍa," ADAJ 35 (1991): 291, fig. 12; 293, pl. 16, no. 2.

ⲧⲏⲣⲓⲟⲏ ⳾

   1. ḤRTT 'BRK 'NT (?) B'W(?) . . .
   1. O Aretas, you are most blessed . . .

The person named is Aretas IV. The expression 'brk is a form of the passive participle bryk, or "blessed," typically used to indicate the absolute superlative (called the elative case).

Fragmentary inscription found in the temenos of the Qasr, near the monumental gateway. It dates from the reign of Malichus II (40–70 C.E.) and, like the preceding inscription, it is valuable for establishing the chronology of the sanctuary. Made with a drill on a marble plaque, it speaks of gold and silver objects.

The Temple of the Winged Lions

Excavation of the Temple of the Winged Lions was carried out in a series of campaigns from 1974 to 1978 under the direction of Philip C. Hammond. The construction extends along the hill to the north of the Colonnaded Street, overlooking the western portion of the street. A bridge over the Wadi Musa led to a road some eighty meters long, rising from the street to the terrace of the temple. This street, somewhat like a *via sacra*, was originally lined on either side with porticoes richly decorated with colored stucco.

Access to the sacred edifice was through two narrow passageways preceded by stairs that led to a portico *in antis* supported by arcades, and from there to a large entrance to the cella. The cella was square, and its rear half was occupied by a *motab*, or platform altar. The perimeter walls were constructed with a double facing of stone blocks, laid in regular courses on the outside but smaller in size and less regular on the inside walls, which were originally clad in marble on their lower surfaces and stuccoed and painted above. The cella pavement was made of white and brown marble chips. A rich architectural

decoration enlivened the internal walls, which contained deep niches framed by strongly protruding engaged columns, doubled at the corners, in the Nabatean style, by quarter-columns. Five freestanding columns stood along each sidewall, forming something like an internal peristyle. The shafts of these columns were covered with stucco, as were the Nabatean capitals, the vine tendrils of which were coupled with an appliquéd stucco flower. Paintings with geometrical, floral, and figured themes (putti, dolphins, human busts, masks), together with frescoes with more complex representations, decorated the niches and probably also the ceiling of the cella.

The altar, which was clad with black and white marble, was surrounded on three sides by engaged columns with two freestanding columns

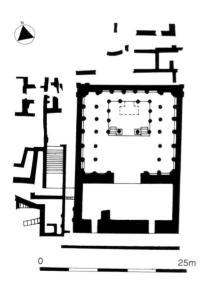

Plan of the temple and its annexes. The ground plan of the building, with a truncated portico in antis, a square cella, and a *motab*, is typically Nabatean.

Top: The cella of the temple from the west, showing the internal peristyle and part of the outside walls.

Betyl found in the Temple of the Winged Lions. It bears an inscription of the "classical" period (late first century B.C.E.–first century C.E.). The idol has been identified as al-'Uzza. The inscription calls the female deity "the goddess of Hayyan" (a personal name).

to the front, all surmounted by figured capitals depicting the crouching winged lions that gave the temple complex its name. To either side of the two columns at the front, staircases permitted access to the platform, and a niche with a door, hollowed out of the rear wall, probably served as a sacristy and a depository for cult objects.

A number of annexes surrounded the temple. Those on the north side have been identified as lodgings for the priests and temple personnel, while three rooms to the west were certainly workshops for craft activities connected with the temple construction. One of these served for refinishing metal objects; another, where jars for colors have been found, was a paint shop; a third was used for marble work. Over a thousand marble fragments in various stages of the finishing process have been found in the third room, among them four plaques that make up a votive epigraph in Nabatean dating to the thirty-seventh year of the reign of Aretas IV (27–28 C.E.) that is considered to be the dedicatory inscription of the sacred complex. According to that chronological reconstruction, the temple was built during the second quarter of the first century C.E., following a ground plan and an internal architectonic articulation common throughout Nabatean territory.

The presence of a square cella with a *motab* at its center, embellished by engaged columns and other decorative elements, links the structure to the temple of Atargatis at Khirbet et-Tannur, for example, which dates from the late first century B.C.E., or to the temple dedicated to the goddess Seia (the local form of Tyche) at Si' in the Hauran, or even to the Nabatean temple at the Wadi Ramm, south of Petra, for which the most significant phase of construction seems to have been during the reign of Rabbel II.

Although the plan of the Temple of the Winged Lions shows indisputable affinities with those structures, its architectural details, and above all the motifs of its painted and stucco decoration, are Greco-Hellenistic in inspiration, and as a whole the temple clearly exemplifies the multiplicity of influences and the eclecticism found in religious architecture at Petra.

According to data that have emerged from excavation, the decoration of the temple underwent a radical transformation during the reign of Malichus II or his successor Rabbel II in which the representational paintings that decorated the niches of the cella were deliberately obliterated by monochromatic designs and the figured capitals were smoothed and stuccoed, perhaps as a result of a revival of the Nabatean aniconic tradition. This change was still ongoing, as material found in the crafts shops seems to indicate, when a fire broke out that led to the abandonment of the temple some time around 110–114 C.E.

Once again, there is a problem concerning

Temple of the Winged Lions. Platform altar in the rear portion of the cella. The altar had engaged columns at either side and was accessible by flights of steps placed next to the front columns.

the identity of the deity venerated in the temple. The discovery of a large stele of an anthropomorphized idol bearing an inscription that refers to a female deity, as well as affinities between this temple and the one at Khirbet et-Tannur once suggested that the Temple of the Winged Lions was dedicated to the goddess Atargatis. Today it seems more plausible that the idol refers to al-'Uzza, while lions as an attribute is also characteristic of the goddess Allat.

Among the many cult objects found during the course of excavation were two statuettes of Isis and a fragmentary image of a priest holding up a statuette of the god Osiris. These are evidently imported objects, and they appear to be much older than the temple. They may have been reused by the Nabateans as votive objects, but we cannot exclude the notion that one of the deities venerated in the temple was Egyptian—probably Isis, who enjoyed a particular veneration at Petra.

The Inscriptions

During the course of the excavation of the temple, a number of inscriptions came to light, many of them fragmentary. The best known of these is an inscription on a narrow band at the base of a betylic stele made of light-colored limestone and measuring 32 cm × 14 cm. This base is framed by a molding, and the central portion of the stele is flanked by two pilasters with carved decoration in geometric relief and surmounted by a dentiled architrave. Above the betyl, represented inside its cult chapel, there is a garland. The betyl's large concave eyes are surmounted by eyebrows, done in high relief, that meet at the bridge of the nose, which is delineated as a round stick, also in relief. The mouth, in relief as well, is split horizontally to define lips. Stylized branches bracket the inscription to either side. This stele is now in the Archaeological Museum in Amman (inventory no. J 13483).

Bibliography: Philip C. Hammond, "Ein nabatäisches Weihrelief aus Petra," in *Die Nabatäer: Erträge einer Ausstellung im Rheinischen Landesmuseum Bonn, 24 Mai–9 Juli 1978*, ed. Gisela Hellenhemper Salies (Cologne: Rheinland-Verlag; Bonn: Habelt, 1981), 137–141; Fawzi Zayadine and Jean Starcky, "Idole d'al-Ozzâ," in *Inoubliable Pétra: Le royaume nabatéen aux confins du désert*,

exhibition catalogue, (Brussels: Musées Royaux d'Art et d'Histoire, 1980), 84–85, no. 55; François Baratte and Fawzi Zayadine, "Anthropomorphes Idol," in *Der Königsweg: 9000 Jahre Kunst und Kultur in Jordanien und Palästina* (Maintz: Philipp von Zabern, 1987), p. 213, no. 201.

'LHT ḤYN BN NYBT
The goddess of Hayyan, son of Naybat.

Similar betyls are well known in the Nabatean sphere, in particular in the sanctuary of Gebel Ramm; the inscriptions identify the representations with al-'Uzza or with Allat. A similar betyl in the zone to the northwest of Petra has been identified, on the basis of the inscription, as Atargatis. In the present case the goddess is designated, as is often true, not with her own name, but as "the goddess of" followed by the name of the devotee, here Hayyan, an Aramaic name already attested in Nabatean that is derived from the same root as the verb "to live." The goddess may possibly be identifiable as al-'Uzza, whose cult is well documented at Petra.

During the course of Hammond's 1981 campaign, a fragmentary plaque was found among the marble fragments in the locality identified as the workshop of a craftsman. It measures 33.5 cm × 10.2 cm and is 3.25 cm thick, hence it was evidently intended to be affixed to a wall, probably in the temple. The lines of the inscription are complete on the right-hand side, where they are marked off by an incised vertical line, but they are broken off on the left. This makes it likely that other contiguous inscribed plaques continued to the left.

Bibliography: Philip C. Hammond, David J. Johnson, and Richard N. Jones, "A Religio-Legal Nabataean Inscription from the Atargatis/Al-'Uzza Temple at Petra," *BASOR* 263 (1986): 77–80.

1. MH DY Y'T' LH MN KSP WDHB WQRB-WN WZWN KLH WMN KSP' WNḤ [Š' . . .

Fragment of an inscription on marble (27–28 C.E.) found in a room next to the Temple of the Winged Lions and intended to be fixed to a wall. This is the earliest text containing legal phraseology found to date.

2. WLKMRY' PLG' 'ḤRN' 'M 'KLT 'KRYZ 'WN QDM DNH PYTHLQWN[. . .
3. 'LWHY DY 'BD K'YR KL DY 'L' KTYB PYPR' MH DY YŠTKḤ [. . .
4. BYWM 'RB'H B'B ŠNT TLTYN WŠB' LḤRTT MLK NBṬW RḤM 'MH WTW [. . .

1. Whatever comes to him of silver, or gold, or offering, or provisions, altogether [all of it], or of silver (coinage) or bronze (coinage) [
2. And to the priests, the other portion [will be allotted]; on the condition that a proclamation of delinquency be completed before this (time), then shall they allot [
3. Concerning the one who did other than all of that which is written above, then shall be repay that which was discovered ["neglected/forgotten"] [
4. On the fourth day of 'Ab, the 37th year of Aretas, [A.D. 27/28], king of the Nabataeans, who loves his people. And [

The formula dating the inscription contained on line 4 permits attribution of this inscription to 27–28 C.E., during the month of Ab, or spanning the end of July and the beginning of August.

This fragmentary inscription is the earliest example of a text that, although certainly religious in nature, is not a simple dedication. In all likelihood, it contained prescriptions regarding various types of offerings: the final section of the text must have stipulated fines to be paid in cases of failure to observe specific norms.

The mention of priests on line 2 leads to the supposition, as attested in Carthaginian texts, that a portion of the offerings carried to the sanctuary, particularly foodstuffs, went to the priests. Unlike the inscriptions from the Carthaginian sphere, which speak of animal and plant sacrifices, this text names offerings in gold and in silver. According to the scholars who published the text, the silver and bronze named at the end of line 1 are to be understood as sums of money in coin.

From the linguistic point of view, the inscription contains new verb forms and a more complex syntax than previously attested. The most significant comparisons are to be found in the inscriptions on the facades of rupestrian tombs (the Turkmaniya Tomb and tombs at Hegra), which also include normative clauses.

The Khazneh el-Far'un

The first monument that one encounters upon emerging from the narrow access of the Siq is the imposing edifice—the best-known of Petra—of the Khazneh el-Far'un, or the "Treasury of the Pharaoh." Its highly decorated, two-story facade, twenty-eight meters in width and over thirty-nine and a half meters in height, makes a striking architectonic impression. The rear walls of the facade are set back, which means that rather than protruding from the rock face, the building appears as if framed by a vast rock cornice. This arrangement probably has contributed to the fairly good state of conservation of the figured reliefs that decorate the front of the building—a rare occurrence among the monuments at Petra. The lower story has a portico made of six free-standing columns with floral capitals, surmounted by a pediment that functions as a pronaos. The second story is divided into three parts: at the center is a round tholos with a conical roof topped with an urn; to either side two half-pediments supported by projecting columns frame aedicules. The spaces on the rear wall to either side of the tholos are occupied by niches bracketed by pairs of engaged columns, with the corners marked by coupled engaged columns.

Architectural and sculptural decorations of extremely high quality enliven these architec-

tonic elements. On the ground level, sculptures in relief, still legible in spite of their mediocre state of conservation, occupy spaces on the rear wall behind the pairs of external columns. They represent the Dioscuri, depicted according to the traditional iconography established in the Hellenistic period and diffused in the Roman age: the two larger-than-life figures stand close to their horses, in heroic nudity save for chlamyses draped across their bodies.

The frieze running above the line of columns is decorated with vine branches and volutes, alternating with paired vases framed by face-to-face griffins. The pediment above the frieze is also decorated with motifs of flowers and tendrils, and the tympanum contains a female bust (in a very poor state of conservation) that may be a gorgon, on a leafy background.

The attic dividing the lower order from the upper is topped by a band of rosettes; a sphinx stands at either end; above the second story two eagles rise from the broken pediment as acroteria. A frieze composed of garlands of leaves and berries runs along the two pavilions and the tholos of the upper story.

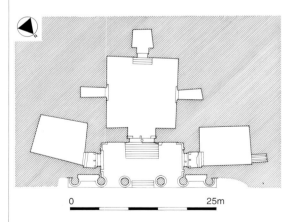

The ground plan of the monument shows a vestibule with columns, a large hall with open niches in its walls (obviously destined to contain sarcophagi), and two secondary rooms opening off the side walls of the portico.

Top: The upper order of the Khazneh, showing its rich and well-preserved architectonic and sculptural decoration. The iconography of the sculptures and the delicate treatment of the ornamental motifs reveal the presence in Petra of highly specialized master craftsmen of Hellenistic culture.

Detail of the colonnaded pronaos and the richly decorated door giving access to the southwest lateral room.

All of the ornamental motifs and the details of workmanship of this construction recall Alexandrian models and reveal extraordinary affinities with works of late-Hellenistic toreutics (the embossing or chasing of metals). In particular, the capitals, which have two rows of acanthus leaves and intertwined floral volutes out of which a central flower emerges, are considered to be variants of late-Hellenistic Alexandrian models that are also echoed, although with stylistic differences, in the Qasr el-Bint and the Temple of the Winged Lions.

Nine large figures sculpted in relief adorn the niche-like partitions of the upper story, three of them on the tholos, two in the flanking panels, and two more on the face and sides of each of the lateral pavilions. The sculptures between columns in the two recessed areas have been identified as winged Nikes, while the other six (leaving out the central image of the tholos) have quite rightly been identified as Amazons. Their dress—a short tunic—and the presence of an ax (which appears here above the figure on the far north end of the facade), their customary

attribute in iconography, make this interpretation more plausible than a suggested identification as maenads.

The draped female deity sculpted at the center of the tholos is certainly the most important image on the entire facade, and her identity has long been a matter of controversy. Posed on a low pedestal (as are all the figures of the upper story), the goddess holds a cornucopia in her left hand and a patera in her right hand. Beneath the pedestal, the large acroterion that rises from the apex of the pediment of the lower order is decorated by two cornucopias framing a solar disk flanked by ears of wheat, originally the symbol of the Egyptian goddess Hathor and, in the Hellenistic age, the symbol of Isis. The cornucopia, a typical attribute of Tyche/Fortuna, is associated here with the symbol of the Egyptian goddess, stressing the link, even the assimilation, between the two deities. That an identification as Isis/Tyche is plausible is confirmed by a resemblance between the Khazneh figure and some portrait images of Ptolemaic queens (Berenice and Arsinoë) painted on oenochoae from Alexandria. Among the dedicatory inscriptions on vases that accompany such representations,

the most frequent mentiozzns are to Agathe/Tyche and Isis (whose cult was sizable and widespread in late-Hellenistic circles). The many dedications to Isis found at Petra and two rupestrian high reliefs in which Isis is shown enthroned also suggest her assimilation with al-'Uzza, the supreme female deity of the Nabatean pantheon.

The figured reliefs, like the overall plan of the architecture of this monument and its decoration, seem to attest to close connections with the Alexandrian world and with the Hellenistic artistic tradition of the first century B.C.E.

The quality of forms in the Khazneh and the refinement of their execution suggest the presence of skilled artisans from the outside, purposely called to Petra for the realization of this great rupestrian facade. These considerations may help to clarify the much-discussed chronology of the edifice, dated by Rudolf-Ernst Brünnow and Alfred von Domaszewski, and, in more recent years, by G. H. R. Wright and J. B. Ward-Perkins, to the age of Hadrian on the basis of historical considerations—in particular, Hadrian's imperial visit to Petra, during the course of which he is thought to have ordered this temple

Detail of the trabeation of the lower order of columns, showing the delicate frieze of tendrils and volutes and the floral capitals with double rows of acanthus leaves.

Detail of the hall inside the Khazneh. Ornate molded niches are set into walls that show traces of preparation for applied stucco decoration.

built in honor of Isis. They also cite considerations of an architectonic nature.

Some of the unique features of the Khazneh—the broken pediment, for example, and more generally, the oddly "baroque" taste of the facade—do in fact appear in the architecture of imperial Rome in the second century C.E., but that late date seems unlikely. The architectonic scheme of this structure is more composite than baroque, combining a classical and balanced rhythm on the lower order with coloristic exuberance on the upper story. Both the stylistic context and the iconographic program suggest a date for the edifice between the second half of the first century B.C.E. and the end of that century. From the viewpoint of urban planning as well, it seems evident that the siting of this monument in relation to the principal thoroughfare of the city, which begins here and ends at the Qasr, was part of an urban plan established and laid out by the Nabatean kings.

That the Khazneh was intended to be a tomb—another hypothesis that elicits controversy—is suggested both by the figurative program, which is entirely linked to funerary symbolism, and the ground plan and internal arrangements. The vestibule gives access to a central chamber with no architectonic ornamentation, where each of the three walls contains an aedicule or niche (the central one being the largest) obviously intended to hold a sarcophagus. A door surmounted by an elaborate molding capped by an eagle acroterion opens on either side of the vestibule. Each leads to a smaller room, also with completely bare walls, at the end of a short corridor.

The edifice seems to have remained incomplete in some details: the stone surfaces of the walls and the ceilings are not completely smoothed, and they display carefully spaced grooves that may have served as preparation for plastering or for the insertion of some sort of applied decoration, probably of painted stucco.

Although today it seems definitively established that the Khazneh was conceived as a grandiose sepulcher for one of the Nabatean kings, the question remains open and insufficient data makes confirmation unlikely. We will have to await further verification to know the dynasty to which the tomb was dedicated and to judge between its various attributions to Aretas III Philhellene, Obodas II (III), or Aretas IV.

Top: The elaborate molding of the southern door of the Khazneh vestibule, with floral capitals and acroteria decorated with winged figures emerging from vine branches.

Bottom: Reliefs in the intercolumnar areas of the Khazneh vestibule. The two male figures standing before horses depict the Dioscuri, a motif that was particularly widespread in Hellenistic and Roman funerary symbolism.

Ed-Deir

The imposing facade of ed-Deir is situated on the summit of the Gebel ed-Deir, a promontory that dominates the Petra basin to the west, and it is reached by a combination of ramps and steps cut into the rock, like a steep *via sacra* flanked by tombs and cult niches. The front of the two-story edifice is nearly forty meters high and fifty meters wide, and it projects from the recessed rock face in high relief.

Along the lower story there is a line of protruding engaged columns with pseudo-Ionic capitals, flanked at either end by pilasters coupled with quarter-columns. A great entrance portal with a tympanum occupies the space between the two central columns, while at either side niches capped by arches, intended to contain statues, occupy the spaces between the end pilasters and the first column. The upper order repeats the architectonic formula of the Khazneh with slight variations: it contains a central rotunda with a conic roof surmounted by an urn, and two projecting lateral structures topped with a broken pediment. Walls to either side frame the lateral structures like antae and have engaged columns combined with pilasters at the corners. Even the smooth back wall is decorated with engaged columns, making it resemble a peristyled courtyard. A continuous Doric frieze with triglyphs and metopes occupied by disks ties together the architectonic features of the upper story.

The general structure of the facade and the details of its architectural ornamentation provide a clear example of local reelaboration and original transformation of motifs from the Hellenistic tradition. In its composition, the overall layout of ed-Deir is analogous to that of the Khazneh, but here the architect has simply suggested a portico on the lower order, creating an architecture of pure facade rather than a projection and achieving a chiaroscuro effect through a trabeation with segments that advance and

retreat, linking the structural elements. The attic separating the two levels is decorated with dwarf pilasters, and the tridimensional effect of the upper order is somewhat compromised by the two antae, of a later date, that enclose the composition and repeat the scheme of the bas-relief decoration in more monumental form. The proportions of the edifice, with its emphasized width and the austerity and simplicity of the ornamental motifs, show proof of a transformation of the original models. For some features of its architectonic structure, this edifice has been compared with the Library of Celsus in Ephesus, which has been dated to the age of Hadrian.

The interior of ed-Deir, a simple quadrangular chamber cut into the rock, presents no funerary installations, but a platform accessible by means of a double stairway occupies a niche cut into the rear wall. The niche is bordered by pilasters and surmounted by an arch with a cornice in stucco. Traces of a betyl can be seen on the wall, and traces of two benches have recently been found along the lateral walls.

These features have prompted the suggestion that the monument may have been a *heroon*, a commemorative mausoleum intended to serve

Top: The upper order of the monumental rupestrian facade. The architectonic scheme repeats the formula of the Khazneh, but is less fully articulated here and has a weaker chiaroscuro effect and no real dual-plane perspective. Here too, the motifs of the architectonic decoration—horned capitals and Doric frieze—are typically Nabatean.

The great urn, sculpted in the round, that tops the cupola of the tholos.

the cult of a deified Nabatean dynast. This ruler has been identified as King Obodas I on the basis of an inscription found on a rock not far from the site that mentions the cult society of that king. Obodas I was buried in the Negev, near the modern city of 'Avdat, and was deified after his death.

Another hypothesis, still to be confirmed, connects ed-Deir with Rabbel II, the last king of the Nabatean dynasty prior to Roman annexation. One argument for this theory is the wholly Nabatean decoration of the monument, which may have been a deliberate choice on the part of the sovereign who boasted of having "brought life and deliverance to his people." The problem of the date of the edifice remains open, but it is obvious that its function was sacred, as indicated by the processional way leading up to it and by its character as a cult-related triclinium, a meeting place for sacred ceremonies and sacred meals connected with the veneration of a deity. Crosses scratched into the walls of the niche attest that ed-Deir, which is also known as "the Monastery," was used as a Christian chapel in the Byzantine age.

The Inscriptions
A Nabatean inscription is carved into the rock wall over a niche. The facsimile copy gives only the right-hand half.

Bibliography: *RÉS*, no. 1423; Cantineau, *Natabéen*, 2:6–7; Fawzi Zayadine and Suleiman Farajat, "The Petra National Trust Site Projects: Excavation and Clearance at Petra and Beiḍa," *ADAJ* 35 (1991): 283–284.

1. DKYR 'BYDW BR WQYH'L
2. WḤBRWHY MRZḤ 'BDT
3. 'LH
1. Let be remembered, 'Ubaydu, son of Waqiḥel
2. and his associates of the symposium of 'Obodat
3. the god

The date of the inscription cannot be determined. It constitutes a proof of the deification of King Obodas I, about which other sources—the en-Numeir inscription, for instance—also give information. The en-Numeir inscription also states that the confraternity (*mrzḥ*) was founded in honor of the deified sovereign and that it held periodic symposia. The word *ḥbr*, meaning "colleague" or "companion," is certainly the technical term designating the members of the symposium. In the Aramaic of the Talmud, the same word is used to indicate the participants in the paschal banquet. The inscription above permits us to suppose that the hill of ed-Deir was the prime site for the cult of Obodas in Petra.

Ed-Deir. Unlike the projecting colonnaded face of the Khazneh, the lower story of the ed-Deir monument has engaged columns and pilasters backed by quarter-columns framing the central doorway and the lateral niches, clearly intended to contain statues. The interior of the monument contains no funerary elements, but it does have a bench lining its walls. Its purpose may have been to serve a cult, perhaps that of a deified Nabatean dynast, Obodas I or, according to a more recent hypothesis, Rabbel II.

Facsimile of the right-hand portion of an inscription on a rock near the facade of the monument, which emerges near the summit of the ed-Deir hill. The text records a symposium of Obodas I, here called "the god." The inscription has inspired the hypothesis that the rupestrian monument was a *heroon* dedicated to the cult of the deified monarch.

The Urn Tomb

The great funerary edifice known as the Urn Tomb or the Doric Tomb is part of a complex of monumental tombs that includes the Palace Tomb and the Corinthian Tomb and that lines the western slope of the massif of el-Khubtha, facing the city center.

Unlike the facades to either side of it, the face of the Urn Tomb reveals an architectonic design that is highly developed on the vertical plane, which gives it a narrow, stretched-out appearance. The rock space is partitioned according to a familiar scheme: a temple facade is framed by corner pilasters doubled by quarter-columns, while two central engaged columns on a podium frame a doorway surmounted by a Doric frieze and a small pediment. Above, a tripartite attic decorated with dwarf pilasters is topped by a pediment with a central acroterion in the shape of an urn, from which the structure takes its name. The only anomalous elements here are four busts in relief (today in an extremely poor state of conservation), perhaps of deities, sculpted on the lower portion of the attic, immediately above the architrave of the lower order. Although the facade is of a conventional type, the sheer size of the architectonic elements amplifies the charac-

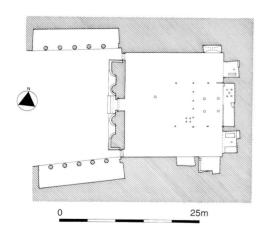

Ground plan and front view of the funerary complex of the Urn Tomb. The tomb's architecture is highly developed on the vertical plane, with a facade divided in a manner typical of the rupestrian tombs of Petra. The disposition of the funerary chambers is more original: they were excavated into the upper half of the face of the monument and closed on the outside with slabs having sculptural decoration.

teristics of the model and accentuates its monumentality.

The same exaggerated proportion and space are reflected in the vast internal chamber, the original disposition of which is unclear due to modifications made when the tomb was transformed into a church.

The funerary complex, which is unique, consists of three burial cells hollowed out of the upper portion of the rock facade, accessible through three entrances placed in the intercolumnar spaces. The central opening is still partially occupied by the slab that originally closed it, which is decorated with a large bust in relief of a male figure who seems to be dressed in a toga. This funerary arrangement is unique: although loculi placed high on the walls of the sepulchral chamber are attested at Petra, the Urn Tomb is the only tomb in which these become an integral part of the architectonic decoration of the facade.

The most original feature of the monument, however, is the great porticoed courtyard that

Top: Portico on the south side of the Urn Tomb, showing the Doric columns perpendicular to the monumental facade. The courtyard faced the Petra basin and the city center.

Bottom: The vast interior chamber, with modifications from the mid-fifth century, when the construction was used as a church and a sort of central apse and lateral arcosolia were cut into the rear wall.

stands before it, bordered on either side by five Doric columns with a pilaster at the front end. The front of the courtyard, which faces the valley below, must once have been closed by a simple balustrade, while a lateral staircase excavated out of the rock led up to the courtyard. The monumental bulk of this great funerary edifice would have dominated the entire valley and the city.

As is often the case, the hypotheses concerning the purpose of this monument and its date are many and various. For example, because it is odd that a funerary edifice of this complexity not have a triclinium hall, and because the principal sepulcher was placed at the center of the facade, it has been suggested that the large internal chamber originally served as a place for gatherings and cult festivities in honor of a deified sovereign. The most commonly accepted opinion is that it was a royal tomb, and given the nature of the edifice, this seems beyond doubt. Although the structure was at first attributed to Malichus II (in theory, the personage figured wearing a toga), a more recent proposal suggests, for architectonic and stylistic reasons, that the monument might be the sepulcher of Aretas IV. Comparisons between the ground plan of this funerary complex and the Forum of Augustus in Rome are less convincing, however, in particular concerning the overall design of the structure and the realization of the porticoed courtyard.

An inscription painted on the rear wall of the chamber, facing the entrance, gives the date at which the tomb was transformed into a church on the initiative of Bishop Jason in the year 446–447 C.E. It was for this later use that something resembling an apse flanked by two arcosolia was cut into the rear wall of the hall, a side door was added, windows were pierced through the facade, and (in all probability) the double rows of arched masonry structures under the great courtyard were created, along with the stairway that has recently been restored by the Department of Antiquities of Jordan.

View of the vaulted constructions and the masonry stairway that underlie the porticoed courtyard of the Urn Tomb, made in the Byzantine era to facilitate use of the structure as a church.

The Tomb of Sextius Florentinus

The dedicatory inscription on the facade of the Tomb of Sextius Florentinus (Brünnow and Domaszewski, Petra, no. 763) identifies it as the tomb of T. Aninius Sextius Florentinus, governor of the province of Arabia. The tomb is located at the extreme northwest end of the cliffs of the Gebel el-Khubtha, and it is the last, topographically speaking, in the series of monumental tombs that occupy the entire western slope of that massif.

That space available for construction was limited can clearly be deduced from the rather narrow, elongated surface that the architect used for the tripartite facade of the tomb. The lower portion, today quite damaged, echoes the shape of a small tetrastyle temple. A large entrance door with a double cornice and a tympanum occupies all the space between the central pair of columns, while the lateral intercolumnar spaces are relatively compressed and bracketed at the corners by pilasters doubled with engaged columns. The columns and the pilasters are set on a continuous podium on either side of the

The interior of the tomb, a vast funerary chamber shaped like an irregular rectangle, is preceded by a small vestibule and decorated by engaged columns. Loculi for burials line the rear wall and the western wall.

entrance. They have Nabatean capitals and are surmounted by a trabeation with a double molding. In the attic a large arch decorated with dentil molding and crowned with an eagle follows the vertical lines of the central columns. The space beneath the arch contains a decoration of branching vines out of which a gorgon head emerges. All of this is surmounted by a trabeation supported by semi-pilasters, which is in turn topped by a triangular pediment with an acroterion at its apex.

The interior consists of one chamber, longer than it is wide, reached through a small vestibule. In contrast to the sobriety characteristic of the majority of tomb interiors at Petra, here the rear wall still bears traces of stucco work and is decorated with engaged columns on a podium that frame five loculi. Other loculi were opened in the right-hand (or western) wall. Both lateral walls appear to have been left completely unfinished.

From the architectural point of view, the facade shows no striking originality; it repeats, in a narrow, elongated form, the model of many

The upper order of the tomb of the Roman governor of the province of Arabia. Inside the broad central arch, a female figure, quite certainly a gorgon, is figured emerging from a background of vine branches, a motif of obvious Hellenistic influence, widespread under the Roman empire as well.

other tombs at Petra (for example, that of the more monumental Urn Tomb). The large central arch that dominates the entire composition is reflected, for example, in the facade of the Bab el-Siq triclinium. A certain Roman influence can be discerned in the semicircular arch (a shape unusual in Hellenistic arched pediment design) and in the alternation of rectilinear and curvilinear architectural forms. As a whole, however, the construction reveals the force and persistence of the Greco-Hellenistic tradition and its translation into the local artistic idiom, even after the Roman annexation of the Nabatean kingdom. The motif of the *gorgoneion* and, more generally, of the figure emerging from a vine-leaf decoration (although not the only instance of the theme in Petra) are obviously of Hellenistic inspiration. The relief's precarious state of conservation does not permit a reading detailed enough to justify dating it to the Augustan age, as has been suggested.

The most interesting feature of this monument is thus the inscription that runs across the lower trabeation. The text of the epigraph, corrected at several points, relates the entire *cursus honorum* of this personage, who was not of aristocratic or senatorial birth, but belonged to the equestrian order, a group politically close to the emperor and placed under his direct control. It reads as follows:

T(ito) . . . ninio L(ucii) fili(io) Pap(iria) Sextio Florentino (trium)viro aur(o) arg(ento) flando trib(uno) milit(um) leg(ionis) I Minerviae quaest(ori) prov(inciae) A[c]haiae trib(uno) pleb(is) leg(ato) leg(ionis) VIIII Hisp(anae) proco(n)[s(uli) pr[ov(inciae)] Narb(onencis) leg(ato) Aug(usti) pr(o) pr(aetore) prov(inciae) Arabiae patri piis[sim]o ex testam[e]nto ipsius.

To [Titus] . . . ninius, Son of Lucius Papirius Sextius Florentinus, Triumvir for coining gold and silver, Military Tribune of Legion I Minerva, Quaestor of the Province of Achaia, Tribune of the Plebs, Legate of Legion VIIII Hispania, Proconsul of the Province of Narbonensis, Legate of Augustus, Propraetor of the Province of Arabia, most dutiful father, in accordance with his own will.

The funerary edifice was thus erected or dedicated by the son of the legate of Arabia in respect of stipulations in the latter's testament. A papyrus found in the Cave of the Letters near the Nahal Hever, by the Dead Sea, tells us that the deceased was governor of the province in 127 C.E. The date of the dedication of the tomb is not given in the inscription, but we gather from documents that Sextius Florentinus could not have arrived in Arabia earlier than the year 126, because in 125 C.E. his predecessor, T. Julius Julianus Alexander, was still in office. Sextius Florentinus was succeeded by Haterius Nepos in 130. If Sextius Florentinus died while he was still in office—which seems plausible, given that he is buried at Petra—the tomb must have been constructed in the age of Hadrian. There seems to be no objective reason for not accepting that date.

The Aṣlaḥ Inscription, Magharet et-Tnub

The Aṣlaḥ inscription is one of the oldest in Petra. It is located at Bab el-Siq, facing the Tomb of the Obelisks, in the cave catalogued as Brünnow and Domaszewski, Petra, no. 21. The inscription is carved into the rear wall of a triclinium that is flanked by two small rooms. The name by which it is designated comes from the donor. Jean Starcky has dated it to between the end of the second century B.C.E. and the beginning of the first century B.C.E.

Bibliography: *RÉS*, no. 1432; Cantineau, *Nabatéen*, 2:2–3, no. 2; Fawzi Zayadine and Suleiman Farajat, "The Petra National Trust Site Projects: Excavation and Clearance at Petra and Beiḍa," *ADAJ* 35 (1991): 275–276.

אלקין חלפאכרבחלפא יויזגנאכׂחייקלא
ונה קיראא ד עבד׳ד חלפא טבאה חלפה
להׂ שרא אלה מנכׂתו עלהׂ׳׳ עבׂדׂתמׂלך
נכׂתו בר חׂרׂתׂתׂמׂלך נבׂטׂו שׂנׂת 1בׂ

1. 'LN ṢRYḤY' WGB' ZY 'BD 'ṢLḤ BR 'ṢLḤ
2. DNH ṢRYḤ' DY 'BD 'ṢLḤ BR 'ṢLḤ
3. LDWŠR' 'LH MNK̇TW 'L ḤYY 'BDT MLK
4. NBṬ W BR ḤRTT MLK NBṬW ŠNT 1.
1. These are the halls and the cistern made by Aṣlaḥ, son of Aṣlaḥ
2. This is the hall made by Aṣlaḥ, son of Aṣlaḥ
3. To honor Dhu-Sharä, the god of Mankatu, during the reign of 'Obodat, king
4. of the Nabataeans, son of Ḥaretat, king of the Nabataeans, year 1.

Linguistically, this inscription reflects a transitional phase: the relative is given as *zy* on line 1, as it is in imperial Aramaic, whereas it is *dy* on line 2, as in classical Nabatean.

Line 2 almost exactly repeats line 1. Line 1 seems a heading, which opens the possibility that a second text may have been repeated next

to the well in an inscription that did not mention the halls. Ṣryḥy', the hall or halls, have been identified by J. T. Milik as the room in which the inscribed text is located, plus the two rear rooms, which together constitute the monument. The epithet of Dushara given here, "god of Mankatu," is attested nowhere else. That reading was proposed by Jean Starcky because he supposed the term to be related to the dynastic name, Malichus, which is almost always written in Nabatean with an *n* rather than an *l*. The ending -*at* is frequent, and it can be compared to the endings of the names Aretas (*hrtt*) and Obodas (*'bdt*), to which -*w*, the suffix typical of Nabatean onomastics, would be added. The epithet of the god would thus link Dushara with the reigning dynasty. Earlier readings gave *mnbtw*, a term that was not explained, however.

According to F. M. Cross, the King Obodas named here is probably the sovereign of that name who defeated Alexander Jannaeus at Gadara in 93 B.C.E., fought Antiochus XII in 85 B.C.E., and was buried at Oboda ('Avdat), in the Negev, and subsequently deified. He is remembered at Petra in the inscriptions of ed-Deir and en-Numeir. For this reason, Jean Starcky has dated this inscription to approximately 95 B.C.E.

The en-Numeir Inscription

The en-Numeir inscription, discovered in 1898, is incised on a projecting cornice carved into the ceiling of a chapel that has a niche at the rear for a cult statue, no longer extant. The inscription, which is still in situ, now measures 1.01 m in length; it is painstakingly carved into a carefully prepared surface on the side of the cornice. The final letters of the lines are missing.

Bibliography: CIS II, 354; Cantineau, Nabatéen, 2:5–6, no. 4; Nicolò Marchetti, "L'iscrizione della cappella rupestre di en-Numêr a Petra e la paleografia nabatea," Vicino Oriente 8, no. 2 (1992): 157–177.

1. DNH ṢLM' DY 'BDT 'LLH DY 'BDW BNY ḤNYNW BR ḤṬ YŠW BR PṬMWN [
2. DY LWṬ DWTR/D' 'LH ḤṬYŠW DY BŠHWT PṬMWN 'MHM 'L ḤYY ḤRTT MLK NBṬW RḤM '[MHWŠ]
3. [Q]YḶṮ 'ḤTH MLKT NBṬW WMNKW W'BDT WRB'L WPŞ'L WŠ'WDT WHGRW BNWHY WḤRTT BR HG[RW . . .
4. [BYRḤ . . . Š]NT 29 LḤRTT MLK NBṬW RḤM 'MH [. . .

1. This is the statue of Obodas the god, which the sons of Ḥonainu, son of Ḥoṭaishu, son of Peṭammon have made . . .
2. Which (is placed) next to (?) Du Tar/da god of Ḥoṭaishu, who is in the chapel of Peṭammon, their great-grandfather, for the life of Aretas, king of Nabaṭu who loves his [people, and of
3. Sha]qilat, his sister, the queen of Nabaṭu, and of Malichus and of Obodas and of Rabel and of Faṣael and of Sha'udat and of Hagiru, his offspring, and of Aretas, son of Hagi[ru . . .
4. [in the month . . . in the year] 29 of Aretas king of Nabaṭu, who loves his people.

Based on the year of reign of Aretas IV, this inscription can be dated to 20 c.e. In "Notes d'épigraphie et de topographie palestiniennes," (RB 66 [1959]: 559–560), J. T. Milik proposes a reading of the beginning of line 2 that would give the translation "which is placed (the statue) next to Du-Tara, the god of Ḥoṭaishu, which are found in the chapel of Peṭammon," an interpretation that modifies the reading given above but is less convincing. The Nabatean term translated as "chapel," shwt, is given here in the form that takes a complement of specification. It indicates a small sanctuary or cella, and it recurs, in the plural, on line 2 of the Turkmaniya inscription. Milik reconstructs the history of the chapel, on the basis of this text, thus: it was founded by Peṭammon, the great-grandfather of the "offspring of Ḥonainu," a name that should probably be interpreted as a family group or a clan. The son of this personage installed a statue of the family god, Du-Tada (or Du-Tara), not otherwise securely attested, in the niche. The descendants then placed a statue of the deified Obodas next to it.

Some scholars have restored the name of the queen, Shaqilat, at the end of line 2. As a result of direct examination of the inscription, Nicolò Marchetti proposed instead to read that name between the end of line 2 and the beginning of line 3, but dividing a word between two lines was contrary to the Nabateans' normal epigraphic habits. Shaqilat, whose complete title was "sister and queen" of the Nabateans, was the second wife of Aretas; the previous queen was named Ḥaldu.

Inscription of the Qabr at-Turkman, or Turkmaniya Tomb

The inscription of the Turkmaniya Tomb was first located and photographed in 1896. It is incised over the entrance to the tomb, between two columns, on a carefully smoothed rectangular space 3.90 m × 1.20 m, set 6.35 m above ground level. It is the only funerary inscription of Petra of a certain length that contains phraseology similar to that of the thirty-seven funerary inscriptions of Hegra. Unlike the Hegra inscriptions, however, its text does not record the name of the tomb's proprietor.

Bibliography: CIS II, 350; Cantineau, Nabatéen, 2:3–5, no. 3; J. T. Milik, "Notes d'épigraphie et de topographie palestiniennes," RB 66 (1959): 555–560; John F. Healey, ed., "The Nabataean Tomb Inscriptions of Mada'in Salih," Journal of Semitic Studies, suppl. no. 1 (1993): 238–242.

1. QBR' DNH WṢRYH' RB' DY BH WṢRYH Z'YR' DY GW' MNH DY BH BTY MQBRYN 'BYDT GWHYN
2. WKRK' DY QDMYHM W'RKWT' WBTY' DY BH WGNY' WGNT SMK' WB'RWT MY' WŠHWT' WṬWRY'
3. WŠRYT KL 'SL' DY B'TRY' 'LH ḤRM WHRG DWŠR' 'LH MR'N WMWTBH ḤRYŠ' W'LHY' KLHM
4. BŠṬRY ḤRMYN KDY BHM PPQDWN DWŠR' WMWTBH W'LHY' KLHM DY KDY BŠṬRY ḤRMY' 'NW YT'BD WL' YTŠN'
5. WL' YTPŞŞ MN KL DY BHM MND'M WL' YTQBR BQBR' DNH 'NWŠ KLH LHN MN DY KTYB LH TN' MQBR BŠṬRY ḤRMY' 'NW 'D 'LM

1. This tomb and the large burial-chamber within it and the small burial-chamber beyond

Fragmentary inscription of 10 B.C.E. carved on pink limestone, found at Sabra, near Petra. It was the gift of a "chief of the horsemen" named Diodoros, "for the life" of King Aretas IV and his family. It mentions a queen named Hagiru, perhaps the daughter of Malichus. If so, this might link Aretas, who is recorded as a usurper, with the family of his predecessor, Obodas II (III), thus legitimizing his sovereignty.

klinai (that is, the seats of the banqueting hall on the basis of the root meaning of the Aramaic word. The room mentioned must have been the triclinium, and we can suppose that it was located in front of the entrance to the tomb, on a slightly elevated platform. The term *šhwt'*, which should be in the plural, refers here, according to Milik, to the facade of the tomb, whereas in the inscription of en-Numeir it seemed to refer to a small cult building.

The tomb and all its constituent parts are placed under the care of the deity thanks to two nouns, *hrm* and *hrg*, which have a very strong sacred significance. Whatever is thus designated is truly the sacred property of the god and must not be touched. The gods are, in the first place, Dushara, with his throne or seat: the term *mwtb*, the term that designates the throne, derives from an element that signifies "to dwell," "to be," or "to stay." It is probably used here in a broad sense to indicate the place in which the idol of the god could be found. Thus it might be a cult platform, an actual throne, or even a small chapel. The place in which the image of the god lodges is deified and qualified by the term *hryš'*, which Jean Starcky and J. T. Milik both consider to be a proper name. More recently, John F. Healey has stated that it is instead an adjective qualifying the throne, and that it means "sacred." The epithet of Dushara, "god of our lord," designates him as god of the reigning sovereign. From the most ancient northwest Semitic documents regarding kingship, the king always had the title of "our lord," that is, lord of his subjects. It should also be observed that the deity received the same title from his devotees. The "documents of consecration" mentioned on lines 4 and 5 are the acts sanctioning the inviolable ownership of the items listed, in the present case, the funerary edifice and its annexes. Such ownership is indivisible and can be held only by the persons specifically designated in the documents. The inscriptions on the tombs of Hegra list those who have the right to be buried in the edifice, naming them one by one. The privilege was usually extended to the descendants of the owner and to predetermined kin (for example, sisters and their descendants), and in some cases there is the possibility that anyone who held written authorization from the owner of the tomb or his descendants could be buried there.

it, in which are burial-places, niche-arrangements,
2. and the enclosure in front of them and the porticos and rooms within it (that is, the enclosure) and the gardens (?) and triclinium-garden (?) and the wells of water and the cisterns (?) and walls
3. and all the rest of the property which is in these places are sacred and dedicated to Dushara, the god of our lord, and his sacred throne and all the gods, (as) in the documents of consecration according to their contents. And it is the responsibility of Dushara and his throne and all the gods

4. that it should be done as in these documents of consecration and nothing of all that is in them shall be changed
5. or removed and none shall be buried in this tomb except whoever has written for him an authorization for burial in these documents of consecration forever.

The inscription contains no elements that can date it, but Jean Starcky places it, on the basis of the characteristics of the writing, around 50 C.E.

It is probable that this inscription reproduced on the facade of the tomb part of a juridical act that, as is attested by an inscription from Hegra, was deposited in the public archives to guarantee ownership. The first part of the inscription details the various parts of the tomb. The meanings of some of the technical terms are unknown, and some installations mentioned in the inscription as attached to the tomb (a triclinium and other constructions) have not been conserved. On line 2, the term *krk'*, here translated as "enclosure," literally indicates a walled enclosure, but, according to the interpretation given by J. T. Milik, it must refer to the courtyard in front of the tomb, a space marked off by an enclosing wall.

The term *'rkwt'*, here translated as "porticos," is read differently by Milik, who proposes the reading *w'd kwt'*, an expression he interprets as "and also the openings," or windows. This is not an obligatory reading, however. Milik interprets the term translated here as "gardens" as seats or

Apparatus

Abbreviations

ADAJ	*Annual of the Department of Antiquities of Jordan*
BASOR	*Bulletin of the American Schools of Oriental Research*
Bowersock, *Roman Arabia*	Bowersock, G. W. *Roman Arabia*. Cambridge, Mass.: Harvard University Press, 1983
Brünnow and Domaszewski	Brünnow, Rudolf-Ernst, and Alfred von Domaszewski. *Die Provincia Arabia auf Grund Zweier in den Jahren 1897 und 1898 unternammenen Reisen und der Berichte früherer Reisender*. 3 vols. Strassburg: K. J. Trübner, 1904–1909
Cantineau, *Nabatéen*	Cantineau, Jean. *Le nabatéen*. 2 vols. Paris: Ernest Leroux, 1930–1932
CIL	*Corpus inscriptionum latinarum*
CIS	*Corpus inscriptionum semiticarum*
DBS	Starcky, Jean. "Pétra et la Nabatène." *Dictionnaire de la Bible*, suppl. no. 7, cols. 886–1017. Paris: Letouzey et Ané, 1966
JS	Jaussen, Antonin, and Raphaël Savignac. *Mission archéologique en Arabie*. 3 vols. Paris: Ernest Leroux, 1909, vol. 1; reprint, 5 vols. Cairo: Institut Français d'Archéologie Orientale, 1997
PEQ	*Palestine Exploration Quarterly*
PL	Migne, Jacques-Paul, ed. *Patrologia cursus completus. Series Latina*. Paris, 1844–1864
RÉS	*Répertoire d'épigraphie sémitique*. Paris, 1900–
RTP	Ingholt, Harald, Henri Seyrig, Jean Starcky, and André Caquot. *Recueil des tessères de Palmyre*. Bibliothèque archéologique et historique, no. 58. Paris, 1955
Wenning, *Nabatäer*	Wenning, Robert. *Die Nabatäer: Denkmäler und Geschichte: Eine Bestandesaufnahme des archäologischen Befundes*. Freiburg (Switzerland): Universitätsverlag; Göttingen: Vandenhoech and Ruprecht, 1987
RB	*Revue biblique*

Selected Bibliography

General Works

Hammond, Philip C. *The Nabateans: Their History, Culture, and Archaeology.* Studies in Mediterranean Archaeology, no. 37. Gothenburg: P. Åström, 1973.

Bowersock, *Roman Arabia.*

Wenning, *Nabatäer.*

Aram 2 (1990), an issue dedicated to the Nabateans and containing a bibliography by Jean Starcky.

Zayadine, Fawzi, ed. *Petra and the Caravan Cities: Proceedings of the Symposium Organized at Petra in September 1985.* Amman: Department of Antiquities, Jordan, 1990.

Graf, David F. "Nabateans." In *Anchor Bible Dictionary,* ed. David Noel Freedman, 4:970–973. New York: Doubleday, 1992.

Graf, David F. "Nabateans." In *Oxford Encyclopedia of Archaeology in the Near East,* ed. Eric M. Myers, 4:82–84. New York: Oxford University Press, 1997.

The Region

Bowersock, *Roman Arabia,* 1–11.

The Nabateans

Origins

Bartlett, John R. "From Edomites to Nabateans: A Study in Continuity." *PEQ* 111 (1979): 53–66.

Malbran-Labat, Florence. "Éléments pour une recherche sur le nomadisme in Mésopotamie au premier millénaire av. J.-C.: L'image du nomade." *Journal asiatique* 268 (1980): 11–33.

Milik, J. T. "Origines des Nabatéens." In *Studies in the History and Archaeology of Jordan,* vol. 1, ed. Adnan Hadidi, 261–265. Amman: Department of Antiquities, 1982.

Knauf, Ernst Axel. "Nabataean Origins." In *Arabian Studies in Honour of Mahmoud Ghul: Symposium at Yarmouk University, December 8–11, 1984,* ed. Moawiyah Ibrahim, 56–62. Weisbaden: Harrassowitz, 1989.

Bartlett, John R. "Edom and the Edomites." *Journal for the Study of the Old Testament,* suppl. series, vol. 77 (1989).

Bartlett, John R. "From Edomites to Nabateans: The Problem of Continuity." *Aram* 2, nos. 1–2 (1990): 25–34, which supports the notion of continued settlement.

Bienkowski, Piotr. "The Chronology of Tawilan and the 'Dark Age' of Edom." *Aram* 2, nos. 1–2 (1990): 35–44, which supports the notion of a break in habitation.

Mattingly, Gerald L. "Settlement on Jordan's Kerak Plateau from the Iron Age IIC through the Early Roman Period." *Aram* 2, nos. 1–2 (1990): 309–335, which supports continued settlement.

Edelman, Diana Vikander, ed. *You shall not abhore an Edomite for he is your brother: Edom and Seir in History and Tradition.* Archaeology and Biblical Studies, no. 3. Atlanta: Scholars Press, 1995.

Eph'al, Israel, and Joseph Naveh. *Aramaic Ostraca of the Fourth Century B.C. from Idumaea.* Jerusalem: Magnes Press, Hebrew University, Israel Exploration Society, 1996.

Graf, David F. "The Origin of the Nabataeans." *Aram* 2, nos. 1–2 (1990): 45–75.

Knauf, Ernst Axel. "Bedouin and Bedouin States." In *Anchor Bible Dictionary,* ed. David Noel Freedman, 2:634–638. New York: Doubleday, 1992.

Lemaire, André. "Nouvelles inscriptions Araméenes d'Idumée au Musée d'Israël." *Transeuphratène,* suppl. no. 3 (1996).

Macdonald, M. C. A. "Nomads and the Ḥowrān in the Late Hellenistic and Roman Periods: A Reassessment of the Epigraphic Evidence." *Syria* 70, nos. 3–4 (1993): 303–413.

Bowls from Tell el-Maskhuta

Rabinowitz, Isaac. "Aramaic Inscriptions of the Fifth Century B.C.E. from a North-Arab Shrine in Egypt." *Journal of Near Eastern Studies* 15 (1956): 1–9.

Rabinowitz, Isaac. "Another Aramaic Record of the North-Arabian Goddess Han-'Ilat." *Journal of Near Eastern Studies* 18 (1959): 1954–1955.

Dumbrell, William J. "The Tell el-Maskhūṭa Bowls and the 'Kingdom' of Qedar in the Persian Period." *BASOR* 203 (l971): 33–44.

The Nabatean Kingdom between Arabia and Syria

General Works: See also under General Works, above

Sartre, Maurice. "Rome et les Nabatéens à la fin de la République (65–30 av. J.C.)." *Revue des études anciennes* 81, nos. 1–2 (1979): 37–53.

Khurt, Amélie, and Susan Sherwin-White, eds. *Hellenism in the East: Interaction of Greek and non-Greek Civilizations from Syria to Central Asia after Alexander.* Berkeley: University of California Press, 1987.

Bowersock, G. W. *Hellenism in Late Antiquity.* Ann Arbor: University of Michigan Press, 1990.

Sartre, Maurice. *L'Orient romain: Provinces et sociétés provinciales en Méditerranée orientale d'Auguste aux Sévères (31 avant J.-C.–235 après J.-C.).* Paris: Seuil, 1991.

Elliott, Jack D., Jr. "The Nabataean Synthesis of Avraham Negev: A Critical Appraisal." In *Retrieving the Past: Essays on Archaeological Research and Methodology in Honor of Gus W. Van Beek,* ed. Joe D. Seger, 47–57. Winona Lake, Ind.: Eisenbrauns, 1996.

The First Period of the "Kingdom"

Negev, Avraham. "The Early Beginnings of the Nabatean Reign." *PEQ* 108 (1976): 125–133. See also the reservations of Jack D. Elliott, Jr., in "The Nabataean Synthesis," cited above.

The Succession and Chronology of Kings

Fiema, Zbigniew, and Richard N. Jones. "The Nabatean King-List Revised: Further Observations on the Second Nabatean Inscription from Tell esh-Shuqafiya, Egypt." *ADAJ* 34 (1990): 239–248.

Numismatics

Meshorer, Ya'akov. *Nabatean Coins.* Trans. I. H. Levine. Qedem, no. 3. Jerusalem: Institute of Archaeology, Hebrew University of Jerusalem, 1975.

Schmitt-Korte, Karl, and Michael Cowell. "Nabataean Coinage, Part 1: The Silver Content Measured by X-Fluorescence Analysis." *Numismatic Chronicle* 149 (1989): 33–58.

Kushner-Stein, A., and H. Gilter. "Numismatic Evidence from Tel Beer Sheba and the Beginning of Nabataean Coinage." *Israel Numismatic Journal* 12 (1992–1993): 13–20.

Schmitt-Korte, Karl. "Nabataean Coinage, Part 2: New Coin Types and Variants." *Numismatic Chronicle* 150 (1990): 105–133.

Schmitt-Korte, Karl, and Martin Price. "Nabataean Coinage, Part 3: The Nabataean Monetary System." *Numismatic Chronicle* 154 (1994): 67–131.

History

The Roman Province of Arabia

Negev, Avraham. "The Nabateans and the Provincia Arabia." *Aufstieg und Niedergang der Römischen Welt* 2, no. 8 (1977): 520–686.

Graf, David F. "The Saracens and the Defense of the Arabian Frontier." *BASOR* 229 (1978): 1–26.

Russell, Kenneth W. "The Earthquake of May 19, A.D. 363." *BASOR* 238 (1980): 47–64.

Kettenhofen, Erich. "Zur Nordgrenze der Provincia Arabia im 3. Jahrhundert n. Chr." *Zeitschrift des Deutschen Palästina-Vereins* 97 (1981): 62–73.

Kennedy, D. L., D. N. Riley, and Sir Aurel Stein. *Archaeological Explorations on the Roman Frontier in North-East Jordan: The Roman and Byzantine Military Installations and Road Network on the Ground and from the Air.* BAR International Series, no. 134. Oxford: BAR.

Parker, S. Thomas. *The Roman Frontier in Central Jordan: Interim Report on the Limes Arabicus Project 1980–1985.* 2 vols. BAR International Series, no. 340, pp. 793–823. Oxford: BAR, 1987.

Zayadine, Fawzi, and Zbigniew T. Fiema. "Roman Inscriptions from the Siq of Petra: Remarks on the Initial Garrison of Arabia." *ADAJ* (1986): 199–206.

Parker, S. Thomas. "The Roman *Limes* in Jordan." In *Studies in the History and Archaeology of Jordan,* vol. 3, ed. Adnan Hadidi, 151–164. Amman: Department of Antiquities (Jordan), 1987.

MacAdam, Henry Innes. *Studies in the History of the Roman Province of Arabia: The Northern Sector.* BAR International Series, no. 295. Oxford: BAR, 1986.

Isaac, Benjamin. *The Limits of Empire: The Roman Army in the East.* Oxford: Clarendon Press; New York: Oxford University Press, 1990; rev. ed. 1992.

Parker, S. Thomas. "The Limes Arabicus Project: The 1989 Campaign." *ADAJ* 34 (1990): 357–376.

Caravan Routes

Glueck, Nelson. "Wâdī Sirhân in North Arabia." *BASOR* 96 (1944): 7–17.

Bowersock, G. W. "Nabataeans and Romans in the Wadi Sirhan." *Second International Symposium on Studies in the History of Arabia.* Riyad, 1979.

Isaac, Benjamin H. "Trade Routes to Arabia and the Roman Army." In *Roman Frontier Studies 1979,* ed. W. S. Hanson and L. J. F. Keppie. BAR International Series, no. 71, pp. 889–901. Oxford: BAR, 1980.

Groom, Nigel. *Frankincense and Myrrh: A Study of the Arabian Incense Trade*. London: Longman, 1981.

Zayadine, Fawzi. "Caravan Routes between Egypt and Nabataea and the Voyage of Sultan Baibars to Petra in 1276 A.C." In *Studies in the History and Archaeology of Jordan*, vol. 2, ed. Adnan Hadidi, 159–174. Amman: Department of Antiquities (Jordan), 1985.

Sidebotham, Steven E. *Roman Economic Policy in the Erythra Thalassa, 30 B.C.–A.D. 217*. Mnemosyne, Bibliotheca Classica Batava, suppl., no. 91. Leiden: E. J. Brill, 1986.

Potts, Daniel T. "Trans-Arabian Routes of the Pre-Islamic Period." In *L'Arabie et ses mers bordières*, vol. 1, *Itinéraires et voisinages*, ed. Jean-François Salles, 127–137. Lyon: GS/Maison de l'Orient, 1988.

Rey-Coquais, Jean-Paul. "L'Arabie dans les routes de commerce entre le monde méditerranéen et les côtes indiennes." In *L'Arabie Préislamique et son environnement historique et culturel*, ed. T. Fahd, 225–240. Strasbourg: Université des Sciences Humaines de Strasbourg, 1989.

Rougé, J. "La navigation en mer Erythrée dans l'Antiquité." In *L'Arabie et ses mers bordières*, vol. 1, *Itinéraires et voisinages*, ed. Jean-François Salles, 59–74. Lyon: GS/Maison de l'Orient, 1988.

Potts, Daniel T. *The Arabian Gulf in Antiquity*. 2 vols. Oxford: Clarendon Press; New York: Oxford University Press, 1990.

Zayadine, Fawzi. "L'espace urbain du grand Pétra, les routes et les stations caravanières." *ADAJ* 36 (1992): 217–239.

Graf, David F. "The Roman East from the Chinese Perspective." In *Palmyra and the Silk Road*. Annales d'Archéologie Arabe Syrienne, no. 42, pp. 199–216. Damascus: Directorate General of Antiquities and Museums, 1996.

Zayadine, Fawzi. "Palmyre, Pétra, la Mer Erythrée, et les routes de la soie." In *Palmyra and the Silk Road*. Annales d'archéologie Arabe Syrienne, no. 42, pp. 167–177. Damascus: Directorate General of Antiquities and Museums, 1996.

Fiema, Zbigniew T. "Nabatean and Palmyrene Commerce: The Mechanisms of Intensification." In *Palmyra and the Silk Road*. Annales d'archéologie Arabe Syrienne, no. 42, pp. 189–195. Damascus: Directorate General of Antiquities and Museums, 1996.

Nabatean Society
Language and Writing
Cantineau, *Nabatéen*.

Contini, Riccardo. "Il Ḥawrān preislamico: Ipotesi di storia linguistica." *Felix Ravenna*, 4th series, nos. 1–2 (1987): 25–79.

O'Connor, M. "The Arabic Loanwords in Nabataean Aramaic." *Journal of Near Eastern Studies* 45 (1986): 213–229.

Ethnicity
Healey, John F. "Were the Nabataeans Arabs?" *Aram* 1 (1989): 38–44.

Dictionaries
Cantineau, *Nabatéen*, 2:53–161.

Hoftijzer, Jacob, and Karel Jongeling. *Dictionary of the North-*

West Semitic Inscriptions. 2 vols. Handbuch der Orientalistik. Leiden: E. J. Brill, 1995.

Onomastics
Wuthnow, Heinz. *Die semitischen Menschennamen in griechischen Inschriften und Papyri des Vorderen Orients*. Studien zur Epigraphik und Papyruskunde, vol. 1, no. 4. Leipzig: Dietrich, 1930.

Harding, G. Lankester. *An Index and Concordance of Preislamic Arabian Names and Inscriptions*. Toronto: University of Toronto Press, 1971.

Al-Khraysheh, Fawwaz. *Die Personennamen in den nabatäischen Inschriften des Corpus Inscriptionum Semiticarum*. Marburg: Lahn, 1986.

Negev, Avraham. *Personal Names in the Nabatean Realm*. Qedem, no. 32. Jerusalem: Institute of Archaeology, Hebrew University of Jerusalem, 1991.

Inscriptions
Cantineau, *Nabatéen*, 2:1–51.

Negev, Avraham. "Nabataean Inscriptions." In *Oxford Encyclopedia of Archaeology in the Near East*, ed. Eric M. Meyers, 4:81–82. New York: Oxford University Press, 1997. A very general treatment.

Briquel-Chatonnet, Françoise. "La pénétration de la culture du croissant fertile en Arabie: À propos des inscriptions nabatéens." In *Présence arabe dans le Croissant fertile avant l'Hégire: Actes de la table ronde internationale* (Paris, 13 November 1993), ed. Hélène Lozachmeur, 133–141. Paris: Éditions Recherche sur les Civilisations, 1995.

Critical Surveys
Teixidor, Javier. *Bulletin d'épigraphie sémitique (1964–1980)*. Bibliothèque archéologique et historique, no. 127. Paris: Librairie Orientaliste Paul Geuthner, 1986.

Littmann, Enno. *Nabataean Inscriptions from Southern Haurân*. Publications of the Princeton University Archaeological Expedition to Syria (1904–1905 and 1909), Division 4, Section A. 4 vols. Leiden: E. J. Brill, 1914–1949.

Littmann, Enno. "Nabataean Inscriptions from Egypt," parts 1 and 2. *Bulletin of the School of Oriental Studies* 15 (1953): 1–28; 16 (1954): 212–246.

Starcky, Jean. "Un contrat nabatéen sur papyrus." *RB* 61 (1954): 161–181.

Starcky, Jean. "Une inscription nabatéenne provenant du Djôf." *RB* 64 (1957): 196–217.

Milik, J. T. "Nouvelles inscriptions nabatéennes." *Syria* 35 (1958): 227–251.

Strugnell, John. "The Nabataean Goddess al-Kutba' and Her Sanctuaries." *BASOR* 156 (1959): 29–36.

Starcky, Jean. "Nouvelles stèles funéraires à Pétra." *ADAJ* 10 (1965): 43–49.

Starcky, Jean. "Nouvelle épitaphe nabatéenne donnant le nom sémitique de Pétra." *RB* 72 (1965): 95–97.

Milik, J. T., and Jean Starcky. "Nabatean, Palmyrene and Hebrew Inscriptions." In *Ancient Records from North Arabia*, ed. F. V. Winnett and W. L. Reed. Near and Middle East Series, no. 6. Toronto: University of Toronto Press, 1970.

Milik, J. T. "Inscriptions grecques et nabatéennes de

Rawwafah." In *Preliminary Survey in North-West Arabia, 1968*, ed. Peter J. Parr, G. Lankester Harding, and J. E. Dayton. *Bulletin of the Institute of Archaeology* 10 (1971): 36–61.

Starcky, Jean. "Une inscription nabatéenne de l'an 18 d'Arétas IV." In *Hommages à André Dupont-Sommer*, 151–159. Paris: Adrien-Maisonneuve, 1971.

Milik, J. T., and J. Starcky. "Inscriptions récemment découvertes à Pétra." *ADAJ* 20 (1975): 111–130.

Milik, J. T. "Une inscription bilingue nabatéenne et grecque à Pétra." *ADAJ* 21 (1976): 143–152.

Starcky, Jean. "Les inscriptions nabatéennes du Sinaï." *Le monde de la Bible* 10 (1979): 37–41.

Negev, Avraham. *The Inscriptions of Wadi Ḥaqqaq, Sinai*. Qedem, no. 6. Jerusalem: Institute of Archaeology, Hebrew University of Jerusalem; distributed by Israel Exploration Society, 1977.

Naveh, Joseph. "A Nabatean Incantation Text." *Israel Exploration Journal* 29 (1979): 111–119.

Milik, J. T. "La tribu des Bani 'Amrat en Jordanie de l'époque grecque et romaine." *ADAJ* 24 (1980): 41–54.

Khairy, Nabil I. "A New Dedicatory Inscription from Wadi Musa." *PEQ* 113 (1981): 19–25.

Starcky, Jean. "Les inscriptions nabatéennes et l'histoire de la Syrie du Sud et du Nord de la Jordanie." In *Hauran I: Recherches archéologiques sur la Syrie du Sud à l'époque hellénistique et romaine*, ed. J.-M. Dentzer. Bibliothèque archéologique et historique, no. 124, pt. 1, pp. 167–182. Paris: P. Geuthner, 1985.

Negev, Avraham, with J. Naveh and S. Shaked. "Obodas the God." *Israel Exploration Journal* 36 (1986): 56–60.

Jones, Richard N., David J. Johnson, Philip. C. Hammond, and Zbigniew T. Fiema. "A Second Nabataean Inscription from Tell esh-Shuqafiya, Egypt." *BASOR* 269 (1988): 47–57.

Healey, John F., and G. Rex Smith. "Jaussen-Savignac 17: The Earliest Dated Arabic Document (A.D. 267)." *Atlal* 12 (1989): 77–84.

Yadin, Yigael, and Jonas C. Greenfield. "Aramaic and Nabataean Signatures and Subscriptions." In *Documents from the Bar Kokhba Period in the Cave of Letters*, ed. Naphtali Lewis (Greek papyri) and Yigael Yadin and Jonas C. Greenfield (Aramaic and Nabatean signatures and subscriptions). Jerusalem: Israel Exploration Society, Hebrew University of Jerusalem, Shrine of the Book, 1989.

Kropp, Manfred. "Grande re degli Arabi e vassallo di nessuno: Mar'al Qays ibn 'Amr e l'iscrizione di En-Nemara." *Quaderni di Studi Arabi* 9 (1991): 3–28.

Bellamy, James A. "Arabic Verses from the First/Second Century: The Inscription of 'En 'Avdat." *Journal of Semitic Studies* 35 (1990): 73–79.

Healey, John F., ed. *The Nabatean Tomb Inscriptions of Madā'in Ṣaliḥ*. *Journal of Semitic Studies*, suppl. no. 1 (1993).

Writing
Cross, F. M. "The Development of the Jewish Scripts." In *The Bible and the Ancient Near East: Essays in Honor of William Foxwell Albright*, ed. G. Ernest Wright, 132–202. Garden City, N.Y.: Anchor Books, 1961.

Naveh, Joseph. *The Development of the Aramaic Script*. Jerusalem: Israel Academy of Sciences and Humanities, 1970.

Healey, John F. "The Nabataean Contribution to the Development of the Arabic Script." *Aram* 2, nos. 1–2 (1990): 93–98.

Healey, John F. "Nabataean to Arabic: Calligraphy and Script Development among the Pre-Islamic Arabs." *Manuscripts of the Middle East* 5 (1990–1991): 41–52.

Gruendeler, Beatrice. *Development of the Arabic Scripts: From the Nabatean Era to the First Islamic Century according to Dated Texts*. Harvard Semitic Studies, no. 43. Atlanta: Scholars Press, 1993.

The Gods and Their Cults

Sourdel, Dominique. *Les cultes du Hauran à l'époque romaine*. Bibliothèque archéologique et historique, no. 53. Paris: Imprimerie nationale, 1952.

Glueck, Nelson. *Deities and Dolphins: The Story of the Nabataeans*. New York: Farrar, Straus, and Giroux, 1965.

Tran, V. Tam Tin. *Le culte des divinités orientales in Campanie en dehors de Pompéi, de Stabes et d'Herculanum*. Études préliminaires aux religions orientales dans l'Empire romain, no. 27. Leiden: E. J. Brill, 1972.

Teixidor, Javier. *The Pagan God: Popular Religion in the Greco-Roman Near East*. Princeton: Princeton University Press, 1977.

Starcky, Jean. "Allath, Athéna et la déesse syrienne." In *Colloques internationaux du CNRS, Paris 1979*, 119–130. Paris: Centre National de la Recherche Scientifique, 1981.

Starcky, Jean. "Allath." In *Lexicon Iconographicum Mythologiae Classicae*, vol. 1, pt. 1, pp. 564–570. Zurich: Artemis, 1981.

Zayadine, Fawzi. "L'iconographie d'Al-Uzza-Aphrodite." In *Colloques internationaux du CNRS, Paris 1979*, 113–118. Paris: Centre National de la Recherche Scientifique, 1981.

Zayadine, Fawzi. "Les sanctuaires nabatéens." In *La Jordanie de l'âge de la pierre à l'époque byzantine*, 93–108. Rencontres de l'École du Louvre. Paris: Documentation Française, 1987.

Lindner, Manfred. "Eine al-'Uzzā-Isis Stele und andere neu angefundene Zeugnisse der al-'Uzzā-Verherung in Petra (Jordanien)." *Zeitschrift des Deutschen Palästina-Vereins* 104 (1988): 84–91.

Zayadine, Fawzi. "Die Götter der Nabatäer." In *Petra und das Königreich der Nabatäer: Lebensraum, Geschichte, und Kultur eines arabischen Volkes der Antike*, 5th ed., ed. Manfred Lindner, 108–117. Munich: Delp, 1989.

Tarrier, Dominique. "Baalshamin dans le monde nabatéen: À propos de découvertes récentes." *Aram* 2, nos. 1–2 (1990): 197–203.

Zayadine, Fawzi. "L'iconographie d'Isis à Pétra." *Mélanges de l'École française de Rome: Antiquité* 103 (1991): 283–306.

Zayadine, Fawzi. "The Pantheon of Nabataean Inscriptions in Egypt and the Sinai." *Aram* 2, nos. 1–2 (1990): 151–174.

Lindner, Manfred, and Jürgen Zangenberg. "The Re-Discovered Baityl of the Goddess Atargatis in the Siyyag Gorge of Petra (Jordan)." *Zeitschrift des Deutschen Palästina-Vereins* 109 (1993): 141–149.

Society

Höfner, Maria. "Die Stammesgruppen Nord- und Zentralarabiens in vorislamischer Zeit: Mit Beiträgen aus griech. und röm. Quellen von E. Merkel." In *Götter und Mythen im Vorderer Orient*, ed. H. W. Haussig. Wörterbuch der Mythologie, no. 1, pp. 407–481. Stuttgart: E. Klett, 1965.

Starcky, Jean. "La civilisation nabatéenne: État des questions." *Annales archéologiques Arabes Syriennes* 21 (1971): 79–86.

Knauf, Ernst Axel. "Dushara and Shai' Al-Qaum." *Aram* 2, nos. 1–2 (1990): 175–183.

Macdonald, M. C. A. "Was the Nabataean Kingdom a 'Bedouin State'?" *Zeitschrift des Deutschen Palästina-Vereins* 107 (1991): 102–119.

Knauf, Ernst Axel. "Bedouin and Bedouin States." In *Anchor Bible Dictionary*, ed. David Noel Freedman, 1:634–638. New York: Doubleday, 1992.

Culture and the Figurative Arts

Patrich, Joseph. *The Formation of Nabatean Art: Prohibition of a Graven Image among the Nabateans*. Jerusalem: Magnes Press; Leiden: E. J. Brill, 1990, 185–196.

Patrich, Joseph. "Prohibition of a Graven Image among the Nabataeans: The Evidence and Its Significance." *Aram* 2, nos. 1–2 (1990): 185–196.

Agriculture at Petra

Al-Muheisen, Zeidoun. "Maîtrise de l'eau et agriculture en Nabatène: L'exemple de Pétra," *Aram* 2, nos. 1–2 (1990): 205–220.

The City
General Studies
Brünnow and Domaszewski

Dalman, Gustaf. *Petra und seine Felsheiligtümer*. Leipzig: J. C. Hinrichs, 1908.

Dalman, Gustaf. *Neue Petra-Forschungen und der heilige felsen von Jerusalem*. Leipzig: J. C. Hinrichs, 1912.

Bachmann, Walter, Carl Watzinger, and Theodor Wiegand. *Petra*. Wissenschaftliche Veröffentlichung des Deutsch-Türkischen Denkmalshutz Kommandos, no. 3. Berlin: Vereinigung Wissenschaftlicher Verlager, 1921.

Kennedy, Alexander B. W. *Petra: Its History and Monuments*. London: Country Life, 1925.

Negev, Avraham. "Petra and the Nabateans." *Qadmoniot* 7 (1974): 71–93.

Lindner, Manfred, ed. *Petra: Neue Ausgrabungen und Entdeckungen*. 5th ed. Munich: Delp, 1986.

Lindner, Manfred, ed. *Petra und das Königreich der Nabatäer: Lebensraum, Geschichte, und Kultur eines arabischen Volkes der Antike*. 5th ed. Munich: Delp, 1989.

Browning, Iain. *Petra*. 3d ed. London: Chatto and Windus, 1989.

Summary of Research and Excavation

Parr, Peter J. "Sixty Years of Excavation in Petra: A Critical Assessment." *Aram* 2, nos. 1–2 (1990): 7–23.

Architecture and Art

Lyttelton, Margaret. *Baroque Architecture in Classical Antiquity*. Ithaca, N.Y.: Cornell University Press, 1974.

Zayadine, Fawzi. "Decorative Stucco at Petra and Other Hellenistic Sites." In *Studies in the History and Archaeology of Jordan*, vol. 3, ed. Adnan Hadidi, 131–142. Amman: Department of Antiquities (Jordan). 1987.

McKenzie, Judith. *The Architecture of Petra*. British Academy Monographs in Archaeology, no. 1. Oxford: Oxford University Press, 1990.

Bienkowski, Piotr. "The Architecture of the Petra Beduin, A Preliminary Report." *ADAJ* 33 (1989): 335–343.

Patrich, Joseph. *The Formation of Nabatean Art: Prohibition of a Graven Image among the Nabateans*. Jerusalem: Magnes Press; Leiden: E. J. Brill, 1990.

Schmidt-Colinet, Andreas. "Aspects of 'Hellenism' in Nabatean and Palmyrene Funerary Architecture." In Ο Ελληνισμος στην Ανατολη; Δελφοι, 1985 (Athens, 1991), 131–144.

Parr, Peter J. "The Architecture of Petra: Review Article." *PEQ* 128 (1996): 63–73.

Urban Plan

Hammond, Philip C. "Nabatean Settlement Patterns inside Petra." *Ancient History Bulletin* 5 (1991): 36–46.

Dentzer, Jean-Marie, and Fawzi Zayadine. "L'espace urbain de Pétra." In *Studies in the History and Archaeology of Jordan*, vol. 4, ed. Muna Zaghloul, 233–251. Amman: Department of Antiquities (Jordan), 1992.

The Siq and Water Distribution

Parr, Peter J. "La date du barrage du Sîq à Pétra." *RB* 74 (1967): 45–49.

Zayadine, Fawzi. "Tempel, Gräber, Töpferöfen." In *Petra: Neue Ausgrabungen und Entdeckungen*, 5th ed., ed. Manfred Lindner, 214–223, esp. pp. 221–223 ("Ausgrabugen im Siq"). Munich: Delp, 1986.

Walls and Fortifications

Albright, W. F. "The Excavation of the Conway High Place at Petra." *BASOR* 57 (1935): 18–26.

Cleveland, Ray L. "The Excavations of the Conway High Place (Petra) and Soundings at Khirbet Ader." *Annual of the American Schools of Oriental Research* 34–35 (1960): 57–97, esp. pp. 57–74.

Parr, Peter J. "Le 'Conway High Place' à Pétra: Une nouvelle interpretation." *RB* 69 (1962): 64–79.

Hammond, Philip C. *The Crusader Fort on El-Habis at Petra: Its Survey and Interpretation*. Salt Lake City: Middle East Center, University of Utah, 1970.

Parr, Peter J., K. B. Atkinson, and E. H. Wickens. "Photogrammetric Work at Petra, 1965–1968: An Interim Report." *ADAJ* 20 (1976): 31–45.

Zayadine, Fawzi. "Les fortifications pré-helléniques et hellénistiques en Transjordanie et en Palestine." In *La fortification dans l'histoire du monde grec*, ed. Pierre Leriche and Henri Tréziny, 149–156, esp. pp. 153–154. Paris: Éditions du Centre National de la Recherche Scientifique, 1986.

Parr, Peter J. "Vierzig Jahre Ausgrabungen in Petra." In *Petra und das Königreich der Nabatäer: Lebensraum, Geschichte, und Kultur eines arabischen Volkes der Antike*, 5th ed., ed. Manfred Lindner, 139–149. Munich: Delp, 1989.

Scheck, Frank Rainer. *Jordanien: Völker und Kulturen swischen Jordan und Rotem Meer.* DuMont Kunst-Reisefürer. Cologne: DuMont, 1985.

The Theater
Hammond, Philip C. *The Excavation of the Main Theatre at Petra, 1961–1962: Final Report.* London: Quaritch, 1965.

The Colonnaded Street and the Triple-Arched Gateway
Parr, Peter J. "The Beginnings of Hellenisation at Petra." In *Huitième Congrès International d'Archéologie Classique: Rapports et communications*, 527–533. Paris: E. de Boccard, 1963.

Kirkbride, Diana. "A Short Account of the Excavations at Petra in 1955–56." *ADAJ* 4–5 (1960): 117–122.

Parr, Peter J. "A Sequence of Pottery from Petra." In *Near Eastern Archaeology in the Twentieth Century: Essays in Honour of Nelson James Glueck*, ed. A. Sanders, 348–373. Garden City, N.Y.: Doubleday, 1970.

Wright, G. R. H. "Petra: The Arched Gate, 1959–60." *PEQ* 93 (1961): 124–135.

Wright, G. R. H. "Structure et date de l'Arc monumental de Pétra: Étude comparative." *RB* 73 (1966): 404–449.

Recent Excavation of the Southern Temple
Joukowski, Martha Sharp. "Excavations and Survey of the Southern Temple at Petra, Jordan." *ADAJ* 38 (1994): 293–332.

Joukowski, Martha Sharp. "Archaeological Survey of the Southern Temple at Petra." *Syria* 72, 1–2 (1995): 133–142.

Residential Areas
Horsfield, George, and Agnes Horsfield. "Sela-Petra, the Rock, of Edom and Nabatene; IV The Finds." *Quarterly of the Department of Antiquities in Palestine* 9 (1942): 105–204. This article summarizes finds that were discussed in previous articles.

Zayadine, Fawzi. "Recent Excavations and Restorations of the Department of Antiquities." *ADAJ* 25 (1981): 341–355, esp. p. 355.

Khairy, Nabil I. "Preliminary Report of the 1981 Petra Excavations." *ADAJ* 28 (1984): 315–320.

Khairy, Nabil I. "Nabatäischer Kultplatz und byzantinische Kirche: Die Ausgrabungen in Petra 1981." In *Petra: Neue Ausgrabungen und Entdeckungen*, 5th ed., ed. Manfred Lindner, 58–73. Munich: Delp, 1986.

Parr, Peter J. "The Last Days of Petra." In *Proceedings of the Symposium on Bilad al-Sham during the Byzantine Period*, 2 vols., ed. Muhammad 'Adnan Bakhit and Muhammad Abu al-Mahasin 'Asfur, 192–205. Amman: University of Jordan; Irbid: Yarmouk University, 1986.

Zeitler, John P. "A Private Building from the First Century BC Petra." *Aram* 2, nos. 1–2 (1990): 385–420.

Stucky, Rolf A., ed. *Petra: Ez Zantur I: Ergebnisse der Schweizerisch-Leichtensteinischen Ausgrabungen 1988–1992.* Mainz: von Zabern, 1996.

The Church
Schick, Robert, Zbigniew T. Fiema, and Khairieh 'Amr. "The Petra Church Project, 1992–1993: A Preliminary Report." *ADAJ* 37 (1993): 55–66.

Rupestrian Architecture
Zayadine, Fawzi. "Die Felsarchitektur Petras: Orientalische Tradition und Hellensticher Einfluss." In *Petra und das Königreich der Nabatäer: Lebensraum, Geschichte, und Kultur eines arabischen Volkes der Antike*, 2d ed., ed. Manfred Lindner, 39–69. Munich: Delp, 1974.

Salies, Gisela Hellenkemper, ed. *Die Nabatäer: Ertäge einer Ausstellung im Rheinischen Landesmuseum Bonn, 24 Mai–9 Juli 1978.* Cologne: Rheinland-Verlag; Bonn: Habelt, 1981.

Schmidt-Colinet, Andreas. "Nabatäische Felsarchitektur: Bemerkungen zum gegenwärtigen Forschungsstand." *Bonner Jahrbücher des Rheinischen Landesmuseums in Bonn* 180 (1980): 189–230.

Hadidi, Adnan. "Nabatäishe Architektur in Petra." *Bonner Jahrbücher des Rheinischen Landesmuseums in Bonn* 180 (1980): 231–236.

Balty, Jean Ch. "Architecture et société à Pétra et Hegra: Chronologie et classes sociales, sculpteurs, et commanditaires: De l'archaïsme grec à la fin de la République romaine." In *Architecture et société: Actes du Colloque, Rome 1980*, 303–324. Rome: École Française de Rome; Paris: Centre National de la Recherche Scientifique, 1983.

Schmidt-Colinet, Andreas. "Dorisierende nabatäische Kapitelle," *Damaszener Mitteilungen* 1 (1983): 307–319.

Zayadine, Fawzi. "Tempel, Gräber, Töpferöfen." In *Petra: Neue Ausgrabungen und Entdeckungen*, 5th ed., ed. Manfred Lindner, 214–269. Munich: Delp, 1986.

Lyttleton, Margaret. "Tombs and Funerary Iconography." In *Petra and the Caravan Cities: Proceedings of the Symposium Organized at Petra in September 1985*, ed. Fawzi Zayadine, 19–24. Amman: Department of Antiquities (Jordan), 1990.

Zayadine, Fawzi. "Die Felsarchitektur Petras: Orientalische Tradition und Hellenistischen Einfluss." In *Petra und das Königreich der Nabatäer: Lebensraum, Geschichte, und Kultur eines arabischen Volkes der Antike*, 5th ed., ed. Manfred Lindner, 212–248. Munich: Delp, 1989.

Matthiae, Karl. "Die nabatäische Felsarchitektur in Petra." *Klio* 73, 1 (1991): 226–278.

Sculpture
Parr, Peter J. "Recent Discoveries at Petra." *PEQ* 89 (1957): 5–16.

Toynbee, J. M. C. "A Bronze Statue from Petra." *ADAJ* 8–9 (1964): 75–76.

Lyttleton, Margaret, and Thomas F. C. Blagg. "Sculpture in Nabatean Petra and the Question of Roman Influence." In *Architecture and Architectural Sculpture in the Roman Empire*, ed. Martin Henig. Monograph no. 29. Oxford: Oxford University Committee for Archaeology, 1990.

Lyttleton, Margaret, and Thomas F. C. Blagg. "Sculpture in the Temenos of Qaṣr el-Bint at Petra." *Aram* 2, nos. 1–2 (1990): 267–286.

Roche, Marie-Jeanne. "Bustes fragmentaires trouvés à Pétra." *Syria* 67, 2 (1990): 377–395.

Monuments
Qasr el-Bint Far'un: Principal Studies and Restorations
Parr, Peter J. "Recent Discoveries in the Sanctuary of the Qaṣr Bint Far'un at Petra: 1. An Account of the Recent Excavations." *ADAJ* 12–13 (1967–1968): 5–19.

Wright, G. R. H. "Recent Discoveries in the Sanctuary of the Qaṣr Bint Far'un at Petra: 2. Some Aspects concerning the Architecture and Sculpture." *ADAJ* 12–13 (1967–1968): 20–29.

Zayadine, Fawzi. "Recent Excavations and Restorations of the Department of Antiquities." *ADAJ* 25 (1981): 341–355.

Zayadine, Fawzi. "Recent Excavations and Restoration at Qasr el Bint of Petra." *ADAJ* 29 (1985): 239–249.

Wright, G. R. H. "The Qasr el-Bint Far'un at Petra: A Detail Reconsidered." *Damaszener Mitteilungen* 2 (1985): 321–325.

Zayadine, Fawzi. "Recherches récentes au temple du Qasr el Bint de Pétra." Πρακτικα του XII Διεθνους συνεδριου κλασικης αρχαιολογιας 1 (1985): 309–321.

Zayadine, Fawzi. "Tempel, Gräber, Töpferöfen." In *Petra: Neue Ausgrabungen und Entdeckungen*, 5th ed., ed. Manfred Lindner, 214–269, esp. pages 237–248 ("Die Ausgrabungen des Qasr el-Bint"). Munich: Delp, 1986.

Zayadine, Fawzi, and Suleiman Farajat. "The Petra National Site Projects: Excavation and Clearance at Petra and Beiḍa." *ADAJ* 35 (1991): 275–311.

The Temple of the Winged Lions
Hammond, Philip C. "Survey and Excavation at Petra, 1973–1974." *ADAJ* 20 (1975): 5–30.

Hammond, Philip C. "Excavations at Petra, 1975–1977." *ADAJ* 22 (1977–1978): 81–101.

Hammond, Philip C. "Excavations at Petra, 1974: Cultural Aspects of Nabatean Architecture, Religion, Art and Influence." In *Studies in the History and Archaeology of Jordan*, vol. 1, ed. Adnan Hadidi, 231–238. Amman: Department of Antiquities (Jordan), 1982.

Hammond, Philip C. "Die Ausgrabung des Löwen-Greifen Tempels in Petra (1973–1983)." In *Petra: Neue Ausgrabungen und Entdeckungen*, 5th ed., ed. Manfred Lindner, 16–30. Munich: Delp, 1986.

Hammond, Philip C. "Three Workshops at Petra (Jordan)." *PEQ* 119 (1987): 129–141.

Hammond, Philip C. "The Goddess of the 'Temple of the Winged Lions' at Petra." In *Petra and the Caravan Cities: Proceedings of the Symposium Organized at Petra in September 1985*, ed. Fawzi Zayadine, 115–130. Amman: Department of Antiquities (Jordan), 1990.

Meza, Alicia I. "An Egyptian Statuette in Petra." *ADAJ* 37 (1993): 427–432.

Hammond, Philip C., and D. J. Johnson. "American Expedition to Petra, the 1990–1993 Seasons." *ADAJ* 38 (1994): 333–344.

The Khazneh el-Far'un
McKenzie, Judith. *The Architecture of Petra*. British Academy Monographs in Archaeology, no. 1. Oxford: Oxford University Press, 1990.

Lyttleton, Margaret. "Aspects of the Iconography of the Sculptural Decoration of the Khasneh at Petra." In *Petra and the Caravan Cities: Proceedings of the Symposium Organized at Petra in September 1985*, ed. Fawzi Zayadine, 19–24. Amman: Department of Antiquities (Jordan), 1990.

Ed-Deir
Lindner, Manfred, et al. "New Explorations of the Deir-Plateau (Petra) 1982–83." *ADAJ* 28 (1984): 163–181.

Matthiae, Karl. "Die Fassade von Ed-Der in Petra: Ein Beitrag zur nabatäischen Felsarchitektur." *Klio* 71, 1 (1989): 257–279.

Zayadine, Fawzi, and Suleiman Farajat. "The Petra National Trust Site Projects: Excavation and Clearance at Petra and Beiḍa." *ADAJ* 35 (1991): 275–311, esp. pp. 282–284.

Tomb of Sextius Florentinus

Freyberger, Klaus S. "Zur Datierung des Grabmals des Sextius Florentinus in Petra." *Damaszener Mitteilungen* 5 (1991): 1–8.

Other Sites

Medain Es-Saleh

Negev, Avraham. "The Nabatean Necropolis at Egra." *RB* 83 (1976): 203–236.

Schmidt-Colinet, Andreas. "The Mason's Workshop of Hegra, Its Relation to Petra and the Tomb of Syllaios." In *Studies in the History and Archaeology of Jordan*, vol. 3, ed. Adnan Hadidi, 143–150. Amman: Department of Antiquities (Jordan), 1987.

Schmidt-Colinet, Andreas. "Zur nabatäischen Felsnekropole von Hegra / Madain Salih in Saudi-Arabien." *Antike Welt* 18, 4 (1987): 29–42.

Hauran

Dentzer, J.-M., ed. *Hauran I: Recherches archéologiques sur la Syrie du Sud à l'époque hellénistique et romaine*. Bibliothèque archéologique et historique, no. 124. Paris: P. Geuthner, 1985–1986.

Index

Hit, 53
Ḥonainu (in inscription), 182
Horsfield, George, 106
Horvat Raqiq, 60, 61
Hubalu (Hubal), 75
Hymar, Arabian kingdom of, 49
Hyrcanus II, 27–28, 30, 31, 144

idols, 78, 154, 165, 170–71. *See also* betyls
Idumea, Idumeans, 27, 35. *See also* Edom, Edomites
Ilat. *See* Allat
Imtan, 67, 68
incense, 18, 53; altars for burning, 72, 86, 88; trade in, 20, 32, 49, 53, 72
India, Indies, 32, 39, 46, 49, 50–52, 53
Indian Ocean, 32, 49, 50–52
Iram, 71, 75, 76, 82, 89
Iraq el-Amir, 144
Irby, Charles Leonard, 103
irrigation, 5, 36. *See also* agriculture
Isaac of Antioch, 76, 86
Ishmael, 10
Isidorus of Charax, 70
Isis, 75, 79, 81, 171, 173, 174
Islam, 48, 75, 85. *See also* Muhammed (the Prophet)
Israel, kingdom of, 9
Ituraea, Ituraeans, 27

Jaffa, 25
Jason (bishop of Petra), 47, 179
Jason (high priest of Judea), 21
al-Jawf, 50
Jeremiah, 10
Jericho, 27, 31
Jerome, Saint, 78
Jerusalem, 28, 31, 40, 45, 48, 106
el-Ji, 12, 103. *See also* Gaia (el-Ji)
John Hyrcanus, 24
Jordan Valley, ix, 2–4, 28, 32, 35, 36, 41; plateau, 4–5, 42
Josephus, Flavius, 17, 18, 24, 25–27, 28, 34–35, 39–40, 112, 144
Judah, 11
Judea, 1, 17, 21, 22, 24, 25, 27, 28, 30, 31, 35, 40, 42, 45; kingdom of, 9, 32, 34, 35, 40, 41, 93; Roman province of, 35, 36, 39
Julia Domna, 46
Julius Julianus Alexander, T. (governor of Arabia), 181
Julius Priscus, 46
Justin, 24

al-Kalbi, Ibn, 75, 78
Kamkam (in inscription), 75
Kana, 18, 25
el-Katute, 124, 127
Kedar, Kedarites (Qedar, Qedarites), 10, 11
Kennedy, Sir Alexander, 106
Kerak, 48, 71
Khalasa, 5, 18, 22, 57, 58, 61, 78. *See also* Elusa
Khazrag (tribe), 78
Khirbet et-Tannur, 62, 71, 72, 170, 171

el-Khubtha, 32, 81, 103, 107, 114, 122, 124, 128, 134, 137, 139, 140, 147, 152, 177, 180
Knauf, Ernst Axel, 9, 12–13, 92, 93
Kulamuwa (king of Sam'al), 60
al-Kutba, 72–73, 76

Labienus, Quintus (surnamed Parthicus), 31
Laborde, Léon de, 103, 105, 106
Lagrange, Marie-Joseph, 58
Larché, François, 164
Lat. *See* Allat
law, legal texts, 17, 41, 57, 59, 60, 63, 98–99, 171, 183
Lear, Edward, 105
Lebanon Mountains, 4
el-Leja, 4, 10
Lemaire, André, 12
Lentulus, Marcellinus, 28
Leuke Kome, 52, 53
Leukos Limen (Quseir al Qadim), 53
Lihyanites, Lihyanite language, 11, 65, 72, 76
Li-Kan (Reqem), 50
literary sources, 17, 18, 36, 41, 46, 49, 57, 65, 107. *See also* specific names
Lollius, 28
Lottin de Laval, Pierre Victorien, 76
Lucan, 131
Lucian, 49
Lucius Verus (Roman co-emperor), 45
Lucullus (Roman general), 27
Lycurgus, 73, 74, 90

Maccabees (books of the Bible), 17, 18, 21–22, 57
Maccabees, 21, 24; Simon, 24; Jonathan, 22; Judas Maccabeus, 21, 22
Macdonald, M. C. A., 9, 92
Madrasa, 67
Magharet et-Tnub, 181
Mahalath, 10
Mahoza, 41
Malalas, John, 46–47
Malichus, 181
Malichus (son of Aretas IV), 94
Malichus I (Nabatean king), 28, 30, 31, 34, 94; on coins, 18, 28; in inscriptions, 62, 71, 149
Malichus II ("who loves his people," Nabatean king), 39–40, 52, 93, 94, 140, 179; on coins, 40, 140; in inscriptions, 68, 166, 168; titulary of, 93
Mampsis, 5, 36
Manawat, 75, 78, 99
Mangles, James, 103
Mankatu (in inscription), 181
Maqlabien, 11
Mar al-Qais (Arab king), 64
Marathus ('Amrit), 133
Marchetti, Nicolò, 182
Marcius Philippus, Lucius (governor of Syria), 28
Marcus Aurelius (Roman emperor), 45
Marib, 32
Mark Antony, 30, 31
Mazin (tribe), 98

Mecca, 12, 48, 75, 78
Medaba, 22, 58, 89, 97, 131
Medain es-Saleh, 45, 61, 139. *See also* Hegra (Medain es-Saleh)
Medina, 78
Mediterranean Sea, 20, 27, 32, 34, 49, 50, 53; and land routes, 1, 2–4, 22, 36, 39
Melpomene, 154, 155
Menelaus (high priest, Judea), 22
Mennaeus, 27
Mercury (god), 72, 73, 76; (planet), 72, 73
Meshquq, 68
Mesopotamia, 1, 2, 42, 44, 45, 50
Metellus, Quintus, 28
Miletus, 62, 68, 94
Milik, J. T., 12, 13, 18, 63, 181, 182, 183
Mithridates of Pergamum, 30
Moab, Moabites, 4, 10, 25, 27, 103, 119
Moghar en-Nasara, 137, 152, 158
monsoon winds, 22, 39, 50–52
motab, 78, 85, 166, 169, 170
Mount Nebo, 52
Muhammed (the Prophet), 78
Musil, Aloïs, 105
Myos Hormos (Quseir), 52, 53
myrrh, 18, 20, 49, 53

Nabatean kingdom, ix, 1, 5, 17, 27, 32, 39–40, 41, 42, 54
Nabatean kings, ix, 1, 17, 27, 40, 93, 94, 107, 168; titularies of, 17, 93, 94, 167
Nabatean language, ix, 9, 17, 57–64; written, 17, 18, 59, 63, 65
Nabateans: as Arabs, 9, 18, 22, 28, 31, 34; art and architecture of, ix, 103, 152–53, 154, 157; history of, ix, 17, 57; literary sources on, 17, 18–25, 36, 65; literary texts of, 57; as merchants, intermediaries, ix, 2, 17, 20, 32, 34, 42, 49, 92, 93, 98, 99, 153; origins of, 5, 9–13, 17, 59, 65; political and military functions among, 91, 94–98, 140; population, 12, 57, 65, 93; society, 5, 9, 17, 22, 57, 91–92, 93, 97, 99, 107; trades and occupations of, 17, 22, 53, 90, 98; water systems of, 20, 36
Nabaṭu (as king), 11, 93, 168; (as a people) 13, 28, 59, 92
Nabayati, 10, 11
Nabonidus (Babylonian king), 9, 72
Nabu, 72
Nahal Hever, 76, 98, 181
names, 9, 11–12, 59, 65, 70, 72, 75, 76, 181; place names, 58
Nanai, 167
Narses (Sassanid king of Persia), 47
Natirel (in inscription), 62
Natiru (in inscription), 18
Natnu (king of the Nabayati), 10
Naveh, Joseph, 61, 98
Nbyt, 11
Nebaioth, 10; Nebaioths, 10, 11
Nebuchadnezzar (king of Babylon), 10
necropoli, viii, 13, 124, 130. *See also specific locations*
nefesh, 60, 61, 81, 89, 130–31
Negev, ix, 1, 5, 18, 36, 40, 42, 47, 60, 81; Obodas I buried in, 176, 181